Bon Courage!

BON COURAGE!

First published in 2003
Second edition published in 2013
This edition copyright © Richard Wiles, 2013

Summersdale Publishers Ltd
46 West Street
Chichester
West Sussex
PO19 1RP
UK

www.summersdale.com

Printed and bound by CPI Group (UK) Ltd, Croydon CR0 4YY

ISBN: 978-1-84953-364-5

Although the events, places and people described in *Bon Courage!* are all real, the names of some characters have been changed to respect their privacy.

Bon Courage!

A French Renovation in Rural Limousin

RICHARD WILES

summersdale

'*Bon courage!*' – words used time and again by our French neighbours, often accompanied by a Gallic shrug, as a comment on the magnitude of our renovations; ironically also a byword for the changes in my life.

Dedicated to Herbert Wiles (1919–1996)

List of illustrations

Contents

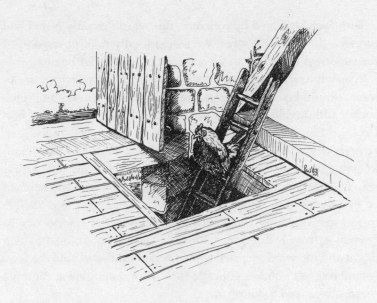

Prologue

Perils of Camping

Not content with nibbling through the groundsheet of our inner sanctum and stealing our supplies of chocolate while we had been shovelling manure from the adjoining barn, the mice were taking liberties now. As I played the meagre beam of the torch along the tent, I traced the shadowy, scurrying bodies of the despicable rodents as they queued up along the apex beneath the flysheet, eagerly awaiting their turn to launch themselves down the canvas sides as if our tent was a giant theme-park slide. The torch flickered and its beam became still dimmer. I whacked it against the palm of my hand and it became bright again.

With eyes blinkered by romance, this wasn't exactly how I had foreseen the first visit when we would finally take possession of the rundown French farm we were in the process of buying.

It was bitterly cold that evening. We each wore two pairs of jeans, several layers of T-shirts and fleeces, hats, scarves and thick socks; additionally, our feet were encased in black plastic bin-bags, held around our ankles with blue binder twine. 'If we keep our feet dry, it'll help us stay warm,' Al had claimed earlier, with knowledge of survival techniques gleaned from her seven-year solo round-the-world trip. I was beginning to doubt the wisdom of her words. My fingers were white and numb. I was unable to feel my nose, and I had to work my jaw from side to side to prevent it from locking shut. Outside, the rain continued to lash down and the wind to howl, while we sat huddled within the tent, assembling yet another gourmet meal with a sputtering camping stove, a wok and a saucepan.

I left the mice to their fun – they were probably only trying to keep warm, after all – set the torch down and scraped some lettuce, peppers, mushrooms and tomatoes from a paper plate into a carrier bag, added a drizzle of *huile de noix* and some ground black pepper, gathered up the neck of the bag and shook it vigorously. The makeshift salad tosser seemed to work quite well I thought, proud of my inventiveness, although I could discern an oily wetness dripping onto my trousers from holes in the bottom of the bag.

'How's that chicken coming along?' I asked, peering around Al's fleecy form to see the slices of chicken sautéing gently in the wok.

'Fine!' said Al, turning to check out my culinary operations. I briefly saw the foot-long blade of the carving knife, held in Al's left hand as she turned to see what I was doing, before it stabbed me squarely and firmly in the forehead. By reflex, my hands shot up to my face, cupping my eyes and forehead as I fell backwards onto the inflatable mattress, emitting a bloodcurdling scream. I lay there groaning, shocked, unsure of the extent of the damage that had been done, while Al – like some manic knife-wielding murderess – screamed in abject panic, thinking that if she hadn't killed me, she'd certainly plunged the blade deeply into an eye socket. A sharp pain throbbed in my forehead as my assailant dropped her weapon and carefully began to prise my hands away.

'No! No!' I moaned, clamping my hands tighter to hold my throbbing skull together, which I feared had been cleaved in two like a nutshell.

'Please,' said Al, wrestling with my wrists. 'Let me look.'

As my hands were parted, I tentatively flickered one eye open and peered through a blurry veil of what I imagined was blood at Al's contorted expression as she studied her handiwork in the torchlight. She wrinkled her nose and swallowed hard. There was a pause. I could hear my heart thumping in my chest.

'Oh, it's nothing,' she stated matter-of-factly, sounding almost disappointed. 'Just a tiny pinprick. There's not even any blood.'

'It bloody well hurts!' I wailed. The mice, who momentarily paused their antics as if they might be called as witnesses to a gory crime, seemed to glower through the canvas at us, before hitting the piste once more, sliding down the sloping walls of the tent.

We consumed our warm chicken salad and half a bottle each of cheap but delicious red French plonk sipped from plastic cups, and huddled together to keep warm while the storm raged outside.

'Damn!' I said after a while. 'I need to go to the loo.' I'd desperately tried to ignore the sensation in my bladder but to no avail. The connotation of my words sent a shiver down my spine.

'Oh,' gasped Al, in full understanding of what this entailed and the horror I felt. 'That means you'll have to go ... outside.'

'It's got to be done,' I said bravely, checking that the sticking plaster I'd insisted on was still firmly fixed over my knife wound (which I still fully expected to gush with blood). 'If I'm not back in five minutes ...' My words trailed away as, bracing myself, I unzipped the tent flap and waved the torch around, hoping that the hordes of mice that surely lurked outside would be temporarily blinded, enabling me to exit without them barging in. 'Close the flap behind me,' I said, crawling out. 'Don't let any of the little buggers get in.'

I emerged from the tent into total darkness and crept for a few feet along the woodworm-infested floor of the barn's upper *grenier*, or granary, to which the guy ropes of our tent had been nailed securely. I played the yellow beam of the torch into the depths of the cavernous barn – which measured some sixteen metres by eleven metres in area – then aimed it up into the exposed oak beams six metres above my head. Trails of cobwebs hung eerily from the timbers. I could hear the rain pelting against the roof slates that protected us from the thunderstorm raging outside.

'You know, this was a really brilliant idea, pitching the tent indoors!' I called out to Al, smiling smugly at my ingenuity. Straightening up, I edged my way forwards in the gloom, and immediately tripped over the guy rope that secured the front of our tunnel tent to the floor, falling face down into the enormous mound of dusty grain that filled the centre of the barn. Mice, which had been nibbling contentedly at this lifetime's store of food, scurried away in all directions.

'Are you OK, darling?' came a quavering voice from within the tent, which had shaken violently as I lunged over the guy rope.

'Yes,' I said, spitting out a mouthful of disgusting chaff. 'Just fine!' I scrambled to my feet, shaking the itchy grain from my sleeves and releasing it from the waistband of my jeans so that it worked its way into my underpants and fell around my legs, collecting in the bin-bags tied to my feet. 'You just stay in there, darling! I can manage!' I noted that my beloved, having already attempted to murder me with a carving knife, hadn't exactly rushed to see what fateful accident had befallen me now.

'If you think I'm coming out, you can dream on!' came the muffled response from beneath the duvet.

Brushing the grain from my clothes, I waded through the mound towards the open trapdoor that gave access to the vast room below. In the feeble illumination of the torch, the trap was like a black pit that threatened to swallow me in its cold darkness. I gingerly stepped onto the rungs of the rickety wooden ladder that poked through the hole and blindly edged down into the abyss. Halfway down I paused and shone the torch into the lower part of the barn. The area was divided into three sections. The central section into which I descended housed a giant circular plastic container filled with grey, floury meal produced by the antiquated contraption on the floor above, which ground the grain to powder and jettisoned it through a hole in the floor. Ranks of what appeared to be half-plucked chickens and a scrawny cockerel lined the rim of the container, clucking in mild irritation at having been disturbed from their nightly roost. The corpses of two of their companions lay in the meal container, where they had pegged out and collapsed, either through malnutrition or some fowl disease that no doubt wracked their scraggy bodies.

The section to my left, beyond the capacious concrete mangers and slatted oak wall, contained several Limousin cows and their emaciated offspring – veal calves chained to the stone wall, never to see the light of day in their short lives. Their big eyes glinted pleadingly in the beam of my torch as they shuffled uncomfortably on the thick bed of hay and their own foul-smelling excrement.

I waved the torch across to the third section, on the right. Beyond the oak beams, worn smooth at the edges by the heads and greasy, leathery necks of the cattle poking through to access the mangers, a solitary black hosepipe dangled from the joists, dribbling water onto the filthy cobbled floor. Slithering amidst this sea of manure and scuttling along the beams above, my torch spotlighted the corpulent bodies of the dozens of rats that infested the barn, their beady eyes staring at me brazenly – the intruder in their lair.

Quickening my descent of the ladder, the rungs of which were pitted with the holes of woodworm – or a much larger boring insect the size of a small bird – I pushed open one of the two huge oak doors that filled the arched cart entrance and stepped out into the pouring rain. The sky flashed with lightning, momentarily revealing the distant tree line in silhouette. Thunder rumbled directly overhead.

Numb fingers negotiating two sets of fly buttons, I relieved myself on the track that ran past the front of the barn, then headed back to the ladder, shinned up as fast as the plastic bags tied to my feet would allow, stumbled across the mountain of grain and returned to the sanctity of our tent.

Al, now sporting a fetching woollen bobble hat, was already asleep, warm beneath the duvet. I crept in beside her, fully clothed, my skin starting to itch from the collection of grain inside my jeans, and clicked the torch off. Almost immediately the darkness was filled with the sound of the mice surveying the perimeter of our tent for a way in. Then, my hearing attuned to the slightest noise, I imagined I heard gangs of rats – bully boys of the rodent world – scrabbling up through the various holes in the floor and pushing aside their playful, diminutive cousins to investigate this strange edifice that had been pitched on their territory. It was going to be a long night.

Chapter One

A Spontaneous Proposal

Camping indoors was infinitely preferable to the traditional outdoor variety, as it had rained incessantly for the past fortnight. We had arrived during that unseasonably cold and wet August of 1998 knowing that the *grange*, or barn, was still occupied by livestock, yet keen to start on the mammoth clearing up procedure that lay before us – despite the fact that the purchase of the farm had not been formally completed. We were blindly confident, nevertheless, that the purchase would proceed without a hitch: because of the binding nature of sale contracts in France there is no possibility of a buyer being gazumped, as can occur in England when an unscrupulous vendor raises the price of the property after it has been verbally agreed with the prospective buyer, or sells it to a higher bidder.

There are two main types of preliminary contract in France: the *Compromis de Vente*, or Contract of Sale, and the *Promesse de Vente*, or Promise to Sell. The *Compromis* binds buyer and seller to the sale at the agreed price and, on signature, the buyer pays a deposit (usually ten per cent of the purchase price), which is held in a special account until completion. One difference with the *Promesse*, however, is that the vendor is committed to sell the property to the purchaser at the agreed price within a period of two to three months, after which the purchaser has the option to withdraw from the sale (although the deposit would be forfeit as damages to the vendor).

In our case, we had signed a *Compromis de Vente* and our ten per cent, non-refundable, stakeholders' deposit was secured in the special holding account at the plush offices of the formidable Madame Marsolet, our appointed *notaire*. The notarial profession in France – under the authority of the Ministre de la Justice – has an effective monopoly in drawing up and authenticating deeds, contracts and acts relating to matters such as purchases, sales, leases, mortgages, marriage settlements, wills and inheritances. The role of this powerful public official in the house-buying process is not to act for either the vendor or the purchaser; the *notaire* is responsible to the state, with the function of ensuring the legal validity of the transaction and the drawing up of the deeds.

At our first meeting with Madame Marsolet, to which we were summoned to sign the *Compromis*, we were immediately struck by her air of authority, her assuredness in the power she wielded and the nobility of her profession. Her well-appointed office was in nearby Le Dorat, medieval capital of the Basse-Marche region, dominated by a darkly brooding Romanesque church, the eleventh-century Collegiate de St Pierre. Madame

Marsolet was a sophisticated lady, immaculately dressed in a smart, pale blue business suit. Her hair was elegantly coiffured and her face expertly made up to accentuate her fine features. Her slender fingers, with manicured nails, glistened with gold and diamond rings.

We sat before her huge antique desk as the process of our prospective purchase was explained with slow deliberation, lest we should enter into an agreement we did not fully understand. Reading from a legal text in precise French, she paused occasionally to peer at us over the rim of her half-moon, gold-framed spectacles as if to add dramatic emphasis to the jargon. Important legal points were delivered in her native tongue, while she slipped seamlessly into faultless English to translate complexities that might be lost on us.

'You are married, yes?' asked Madame Marsolet.

'Er, no. That is, I am, but to someone else. But Al is not. Married, that is,' I mumbled, aware that I was rambling. 'I'm in the process of getting a divorce.'

'You have children?'

'Yes,' I said. 'Two.'

'Ah! Then I must explain something very important to you,' said Madame Marsolet. 'It is for the benefit of you, Madame, er, Winter.' She glared at Al over the top of her spectacles. Al shuffled nervously on her chair like a troublesome schoolgirl hauled before a frightening headmistress, then sat bolt upright, hands neatly on her lap. 'What I say concerns the inheritance laws in France. When buying property, we have a form of contract we call *en division*. It is the normal form of contract. In this, each partner to the purchase is deemed to own fifty per cent of the property. This is clear?'

'Yes, Madame,' we replied in unison.

'If we were to use this contract for your purchase, and this man should die,' she pointed to me, 'his children, they will inherit his fifty per cent. You, Madame Winter, would no longer have sole rights to your own home. It could be very inconvenient for you. On the other hand, if you were to die first, Madame, and you had no children, your proportion of the property would go to surviving parents, brothers or sisters, and Monsieur Wiles would no longer have sole rights to his home. You both understand this?'

'Yes, Madame.'

'While you could make a will in France leaving some of this proportion to the remaining partner – or to anyone else you choose, or to a retirement home for the, how you say, *l'âne*, the little donkey – the children of a previous marriage could always contest this. *Non!*' She placed her fingertips on the desk blotter, as if she was depressing the ivory keys of a piano. '*Non!* Far better for you both to buy this property under what we call in France the clause *en tontine*.' She shuffled papers on her desk. We sat listening attentively, such was this formidable lady's command. 'The clause *en tontine* is the best for people such as yourselves, who have children from separate marriages. In effect it denies the children of the first dying spouse their normal right to inherit the property. This means that the property, on the death of the first partner, will be passed in its entirety to the second partner. I make myself clear?'

'Yes, Madame.'

'There is a threshold on the value of the property that can be passed to the remaining partner, and this rises annually – I believe it is currently approximately 300,000 French francs – but this is usually sufficient to enable the surviving partner not to incur death duties. Under this clause *en tontine*, the property would, on the death of the second partner, pass to his or her heirs.' Madame Marsolet leaned back in her chair and interlaced her fingers. We took that gesture as a sign that her explanation was complete and relaxed a little.

'Well, that sounds like the best option for us,' said Al boldly. I nodded in agreement.

'Ah, but there is, how you say, a requirement,' said the *notaire*.

'And what is that, Madame?' queried Al.

'You must be married.'

Al and I looked at each other for a moment and smiled. Then I shrugged in typical Gallic style, turning my palms up. '*Pas problème*,' I said, reflecting that I had actually asked Al to marry me just two weeks into our relationship, so convinced was I that I had met my soulmate. On the evening of that spontaneous proposal, my feelings had been eagerly reciprocated. Sitting in this plush office just six months later, our intention to marry was confirmed.

We left the offices of Madame Marsolet and headed for the Café de la Poste in the main square for a *café au lait*, quietly confident that we were in eminently capable hands.

During the two to three months after signing that initial contract, there was little we could do but sit back and wait in England for the searches relating to the current title of the property to be carried out to determine that it was free from any restrictions that could reduce its value; to check that the requirements of any *clauses suspensives*, or let-out clauses were met; and that no mortgage or charge existed over the property. We patiently waited to attend the signing of the final contract, the *Acte de Vente*, at which time completion would occur, the balance of the purchase price would be forwarded from England, and we would be the proud owners of a farm in France.

All was not plain sailing, however. Since first viewing the property the previous June, haggling over the price, coming to an agreement and signing a *Proposition d'Achat* prepared by the estate agent, certain worrying conditions had come to light. Because we were purchasing more than one hectare of farmland, it had been necessary to refer the sale of the property to the *Société d'Amenagément Foncier et d'Etablissement Rural* (known by the acronym SAFER), the agricultural commission which has the automatic right of pre-emption. In order to preserve land that it feels should remain in agricultural use, the SAFER would first be obliged to offer the property to the community – often at a lower price than was being asked by the owner. Should any prospective local buyer come forward within a period of two months, our agreement would be rendered null and void and we would lose the farm.

We sat chewing our fingernails nervously back in our East Sussex home, while in France neighbouring farmers were given the opportunity to pull the rug from under us and purchase the land themselves. To our great relief, none did, and the sale was cranked into its next gear and lumbered towards its expected conclusion at the end of August.

We had planned to camp out in the field at the rear of the *grange*. Pitching the tent on a relatively flat patch of grass, clear of cowpats, we had soon found ourselves awash. The leaky asbestos gutter that ran along the length of the barn deluged us with hundreds of litres of water each day, while a drainpipe protruding from the wall discharged a continuous and malodorous slurry from within the barn, which trickled past the tent in a brown river. From this quagmire emerged legions of amphibians: black salamanders with bright yellow blotches, and enormous bullfrogs, whose croaking was more like the call of a ferocious night predator. Both seemed intent on invading our damp shelter. Each morning, too, we would awaken to the sound of the farmer's dogs urinating against the flysheet.

'There's nothing for it but to pitch the tent inside the barn,' I announced decisively one morning. 'At least we'll be dry in there. What could be worse than being continuously drenched in cow shit and dog pee?'

What indeed.

'*Si vous voulez*,' murmured Monsieur Jérôme L'Heureux, the owner of the farm, when we revealed our intention to him. He turned back to his task of administering warm, sugared brandy to a cow with a hacking cough, shaking his head slowly in disbelief. '*Bon courage!*'

Chapter Two

New Directions

I take full responsibility for sowing the seeds that eventually led us to buy the shambolic property that was to dominate our lives thereafter, and with which we would fall madly in love. Holidaying in the Dordogne region of France a year before I met Al, I was, as ever, drawn like a magnet to the windows of local estate agents. Houses and the environments people create within them have always fascinated me; driven, I suppose, by an innate nosiness. I am also a practised devotee of the early evening stroll, during that brief window of opportunity just before dusk when people are wont to turn their lights on before they close their curtains, revealing their rooms for all to see. Luckier than many who admit to these vaguely voyeuristic tendencies, my profession as a writer of interiors features has given me licence to worm my way into a host of chic houses, photographer in tow, to interview proud owners usually only too eager to talk about their homes and their lives for the edification of the magazine-buying public.

But on this particular French holiday, it was not the interior design aficionado but the do-it-yourselfer trapped within me who homed in on the astonishingly cheap prices demanded for quaint cottages, substantial farmhouses and rambling *châteaux* alike. Here were ramshackle properties ripe for the picking – the home renovator's dream! For years I'd written on the subject of DIY for national magazines, cutting my journalistic teeth on the ubiquitous *Do It Yourself Magazine*. During the mid-1970s I moved on to *Ideal Home* magazine, where I swallowed my pride and ghosted as DIY diva Ms Kate McKenzie, with a remit from the chauvinistic male editor to 'keep it simple; it's aimed at women'. In the 1980s I emerged as *Best* magazine's laddish handyman, offering practical advice on a weekly basis; and by the 1990s I had matured as *Traditional Homes* magazine's authoritative expert on period home restoration. Having developed a number of other practical magazines, and written or edited various books on home renovation, I found myself labelled as something of an expert. By the time I was dragged away, twitching, from those French estate agents' windows by my holiday companion, my appetite had been thoroughly whetted.

With hindsight, I believe that I had also subconsciously recognised a lifebelt with which I could haul myself from the whirlpool I had been caught in since the failure of my sixteen-year marriage; a downward spiral that was threatening to suck the life and free will from me. Work was not going well. The home interest magazine business had become sluggish; the do-it-yourself industry was in the doldrums. As a result of this, and with divorce and child maintenance payments to finance, I was stony broke. Feeling the need for stability that life as a freelance writer denied me, I contacted an old acquaintance, the editorial director of a magazine publishing company based in London, and secured for myself a full-time job as Senior Editor. In return for a steady income, a regular holiday allowance, sickness benefits and company pension plan, my remit was to develop new magazine titles for the international market. I considered my new job to be a glint of light in an otherwise gloomy future. But the light was cruelly extinguished after eleven short months when I was made redundant. I felt like the weakly antelope singled out from the herd by a stealthy predator: easy pickings. When a flimsy straw was offered to me, I readily grasped it, enabling me to continue in virtually the same job, but as a freelance, with a drastic cut in salary and no other entitlements.

In another unexpected blow, my 77-year-old father died in mid-swing of a table tennis bat, competing against league players 40 years his junior, in his local village hall. Dying of coronary artery thrombosis in this way was preferable to suffering a long illness, although I was aware of the fine thread that had separated my depressive father from the inner demons that haunted him.

My elder brother Phill and I had been appointed executors of our father's will, and in sorting through mounds of his paperwork, we uncovered a heart-rending series of diaries that revealed the daily torment he had suffered since the loss of our mother some eight years previously. Carefully scripted entries described his inability and unwillingness to cope without her at his side. He was biding his time until he joined her, as he was sure he would. Contrary to my agnostic beliefs, I hoped that he had.

When Phill and I discovered that we had been left a modest inheritance, I began to think seriously about the possibility of buying a property in France, although at that time I had not formulated a plan to up sticks and leave England for good. The venture was, however, one that I was sure my father would have heartily agreed with and something he would have loved to do himself. I researched the subject in detail, scouring the websites of online estate agents, reading the classified advertisements of agents and private vendors in French lifestyle magazines such as *France* and *Living France*, and the property paper *French Property News*. I familiarised myself with the legalities involved in buying abroad, and visited the French Property Exhibition in Hammersmith, London.

It was around that time that I met Al. We were introduced by a fellow train commuter, Lee, with whom we had both independently struck up a friendship. Lee (who later received from Al the appellation 'Birdie') was a vivacious, statuesque and opinionated young lady with long, silky, blonde hair and piercing hazel eyes. She ruled the television executive boss to whom she was a personal assistant with a rod of iron and her raucous tales – and particularly her animated impressions – of the antics of media folk enlivened the otherwise dreary train journeys.

The first time I encountered Al she had leapt onto the train at Charing Cross in a breathless flurry, moments before departure, having run all the way up the escalator from the Tube station. She flopped down onto the seat opposite Birdie and me, next to a corpulent, suited gentleman concealed behind the pages of the *Financial Times*. Refusing to budge an inch even for Al's slender frame, the man merely flicked his paper irritably. Curling a lip at the man behind the pink paper, she placed an unopened can of Coke on the floor between her feet. I glanced down absently and noted that this strange creature was wearing pointy-toed slip-on shoes with Cuban heels and leopard-skin uppers. She wore blue jeans, a black blouse with huge white spots, and two jackets: denim underneath and on top a shiny black quilted bomber jacket with an artificial fur collar. Her horn-rimmed spectacles had steamed up and her shoulder-length auburn hair, gathered at the top in a ponytail, sprouted like the leaves of a pineapple.

'Hiya, doll! Just made it by the skin of my teeth!' she said to Birdie, peering over the top of her misty spectacles with quizzical eyebrows. The man next to her rustled his paper and coughed pointedly: in-carriage talking was frowned upon by some members of the commuting fraternity.

'Hi, Al. This is Richard,' said Birdie by way of introduction. 'Richard, this is Al.' It was the first time I had met a girl called Al but the name seemed appropriately unconventional. Struggling to disentangle herself from the straps of her bag, Al extended a hand for me to shake.

'Hiya, Rich,' she said with warm informality, beaming broadly (Al possesses a disarming Julia Roberts style smile in common with Lee; the two were often mistaken for sisters). 'Lee's told me all about you.' I shot Birdie a questioning look at which she merely smirked. Just then Al's bag slipped from her lap and onto that of her bulky neighbour, who huffed and shook his paper.

'I am sorry, sir!' said Al with what I was to discover was characteristic politeness. She retrieved her bag, stood up and studied the luggage racks. They were fairly full. Ramming the bag into a crevice, she wriggled out of her two jackets and stuffed them under her bag above the man's head. As the train jolted forward, she fell back into her seat, kicking the Coke can over. It rolled across the aisle. Al pursued the can, picked it up and returned to her seat.

'What a goofball, eh? Can't take me anywhere!' she said, twanging at the ring pull. I flinched and gritted my teeth with expectation just as she pulled the ring back fully, showering herself and the pink paper with a fizzy explosion of sticky liquid. At that moment her bomber jacket slithered from the rack and landed squarely on *FT* man's head. After that, he lost interest in tracking the movements of stock in the City, folded his paper and seemed to lapse into a catatonic trance. Al and Birdie proceeded to gabble excitedly in what seemed to me a single sentence that lasted the hour-long journey from Charing Cross to Wadhurst station, where we alighted.

I was immediately entranced and intrigued by this vibrant, humorous young woman and we were instantly drawn to each other, forming a genuine friendship. Eventually, however, when the opportunity arose, I plucked up the courage to ask Al out on a date. Sharing a love for music – particularly jazz – country walking, cooking and homemaking, the romance between us blossomed amidst the unwholesome atmosphere of the filthy, clanking commuter trains that trundled us to and from the City. I found Al to be delightfully unconventional from the outset, bearing more than a passing resemblance to Popeye's girlfriend, Olive Oyl – in my eyes a seamless composite of the actresses Minnie Driver, Shelley Duvall and Andie MacDowell.

The second daughter of a traditional country doctor and his equestrienne wife, Al had spent her childhood and formative years steeped in the world of ponies and horses and, on leaving school, had naturally drifted into the world of showjumping. Eventually, as a qualified trainer and teacher, she travelled and competed extensively on the UK circuit and also visited Holland, Belgium and Germany seeking talented young horses to bring on with her employer, a member of the British showjumping team.

After three or four years, her love for America and a desire to expand her horizons found Al working in Maryland, with the novice and international horses of a US showjumping team member, and subsequently touring the Arizona and Florida circuits. This first stint at travel broadened her horizons beyond the narrow realm of equestrianism, and at the tender age of twenty-two she left home on the start of a tour that would take her to Africa, Australasia, South-East Asia and America, working in numerous diverse jobs. On returning to England seven years later – feeling a wiser and richer person for her experiences – she had entered the frenetic music industry.

Al's elder sister Claire had been ill for some years and Al (endearingly referred to by her sister as 'Sprog', the runt of the litter) left permanent employment, working in a succession of temporary jobs so that she might be readily on hand to attend to the needs of, or simply hang out with her sibling. Claire's frequent periods of confinement in hospital and her constantly frail health had not, however, blunted her rumbustious wit, earning her the nickname 'Lairy Clairey'.

A number of failed relationships had left Al disillusioned and distrustful of men and she openly shared with me that the last thing on her mind when meeting me was a relationship: Claire's health was the most important issue. But after only two weeks of being with Al, I was so certain that I had found my soulmate that I asked her to marry me. She readily agreed, while deeply suspicious of my sanity. 'But I'm a silly goose, Rich,' she said. 'What on earth do you see in me?' What I saw in her was a refreshing honesty, a zany wit and an ability to see the funny side of life's tribulations. Her ever-present smile and lack of embarrassment at her own clumsiness was alluring and admirable. Few things seemed to faze her. On one occasion, she was caught sensuously stroking a female commuter's hand in mistake for mine on a particularly crowded train and, rather than being mortified by the gaff, spent the rest of the journey snorting with unbridled mirth. Al had reawakened my dormant ability to laugh – particularly at myself – to put behind me the angst and pain of the past, to remember the good times, and to greet the uncertain future with optimism. 'Learn to control what you can and let go of what you can't,' she would say sagely.

After our whirlwind romance, Al had moved into the lodge house I rented on the outskirts of Tunbridge Wells. She shared my enthusiasm for a new life in France. She had fond memories of the country, having lived and worked in a small *auberge* while refining her French in preparation for her world tour. Having lived away from England for almost a decade, she relished the chance of departing those shores again in search of adventure.

We sat down together and listed our requirements. Ideally, we wanted a modest cottage or a small farmhouse (rich in oak beams and period features); it should have a sizeable garden (one of my aspirations was to create a cottage-style garden entirely from scratch); it should be in a quiet hamlet or village, well off the tourist track (we valued our privacy and wanted to mingle with the local French community); the property should be sufficiently far south to ensure a warm climate, yet it should be accessible from the UK in less than a day (if we ever decided to move to France permanently, we'd want to make frequent return trips to Sussex to visit Al's parents, her sister, and my children).

Sharing our intentions with my brother, I was somewhat miffed to receive a telephone call from him a few months later announcing: 'Hi, bro! We're off to France to buy a house!' Sure enough, he and his wife Stephie and their daughter Hollie, having blatantly pinched my idea, promptly beat me to it by purchasing a house near the village of Azerables, in the Creuse *département* of central France's Limousin region. It had been the first of several properties they had seen and the one to which they had returned, smitten.

Not one to succumb to petty sibling rivalry, I decided to ignore my brother's shameless effrontery and to turn his one-upmanship to our advantage. Al and I decided to pay him a visit while he was in France carrying out initial renovations, and to use his house as a base while we checked out properties in the surrounding area. Unsure of whether we would even like the region, not being familiar with that part of France, we arranged appointments with various estate agents who would show us a selection of properties within our price range over a period of a few days. We would make no snap decisions. We would take plenty of time to absorb the countryside, the villages, and the properties. We would return to England and think about what we'd seen. At least, that had been our resolve.

The journey from Calais, after a choppy, late-night crossing from Dover, was long, although the French autoroutes were fast, straight and largely traffic-free. Al, who rates sleeping as one of her favourite things, proved this by remaining comatose for virtually the entire eight-hour drive. However, it was necessary for me to rouse her whenever we needed to pluck a toll ticket from the machines at *péage* stations (invariably on the passenger side of our right-hand drive vehicle), or at key roundabouts. Roundabouts in

France have always been a trial for the foreign driver. Revolving anticlockwise has always seemed oddly cack-handed to me and it is only recently that the French have abandoned the curious policy of stopping mid-circuit to admit cars wishing to enter the flow.

'Argh! Al! Roundabout! Which way?' I shrieked, bearing down upon a particularly enormous roundabout with dozens of exits that resembled the spokes of a bicycle wheel. The names of the destinations on the signpost were a blur to me. 'Al, wake up! I'm getting dizzy!' I cried frantically. I performed several giddying circuits before Al came to her senses and rubbed the sleep from her eyes. Haring around again with a queue of irate French drivers on my tail honking their horns angrily, Al finally seemed to locate our position on the map.

'Right!' she said decisively, prodding the map.

'Which right?' I wailed, steering the car around again.

'No, doll. I mean, right as in OK. Right here!'

'Whaat?' We sailed past the junction she had indicated.

'Oh, I meant that right …'

'Which right?'

'The one on the left,' said Al sternly, indicating another turn off on the right.

'On the left? What are you on about? There aren't any lefts! They're all rights!' The car tyres squealed as we careered around again.

'Look, we need to go right around the roundabout and head left.'

'Whaat?'

'Right. Turn right here! Oh, you've missed it! Go around again!'

On the route south, we passed the popular resorts of Boulogne-sur-Mer and Le Touquet, crossing the chain of lofty viaducts, de Quéhen, de Hercquelingue and d'Echinghen, and squeezed between the forest of huge white wind turbines at the Parc Éolien de Widehem, before crossing the vast plains of the Somme. In the half-light, its fields of blood-red poppies seemed to mark the featureless landscape indelibly with the memories of First World War battlefields, its many memorial cemeteries an enduring reminder of those who died. I found it a sombre area, and was glad when the sky began to lighten with the new dawn. Soon I could make out huge fields of crops whose boundaries seemed to merge together, intermittently straddled by automatic watering gantries resembling monster stick insects rolling slowly across the landscape on wheels, irrigating the crops beneath them as they passed.

Drab grey villages came and went without us seeing a living soul (although my sleeping navigator merely grunted when I pointed this out). We headed for the autoroute that would squeeze us through the cathedral city of Rouen, hugging the banks of the broad, languid River Seine, curling its way from Paris in the east towards the coast near Honfleur. South of Rouen, we negotiated a series of roundabouts that took us past the towns of Evreux and Dreux into the lush Loire Valley with its plethora of vineyards and perfectly manicured *châteaux* of ancient kings and nobles.

Motoring on towards Chartres, one of the two spires of the twelfth-century cathedral dominated the horizon, concealing its twin from view. Seemingly all alone in this landscape, in reality the cathedral looms over the centre of a beautiful medieval city. We skirted around the city, watching the second cathedral spire creep into view, joined the A71 *péage* at Allaines and headed for Orléans, once the intellectual capital of the country. The smooth, fast motorway cut a neat swathe through the lush pine forests of the Loir-et-Cher, which concealed it from the surrounding habitations of La Ferté-St-Aubin, Lamotte-Beuvron and Salbris, and us from sight of them. We headed on towards the city of Châteauroux and the verdant Creuse *département*. This is one of the ninety-five administrative divisions of France, broadly similar to English counties, but themselves contained within twenty-two *régions*, such as the Limousin.

The Limousin – composed of the *départements* of Creuse in the north-east, Haute-Vienne in the north-west and Corrèze in the south – is situated on the north-western edge of the Massif Central. This sprawling central plateau of granite and crystalline rock also encompasses the *région* of Auvergne to the east of the Limousin, and the northern tips of the Midi-Pyrénées and Languedoc-Roussillon *régions* to the south. Despite the existence of health-giving spas and the well-known major cities of Clermont-Ferrand, Vichy and Limoges, the Massif Central is not an area generally regarded as a major tourist destination. It is, however, an area of dramatic contrasts.

The Auvergne *région* is noted for its lakes formed of extinct volcanoes and its hot springs at towns including Vichy, Royat and Saint-Nectare, and draws adventurous spirits to its mountainous heights for summer hiking or winter skiing; it also features some of the country's most splendid Romanesque churches and medieval castles. On its eastern fringes are the mountain ranges of Forez, Livardois and Velay; in the west are chains of extinct volcanoes, the Monts Dômes, Monts Dore and the Monts du Cantal.

The Aveyron *département* in the Midi-Pyrénées, spreading south-west from the Monts d'Aubrac, is interlaced with the rivers Lot, Aveyron and Tarn, which meander through vertiginous gorges and valleys where picturesque villages cling impossibly to the rugged cliffs. To the east in the Lozére *département* of Languedoc-Roussillon are the vast, isolated, tabular plateaux of the Grande Causses (Sauveterre, Méjean and Comtal) and the steep declivities of Les Cévennes, a region strewn with metamorphic bedrock that dates from prehistory.

The Limousin, however, is the gentler landscape of the Massif Central. It is the land of a thousand languid lakes; land of the doe-eyed, tan Limousin cattle, whose cowbells chime enchantingly in the breeze as they graze the lush green pasture; land of crumbling farms and houses. The city-dwelling inheritors of these rambling properties, which were built with only mud between the stones, have neither the means nor the will to forsake the excitement of the conurbation to restore the properties of deceased predecessors, in a place where work is scarce and entertainment modest. And so the buildings crumble and collapse. Hence, apart from an influx of foreigners drawn by cheap property prices, the land is populated largely by small pockets of aged farmers toiling for scant reward on the land.

The geology of the terrain is such that beneath shallow, quite infertile topsoil there lies clay and granite. This means that the varieties of crop that can be successfully grown on the land are few. Although wheat is widely grown, the region is characterised by its rustling fields of broad, green-leafed maize, the stems of which reach over two metres tall at the height of the growing season, bedecked with crisp corn cobs in fibrous sheaths; and swathes of vibrant yellow sunflowers, saucer-like faces turned in unison toward the sun. In the autumn their precious seeds are extracted from the dried, wilted husks for the production of oil.

. The rocky soil of the *région* was never ideal for the growth of crops, but offered lush pastureland that was well suited to grazing sheep and cattle. Farmers had come to rely upon rearing the rust-coloured Limousin breed of cattle, not only for the splendid quality of their beef but also because the powerful oxen could be harnessed to pull carts and ploughs and haul heavy loads.

This tough breed's lineage appears to stretch back many thousands of years. It is widely recognised, for example, that today's Limousin cattle are similar to animals painted by our prehistoric ancestors in the Lascaux Cave near the beautiful medieval town of Sarlat in the Dordogne. I had witnessed this similarity myself when visiting the astonishing replica of the cave – a stone's throw from the original, which is no longer open to the public – during that watershed French holiday when I first became lured to the country. I think that for me, the abiding image that will always characterise the *région* is that of herds of Limousin cattle grazing the green pastures.

As we drove on, the relative flatness of the countryside – which, like the plains of Norfolk, I feel offers the eye no relief, no richness or texture – started to form undulations as we motored past Argenton-sur-Creuse towards our exit at Eguzon. An area of green pastures, deep folds and hillocks, with farms nestling in between, the rolling countryside reminded me of parts of Sussex and Kent, where I have lived most of my adult life. Narrow lanes leading to pretty hamlets and villages intersected small hedge- or tree-lined pastures. One difference is that the Limousin lanes are, for the most part, as straight as stair rods, while their Sussex counterparts tend to meander in order to reach their goal.

On arrival at my brother Phill's house in the early morning, we exchanged pleasantries over fresh coffee and croissants and were shown around his property. Nestling at the end of a narrow lane with only an extremely pretty converted mill as its neighbour, Phill's property consisted of a combined pair of characterful stone-built cottages with an attached stone-built barn, another huge separate stone barn and about one acre of garden. The façade of the house, beneath a steeply pitched tile roof, featured red-brick window and door reveals surrounded by *crépi*, roughcast mortar typical of the region. Popularly, the bricks were painted red with the pointing picked out in black and the *crépi* painted grey.

After the tour Al announced that, amazingly, she was still sleepy and retired to bed. During the next ten hours, while I assisted Phill with his preliminary renovations, noisily prising massive nails from the exposed oak ceiling beams in the kitchen, just inches away from where Al lay sleeping in the room above, or scraping trowelfuls of cement render onto the damp walls – the strains of Edith Piaf resounding from the stereo – Al did not rouse. Worried that she had somehow passed away in her sleep, I periodically scaled the ladder to check on her, resisting the urge to test for signs of breathing by holding a mirror to her nostrils, although I did make a visual inspection that the carotid artery in her neck was twitching. Was this person really suited to the labours of restoring a crumbling ruin into a dream home?

The following day, with Al suitably rested but me thoroughly exhausted from the long drive and my subsequent labours, we set off early to meet an estate agent whose office was located in the nearby large town of La Souterraine. Our first sight of the attractive town encouraged us that this region held distinct possibilities for finding our dream property. La Souterraine – built on the site of a Roman way between the cities of Argenton and Limoges – is of great historical, archaeological and ethnological significance and features some remarkable medieval architecture. Dominating the centre of the town is the radically restored L'Eglise Notre-Dame, which contains a Gallo-Roman crypt. Built during the eleventh and twelfth centuries by the monks of L'Abbaye de Saint-Martial de Limoges – with the help of subsidies from King Henry II of England and later from Richard the Lionheart, who financed the construction of the belltower – the church once formed part of a monastery. Built on a site previously occupied by the Sosteranea Villa owned by Gérald de Crozant, Viscount of Bridiers, this was the foundation of the town. Subsequent conflicts between the monks, the Viscounts of Bridiers and the population resulted in the construction of fortified walls in the thirteenth century. Demolished and rebuilt around 1226, the walls divided the town between the monastery, church and cemetery on one side and the habitations of the bourgeoisie on the other. Later, fifteenth-century construction of new walls, reinforced every two hundred metres with a tower or fortified door, doubled the area of the town.

Of the several original *portes*, or gateways, only two remain today: La Porte Saint-Jean, a turreted tower now looming over a pretty square flanked by the church on one side and shops and cafés on the other, and La Porte du Puy Charraud, a simple archway pierced through a humble two-storey building.

We entered the square through the arch of La Porte Saint-Jean and headed for the estate agent's premises. After some preliminary enquiries about our requirements we were taken to view properties that ranged from a small detached stone farmhouse with an attached barn (which lacked any land and was cheek-by-jowl with neighbouring properties); a small picture-postcard cottage, the restoration of which was virtually complete (not for the likes of a committed do-it-yourselfer!); and a vast utilitarian double barn demanding total conversion (but which had been stripped of any character it might once have possessed). As attractive as they were in their own ways, they lacked that certain elusive quality Al and I both looked for, but which we could not quite put our fingers on. We thanked our guide and planned to carry on looking.

The next day we visited the offices of an English-run agency located in the adjoining Haute-Vienne *département* through which my brother had made his purchase and, after scouring their album of properties for sale, narrowed down our selection to several possibilities. For the English purchaser, a company such as this offers more than just an estate agency: their intention is to provide a complete service that steers those people unfamiliar with, or afraid of, the French system through its legal complexities, acting as a kind of bilingual go-between. The prices they quote, therefore, not only include the *notaire*'s fees, taxes and other charges but also their own, usually hefty fee.

The Haute-Vienne is largely an area of open countryside stretching westwards from the Massif Central. Subjected to a generous amount of annual rainfall from the clouds that stream inland from the Atlantic to the west, it is an area of abundant woodland and green pastures. Due to its underlying geology, there is a tradition of stonemasonry in the Limousin – in fact, *limousinage* is the word for 'rough masonry' – and as we drove to the numerous properties I noticed how the majority of the houses were built with strong, rough-hewn granite walls with broad, pitched roofs clad with light-brown Roman tiles, which themselves originated in the south of France. To the south we could see the rounded, barren peat moors of the Monts de Blond and the Monts d'Ambazac, which rise to a modest seven hundred metres yet offer splendid views over the flocks of grazing sheep and Limousin cows that populate the fields of this rural *département*.

It was a hot, cloudless day, spent enjoyably perusing cottages, barns, farmhouses and tumbledown ruins, in the company of the delightful, flame-haired Hero. Fashionably dressed in a summer outfit comprising miniskirt, blouse, jacket and high heels, the statuesque young lady hardly seemed appropriately attired for hacking through the sea of nettles, thistles and rampant grass that invariably surrounded these forlorn properties. Yet, clipboard in hand, she gainfully tottered after us as we delved into every nook and cranny of the vacant, barely habitable properties on her list. But still that certain element we were seeking eluded us.

'Look,' said Hero, near the end of the day, sounding concerned that we had not already been smitten by the treasures we had seen. 'You might as well see this one last property. You've nothing to lose.' Almost reluctantly she handed us a photocopied sheet bearing a murky black and white photograph of what looked like a rubbish tip with some distant, ramshackle buildings in featureless silhouette. I sneered at the prospect. The descriptive details were less than effusive about the property which, judging by the code I interpreted as being a date printed in one corner, had been on the market for some three years.

Loads of buildings and a field! screamed the title proudly. Quantity, not quality, seemed to be the subtext. The details below were scant, but to the point:

Setting: Hamlet.
Type: Detached.
Condition: Basic level.
Sanitation: No.
Outbuildings: Yes.
Land: Field.

'OK,' we shrugged. 'We might as well take a look.'

Chapter Three

Le Mas Mauvis

As we drove down the rutted track that led to the property we were assailed by the sound of dogs barking. Lots of dogs barking. Or perhaps 'howling' would be a more appropriate word. On our right was an assortment of dilapidated buildings. There was a simple cottage, the windows of which were badly rotten and glazed with polythene and fronds of ivy instead of glass, with a substantial tree sprouting jauntily from the base of its front wall. There was also an attached barn with an undulating clay-tiled roof and a gaping cart entrance, its oak doors hanging obliquely from their hinges. Beyond that was a row of two modest barns connected to a much larger stone *grange* with an open-fronted hangar attached to its other side, intended for the storage of hay bales or machinery. Half-hidden behind the barns and the cottage we could just glimpse another small cottage with exposed brick window reveals. Assorted rusty farm machinery and huge plastic bags of white fertiliser littered the ground around the buildings, while the dismembered corpses of unidentifiable animals (fowl apparently, judging by the presence of feathers) lay scattered around. Scrawny chickens pecked at the corpses, having seemingly turned to cannibalism through the effects of starvation.

As we climbed out of the car we were startled by the lithe figure of a black and white border collie, which shot silently from its hiding place beneath an ancient piece of machinery and began to circle around our legs, ears flat against its head, its pointed jaws snapping menacingly at our heels as if it was rounding up a flock of wayward sheep. The dog's nimbleness was not in the least compromised by the fact that it possessed only three legs: two at the back and one at the front. As the tripedal animal wove between us, the odour of manure that clung to its sleek coat told us that this creature was clearly not a cosseted pet but a working cow dog.

The front door of the little house on the opposite side of the track creaked open and a broad-shouldered man with a thatch of black hair emerged, dressed in oil-stained denim jeans and a shirt open to the chest. '*Allez! Allez!*' he snapped at the dog. The animal scuttled back under its hiding place and peered out at us, panting furiously and quivering with nervous excitement.

Had the man's skin been green rather than sun-bronzed, he could easily have been the body double for The Incredible Hulk. In a stance presumably borne of a lifetime of wrestling cows to the ground and hog-tying them, his arms were held bowed at his sides and he walked with his head down. He appeared about to charge and fell us with a rugby tackle. (Indeed, as we learned later, the young man had toyed with a career as a rugby player, but opted for farming.) This giant swaggered over and, introduced by Hero as Monsieur Jérôme L'Heureux, the owner of the farm, gripped our hands in a greeting that left my fingers throbbing. After various formalities were exchanged between Hero and the burly farmer, our redheaded guide turned to us and said: 'Would you like to have a look around, then?'

'Yes. But which property is for sale, exactly?' I queried naively, puzzled by the motley collection of buildings ranged before us.

'All of it,' came Hero's reply.

'All of it?' Al and I squeakily chirped in unison, consulting the agent's details again in disbelief, and homing in on the price: 150,000 francs, including *notaire*'s fees, government taxes and the agent's fee. That equated to about £15,000 at the prevailing exchange rate. For an entire farm? Surely not!

'*Tous les bâtiments,*' said the farmer, pointing in turn at each of the buildings. He showed us around the first house and its attached barn (which contained an ancient, rusting blue Citroën and a splendid antique two-wheeled charabanc), pointing out features he considered selling points sure to impress us, such as the shallow stone sink in a recess near the door of the house and an ancient bread oven, housed in a lobby behind a room crammed with huge fuel storage tanks, the floor slick with oil. Judging by its advanced state of decay, however, the dome-shaped oven, set within a wall rendered with strawed mud, had not yielded a single baguette for many a year. The back elevation of the cottage was clad with mature ivy, the tendrils of which had wormed their way into the joints between the stones, dislodging many.

The small detached cottage that nestled between the first house and the row of barns was undeniably quaint and characterful. Its front façade – with brick reveals typical of the region – had no outlook, facing as it did the back of one of the barns. It comprised two rooms with a beaten earth floor pitted with rat holes, leading from a central front door, and at the rear a corrugated-tin-roofed extension housing four pigpens, *sans cochons*, with a stone-walled terrace beyond. The traditional casement window frames on the front of the house were rotten, the glass long since replaced with plastic, which had discoloured nicotine yellow after prolonged exposure to the sun. Louvre shutters hung at jaunty angles at each side of the windows, held back against the wall with traditional metal *tête bergère*: retainers in the shape of a shepherd's head. Tiny brick-revealed windows peeped from beneath the verge of the tiled roof, which itself was inlaid with two rows of half-round tiles separated by flat tiles as decoration.

During our tour, Monsieur L'Heureux, in a display of male chauvinism, attempted to address me directly with information about the property, with a total disregard of the fact that I obviously had not the foggiest idea of what he was saying. I simply smiled foolishly and nodded or shrugged, hoping that one or other of these gestures would compliment his comments. Al, who speaks what most people would regard as excellent French, but which she considers rusty and ropy, saw me squirming and came to my rescue: '*Pardon Monsieur. Rich, il ne parle pas français.*' She made a slicing motion across her throat – somewhat overdramatically, I thought.

'What was that?' I whispered in her ear.

'I said you speak absolutely no French,' replied Al. Suddenly I felt exposed. Three pairs of eyes appeared to scrutinise me – He Who Speaks No French At All – with a look of equal derision and pity.

'Thanks for that boost of confidence,' I said.

'You speak no French at all?' asked Hero, twisting the knife. 'That's quite unusual for someone of your age, isn't it?'

I tittered girlishly, embarrassed that I could not even draw on a smattering of schoolboy French. Because of my father's job as a high-powered trouble-shooter for Scottish & Newcastle Breweries, a large portion of my childhood seemed to have been spent moving home and changing schools, and consequently I had missed out on the crucial start of French lessons and was forced – by a hideous twist of fate – to be subjected to double periods of Extra Maths while my peers were fast becoming bilingual. Practising their new-found language skills in the playground, the other kids would metaphorically kick sand in my face. Now it was happening all over again!

Rubbing his bristly chin with a leathery palm, Monsieur L'Heureux studied me as if, by allowing women to speak for me, I was a kind of linguistic eunuch. (For years after that, despite the fact that I rapidly learned to understand and converse in French, the macho monsieur continued to regard me with suspicion. Exactly what kind of man was I?)

After my ritual humiliation we continued our survey of the property. We were unable to enter the two ancillary barns attached to the main *grange* due to the presence of a large, vicious looking, coarse-haired, mangy dog of indeterminate pedigree (although his robust stature suggested that his ancestors might have dabbled in interspecies breeding). Secured as he was by a long chain to an iron ring fixed to the wall, the black beast resigned himself to growling, baring his yellow teeth and slavering as we admired his spacious quarters through the open door. Judging by the piles of fetid excrement that covered the floor, he had been incarcerated in the dank cell for many years. By his side was a large tin bowl containing chunks of stale baguette soaked in milk and eggs. The presence of copious gnawed bones and bits of brown fur nearby, however, suggested that unlucky rats that passed within range of his chain supplemented the dog's meagre diet. Monsieur L'Heureux slammed the cell door shut and we moved on.

In the adjoining ancillary barn a pack of about ten floppy-eared hounds – large hunting dogs similar to beagles, although with a more visible skeleton – were attempting to crawl under the smallest of gaps in the rotten doors, which were reinforced with odd bits of wood nailed on. Unlike their mangy cellmate, they appeared keen to escape their confinement. Al and I peered through a gap in the huge barn doors at the scene of squalor within, and the stench that wafted out told us that these wretched creatures were also long-term inmates who shared communal toilet facilities.

The main barn was outwardly nothing more than a utilitarian stone structure: not a period building, being constructed in the early 1900s, yet built in a style that has been traditional in this area of France for hundreds of years. Its symmetry gave it an air of grace and elegance that belied its intended function. Stout and sturdy walls of sand-coloured stone bonded with nothing more than mud, although mortar-pointed, measured over a metre thick; its steeply pitched apex roof was clad on the front elevation with grey *ardoises*, slates, and on the rear with russet-coloured clay tiles. In the middle of the front façade of the barn was a broad, arched access hole large enough to swallow a fully-laden cart. Stout oak doors at each side folded back against the front wall. The pegged joints of the barn doors had sagged and the cladding was rotten at the base. At each side of the barn entrance were two smaller ancillary doorways with stone lintels and weathered oak plank doors through which the animals could pass. On the top floor, original oak shutters – grainy planks bolted to a ledged-and-braced frame – flanked a pair of side openings measuring just over a metre wide by nearly two metres in height. More like doors than windows, these openings were evidently intended for the loading and unloading of materials. A central, broader opening about two metres square and arched with a soldier course of red bricks was fitted with inward-opening shutters, and in its heyday would perhaps have been fitted with a hoist to haul sacks of grain from a wagon to the upper floor for conversion into meal.

We entered the central section – some five metres wide and more than double that dimension from front to back – which was flanked by huge concrete mangers. We peered through the gaps between the thick oak beams that divided the outer sections of the barn, which were about the same floor area as the central section. On our left stood four feeble veal calves, kept permanently in the dark, chained to metal rings attached to the walls: their mothers could be heard bellowing miserably for their offspring from the field at the back of the barn. I was aware of the furore that is constantly levelled at veal production – a by-product of the dairy industry – because of the inhumane treatment the animals are subjected to. Female calves can look forward to a long life in the milking herd, but the short life of the male calf is indeed pitiful. Soon after birth, fragile male calves destined for veal production are separated from their mothers and kept confined by a chain around their necks in a cold, dark byre. Because their movement is restricted, muscle development is inhibited, making the meat tender. A diet of milk substitute purposefully deficient in iron and fibre results in the anaemic flesh that is regarded as a delicacy. The physical and mental torment placed upon these defenceless animals is at least short-lived, as they are slaughtered at about sixteen weeks of age.

The bay at the right-hand side of the barn housed more youngsters. Both Al and I were horrified at the conditions in which the calves were kept and upset about the way the dogs appeared to be permanently locked up in their dark and stinking hovels.

Our view tainted by the sight of the animals, it was not until Al and I emerged through the trapdoor into the vast upper floor of the *grange*, covering a surface area of some 135 metres square, that the intangible feeling we both shared but could not express in words enveloped us. This capacious, church-like space, with its impressive vaulted oak ceiling towering six metres above our heads, its walls of rough stone, its pine-boarded flooring, was so unlike anything we thought we had been looking for. Until that moment I had never considered that I might one day want to live in a barn conversion, being generally of the opinion that the usual practice of arbitrarily partitioning off these spaces into smaller room-sized units destroys the very element that makes them so dramatic: their vastness. But I could see immediately that this barn – if one overlooked the mound of grain that covered virtually all of the floor area, and despite the flimsy roof through which daylight streamed, and the lack of a staircase or windows – needed very little in the way of conversion. This was a space to be savoured. Al, gazing around her in wonderment, was obviously of the same opinion.

'Rich, can you imagine this as one huge open-plan room?' she said, with a look of awe on her face. 'Living room, dining room, kitchen ...' She indicated thirds of the vast space.

'I can!' I replied. 'I can. But think of what it would take to heat such a huge space in the winter.' I added a touch of boring practicality.

'Perhaps, but it's possible. A big open fire at one end and one of those *poulet* things your brother has.'

'Chickens?' I exclaimed, momentarily confused. Then I smiled a wry smile. Al suffers from a debilitating, if humorous condition, which I dubbed 'Alism': a kind of wayward form of malapropism that caused her to select similar-sounding but totally inappropriate words for her intended usage.

'*Poêles*,' I corrected almost automatically, tuned in to her verbal gaffes. 'Wood-burning stoves.' My own severely limited French vocabulary contained a disparate assortment of words gleaned from studying the catalogues of do-it-yourself stores and ironmongers.

'Yes, that's what I said, Lol,' she replied, unperturbed, using one of the many and various randomly selected nicknames she was apt to use for me.

'We'd get through a lot of wood, though,' I countered, reflecting on how amazing it was that Al's challenging command of vocabulary had not hindered her in learning to speak French.

Outside again, we examined the open-fronted hangar that was built onto the short end of the *grange*. Clad with vertical oak boards weathered to an ash grey colour, the hangar housed a rusty, wheel-less combine harvester and various other pieces of farming machinery. We walked around the back of the *grange*, where the ground fell away in a gradual slope. The building loomed over us, its stone wall pierced with four small, frameless windows with red brick reveals and arched tops. The guttering was beyond repair, and its downpipe simply discharged onto the ground at the base of the wall, causing a permanent boggy patch.

'How large is the field that comes with the property, then?' I asked, and Hero posed the question to Monsieur L'Heureux, who pointed dramatically towards the tree line about a hundred metres beyond the building and moved his arm to the left, tracing a broad sweep towards another, distant tree line – it looked like an area of some ten acres. Some field!

'*Voudriez-vous voir toute la terre?*' said the farmer, again addressing his remarks directly to me.

'Monsieur L'Heureux would like to show you the rest of the land,' said Hero, and, joined by the tripedal dog running at its master's heels, we were led past the barn down a little grassy *chemin*, or path, to a murky pond on our left.

As we approached, dozens of frogs leaped from the bank and skimmed off across the water. Electric-blue dragonflies darted hither and thither. The sound of crickets filled the air. A startled heron, which had been wading in the shallows of the pond, launched itself skywards in a cascade of water. The path and the pond, the farmer explained, were *communal*, freely accessed by the villagers; the spring-fed water source had in past times, he revealed, been the place where the villagers would come to wash their clothes. He pointed out the big flat stones at the water's edge, against which bygone inhabitants would beat and scrub their clothes. Judging by the green scum that now covered the entire surface of the pond, this open-air washeteria had been irreversibly superseded by the invention of the electric washing machine.

The dog plunged into the pond, snapping at the frogs, then returned to the path, its long, matted coat dripping wet. I made the fatal error of catching the rangy eyes of the stinking animal, which it mistakenly interpreted as a sign that I wanted to play. As it bounded over, I waved a dismissive hand and the dog leaped into the air, snapping at my outstretched fingers and showering me with what smelled like liquid manure. Landing awkwardly, the dog scrabbled to its three feet and immediately locked its jaws onto the hem of my trouser leg. Shaking its head violently, it emitted a fierce growl. The others, having sauntered after the farmer, were unaware of my plight. I picked up a stick and lobbed it, and the dog released its grip on my jeans and launched itself after the projectile, disappearing with a mournful whimper into the deep drainage ditch that fed into the pond. It emerged filthy, with disgusting silt from the ditch clinging to its coat, the stick clamped in its teeth. As Monsieur L'Heureux turned to investigate the kerfuffle, the wretched dog decided to play for the sympathy vote and hobbled, whining, towards its master. The farmer glowered suspiciously at me and then at his playacting dog.

'Oh, the poor dog!' said Al. 'What did you do to it?'

'Nothing!' I protested. 'The bloody thing attacked me!' At the sound of my voice the devious animal cowered and began to quiver most convincingly. 'Look, the filthy animal's just putting it on! I never touched it. I only threw it a stick.'

'Rich! How could you? The poor animal's only got three legs!'

'Yeah, well it nearly had one of mine, actually!'

'Don't be pathetic, Rich,' said Al, cooing at the phoney canine. 'And watch where you're walking: it smells like you've stepped in something disgusting.'

Now that I had been suitably chastised, we continued along the *chemin*. Half concealed by a barrier of thick gorse and mounds of rough-hewn rock was another expanse of water, in the form of a steep-sided rectangle, which our guide revealed that he had been excavating with the intention of stocking as a fishing lake. Not a particularly attractive feature, Al and I both thought.

'Bit of an ugly-bugly, eh, Boss?' Al whispered. I nodded. I found myself wondering how my three-legged foe would fare trying to scramble out of *that* particular water feature. I glared at the animal, baring my teeth, and he slunk off, tail between his two back legs.

After we had admired the farmer's earthworks – and the pile of old sofas and broken furniture, cardboard boxes, assorted smashed bottles and the rusting hulk of a tractor with only three wheels that languished in an impromptu rubbish heap as a backdrop to the Ugly-Bugly – we were led off the communal path along a leafy walk that passed between an area of dense, bramble-choked woodland on our right, mainly stocked with juvenile oaks, and a marshy area on our left. The little stream that meandered through the marshland was fed, we were told, from a natural spring located on the property. Monsieur L'Heureux indicated the stone trough amongst the reeds where cattle would have been taken to drink. Beyond the woodland, we entered a further field of some two acres in area. An informal path carved through long grass led into a pretty copse of chestnut, hazel and oak trees, with dappled sunlight filtering through the branches.

'And this is all part of the property?' I asked, doubtfully.

Hero consulted our guide. Apparently forgetting again that I was He Who Speaks No French At All, he looked me squarely in the face, tapped a chunky forefinger to one side of his nose as if he was about to impart some secret knowledge to me alone, man to man, and said: '*Écoutez, si vous voulez ce champ aussi, nous pouvons discuter un prix.*' I grinned stupidly and glanced at Al for assistance.

'If we want this field as well, we'll have to discuss the price with him,' Al translated for me.

'How much land is there altogether?' I asked.

'*Combien de terre, Monsieur?*' she asked the farmer.

'*Cinq hectares,*' he replied.

'Five hectares,' she told me.

'That's about thirteen acres, I think,' interjected Hero. 'Whatever would you do with that much land? It's an awful lot to upkeep.'

I recovered my composure and grinned. No problem! 'I'd keep llamas and fly balloons!' I said. I'd always fancied being a landowner and had dreamed of breeding llamas in my dotage (which seemed to have crept ever closer of late).

'Llamas, eh? What do you do with llamas then? Do you ride them?' asked Hero.

'No. No, they can't be ridden,' I explained. 'You can use their fibre – the wool – for spinning, for making knitted clothes. But I'm interested in trekking. Al and I both love long-distance walking and llamas are bred as pack animals. They'll happily carry your tent and belongings.'

'But you still have to walk,' said Hero, raising her perfectly plucked eyebrows in puzzlement. Clearly the concept of hiking was alien to her. She shrugged. 'OK. So you fly hot-air balloons as well? Now that sounds fun!'

'Yes, it is fun! I have my own balloon,' I explained. I was immensely proud of my achievement in gaining a private pilot's licence. Ever since my wife had bought me a birthday flight in a big commercial balloon several years ago I had been hooked on the sport, and the very next day had signed up for an intensive course of instruction with the Sussex-based British School of Ballooning. For the next year I flew as often as I could, clocking up the twenty hours that would enable me to take my flight examinations. To my own surprise I passed with flying colours and immediately commissioned a balloon to be made for me in a striking red and black livery of my own design. I subsequently took to the airways over Kent and Sussex, flying for fun with friends and relatives.

However, flying in England had become a challenge. Many farmers were intolerant of balloons, and pilots' maps were marked with a patchwork of 'sensitive areas' where landing or overflying was inadvisable or prohibited; it had become increasingly difficult to find a place to set one's basket down. However, I still had fond memories of flying in France. A substantial portion of my training had been carried out in Normandy. The attitudes of French and English farmers were starkly different. A common reaction from farmers in the UK, on having a balloon descend uninvited into their field, ranged from mild irritation to intense anger – even illegal impounding of the aircraft at the barrel of a shotgun – while their French counterparts adopted a more laissez-faire attitude, even regarding such a relatively rare event as an honour. The French were aware that ballooning had begun in their country and were rightly proud. On landing, the population of entire villages would turn out to see *la montgolfière* and we aviators were frequently invited back to the farmhouse for breakfast or, after an evening flight, to sample a lethal homebrew. All things considered, I relished the chance to fly again in the clear skies above France.

'Llamas and hot-air balloons, eh?' said Hero, bringing me back to the here and now. 'Well, I've heard it all now!'

Monsieur L'Heureux, who professed to speak no English, smirked cannily as if he understood much more than he let on.

Urged to step over a rickety wire fence at the edge of the copse, we found ourselves enclosed within a tunnel-like, tree-lined pathway, through which the dappled sunlight filtered. This, we were told, was the *route à la Pentecôte*, an ancient communal way of historical and religious significance, which formed part of a pilgrimage held in honour of St Maximin. Each Whit Monday, the longest procession in Europe – *Le Procession des Neuf Lieux* – attracts hundreds of religious devotees who walk more than 50 kilometres, pausing to bless the crosses erected and decorated with flowers by villagers in communes en route. Le Mas Mauvis itself possessed a cross, explained Monsieur L'Heureux proudly, and the hamlet was host each year to many picnickers and other visitors who came to watch the procession pass by.

The farmer parted the overhanging branches of the saplings on the opposite side of the path to reveal a large, dome-shaped rock nestling in the long grass, surrounded by smaller stones.

'*C'est une pierre antique,*' he said.

'An ancient stone?' repeated Al. 'What was its purpose?'

'*Sacrifice,*' said our guide with a theatrical air of mystery and a distinct twinkle in his eye.

'Sacrifice? Animal?' asked Al.

'*Non, pas animal. Sacrifice humain.*'

'Ugh! Human sacrifice!' groaned Al. 'Horrible! Glad that's not part of the property, eh, Rich?'

Without further ado, Monsieur L'Heureux was off, trudging along the pathway, and we scampered after him, little suspecting how the presence of that stone would affect our future lives. Following the swaggering farmer and his reeking three-legged dog, we emerged some minutes later on the little tar road that led through the hamlet, running along the perimeter of an unkempt communal area of grass in the centre of the hamlet.

Several properties ranged around the central grassed area, mainly *petites maisons à la campagne*, humble country cottages with attendant barns and outbuildings, although I could also glimpse a larger, grander *maison* in one corner. The majority of the buildings were partially concealed from view by ancient oak trees, which seemed to encircle the habitation and demarcated most of the surrounding pastures. The prevailing atmosphere was one of intense calm, a scene in which simple farming folk would go about their rural tasks in this quiet corner of the countryside.

As if to emphasise this, as we traipsed along the lane towards the farm, a little red tractor trundled past. Driving was a tall, gaunt man with a drooping moustache, wearing a green boiler suit, and clinging on to the back was a short, slightly hunched man with the same vague expression as his companion. Monsieur L'Heureux raised an arm in greeting, calling out '*Bonjour Cédric! Bonjour Émile!*' but the only sign of acknowledgement either man gave as they rolled past was a simple nod of the head.

Thanking Monsieur L'Heureux profusely for his time, we drove away from Le Mas Mauvis, our minds awhirl with the possibilities offered by owning the farm and its acreage, forcing us to rethink our strategy and to amend our resolve. Impetuous we might have been, but we determined there and then not to leave France without securing this property.

Chapter Four

Baby Wipes and Bureaucracy

So that is how, some three months later, we came to be camping inside the *grange*, awaiting completion of the sale that would make the ramshackle property our very own.

The day after the thunderstorm the constant rain finally abated. We emerged from our tent tired, dishevelled and grumpy after a disturbed sleep. I was also suffering from mild queasiness due to an insufficiently inflated airbed, which threatened to pitch me onto the floor with each slight stir that I made. During the night we had been frequently roused from our slumbers by the sound of the mice squeaking and rummaging around outside the tent.

When we finally gave up trying to sleep and unzipped the tent flap at about seven-thirty in the morning, the rodents made themselves scarce although their pungent smell lingered, a ring of fresh droppings encircling the tent. Descending the ladder, we stepped over the corpse of a hapless chicken that had expired during the night, toppling from its perch on one of the rungs. Pushing the creaky barn doors open, our dark mood lightened when we were greeted with the sight of a cloudless sky of the richest blue and a dazzling sun emitting an intense heat that caused the wet ground, the roof of the barn, and our several layers of damp clothes to steam. We felt a little overdressed.

Impatient to make inroads into the vast clearing up operation the property demanded – the buildings, even the two cottages, had been used as animal houses for a decade or more, and apparently had not been cleaned out in as long – we were hampered by the enduring presence of the cows and their calves, the remnants of the fast-dwindling brood of chickens, and the canine prisoners. Already the date proposed for exchange of contracts had come and gone, due to some unexplained technical hitches. The fact that the farm was not legally ours was all that stayed our hands from letting loose our miserable squatters. Although Monsieur Jérôme (we now addressed our vendor by this vaguely informal name) had promised that the departure of the livestock was imminent, the animals remained entrenched. We were, nonetheless, grateful to be able to camp alongside the livestock.

We were obliged to bide our time, and occupied ourselves by taking copious measurements, drawing up plans for our future home or, at the end of a hectic day, sitting in the barn on our camp chairs, sharing imagined scenarios of the life for which we were laying the foundations.

'Tell me what you're going to be doing when you're a little grey-haired old man living here in Mauvis,' prompted Al dreamily. 'I mean, will you wear dungarees or braces, maybe a straw hat?'

'Definitely braces! Let's see now. I'll be pottering in the garden, I expect,' I responded. 'Tending my vegetables, taking the llamas for a walk, maybe reading a book in the shade of a tree ...'

'While I'm indoors making chutney or vegetable soup,' she offered. 'Or maybe I've taken up knitting.' Now that I just had to see!

Our plans for the main *grange* were to create a somewhat unconventional, upside-down environment, with the main living quarters ranged aloft and guest bedrooms, bathroom and utility room below in the spaces currently occupied by the livestock. This arrangement would enable us to benefit from the splendid westerly views and magnificent sunsets that would be afforded once we had pierced window openings in the back wall of the building – mirroring those in the front wall – overlooking what would eventually become our garden. We were in absolute agreement that we wanted the huge upper storey to form an open-plan space combining the functions of living room, kitchen and dining room. These areas were already visually delineated by an arrangement of roof-supporting trusses that jutted out from the inner faces of the front and back walls, connected at floor level by two stout oak stretcher plates, bracing timbers which we had already become used to stepping over without thinking.

In our plans, a staircase would rise from ground level into the right-hand section, which would also contain a kitchen furnished predominantly with old pine dressers, an island hob unit and butcher's block, and a ceramic butler's sink housed in salvaged pine cupboards. A future stage of the renovation would be to knock a doorway through the thick end wall of the *grange* to connect with the adjoining ancillary barns, which Al had dubbed 'Bill' and 'Ben' for easy identification purposes, but alas, she would constantly confuse the two.

The central section of the main barn was to contain little more than a lengthy dining table, sufficiently large to accommodate a dozen or more diners sitting on an assortment of chairs and benches, while the left-hand section would become a living area furnished with comfortable sofas surrounding a broad, open fireplace of the inglenook design prevalent in medieval English homes. Above this section we proposed to construct a mezzanine floor housing a library and a space for me to write.

Our priority, however, was to elevate the *grange* to a standard of basic habitation that would enable us to carry out further renovations in relative comfort: that is, the installation of electricity, plumbing and sanitation. Of electricity there existed only a rudimentary system within the barn comprising of a few bare, low-wattage light bulbs dangling from the beams. Power was taken from the house on the opposite side of the communal track via an overhead cable (the house, we discovered, was owned and occupied by Monsieur Jérôme's aunt, Madame Véronique Desveaux, and her aged father-in-law). Plumbing consisted of a single black hosepipe that followed the same overhead route as the electric cable, and terminated in the barn at a filthy nozzle that constantly dribbled onto the cobbled floor. Fixed above the mangers were small cast-iron water feeders – *buvettes* – fed by pipework branches taken from the hosepipe, their flow of water controlled (with marginal success) by small internal ball-valves. As for sanitation, there was none on the property – even the cottages pre-dated the advent of the water closet.

Although I am willing to tackle most renovation jobs, I am respectful of electrics and, unfamiliar with the French system, I decided to leave this particular installation to a local tradesman. I likewise fought shy of the initial plumbing work, partly due to the limitations of our vacation and the need to get the renovation work underway. Hero had kindly recommended the services of a local tradesman, Monsieur Cyrille Laborde, who practised both disciplines, and we arranged for him to visit in order to prepare a quotation for carrying out the work. We also contacted another recommended artisan, Monsieur Marcel Fugère, about the installation of a *fosse septique*, or septic tank.

Monsieur Laborde was an excessively jovial man from the outset, a veritable live wire with bulging eyes and an unruly mop of salt-and-pepper hair. His overall demeanour was that of a man who, in the course of his chosen profession, had received one too many electric shocks. Sweeping hyperactively through the barn, he gabbled nonstop in indecipherable French, pausing occasionally to shake his head and shrug, or to slap his forehead and dramatically raise his eyes aloft, as if what we were asking him to do was ludicrous. '*Oh! Non, non, non, non!*' he would cry suddenly. '*C'est impossible!*' Then, scribbling frantically in his notebook, he would look up and fire off a barrage of questions without waiting for a response to any. Whenever Al attempted to elucidate on the wiring diagrams we had carefully prepared for his information, Monsieur Laborde would appear to take no notice, only to interrupt with his own observations. After his energetic performance, however, he merely grinned, tucked our diagrams into his notebook, shook our hands, and with a final '*D'accord! J'comprends! J'comprends! Bon courage!*' was gone, promising to furnish us with a quote before we left for England.

By contrast, Monsieur Fugère – who, in addition to installing *fosses*, was also a stonemason and roofer – was a quiet and unassuming man with a sweet, infectious smile. Unlike the electrically charged Monsieur Laborde, he would listen attentively to Al's faltering description of our sanitary requirements, purse his lips and murmur '*Mais oui, oui, oui, oui, oui! Pas problème!*' With calm professionalism he quietly sketched a diagram on a scrap of paper showing the proposed layout of our sanitation system: a septic tank of some 2,000-litre capacity (adequate to cope with the lavatorial requirements of a small primary school, he assured us) with a herringbone arrangement of underground pipes stemming from it that would filter the waste water away.

Although we had no concrete proof, we suspected that Monsieur Fugère's air of sangfroid was perhaps induced by regular nips from a hip flask, as he would find it necessary to make frequent visits to 'consult papers' in the cab of his van, returning to waft suspiciously alcoholic fumes over us.

Anyone who has experienced the masochistic delights of sleeping under canvas for anything longer than a few nights will appreciate the urgent need to perform more than cursory ablutions. After this duration the term 'roughing it' equates to 'living in squalor'. With no laid-on water supply – the filthy hose dangling in a pool of slurry in the barn simply held no attraction – we cleansed our bodies daily with copious baby wipes. These imbued us with an aroma that evoked the less wholesome aspects of child rearing. The alternative, boiling water in our minuscule camping kettle, produced only enough liquid to wash little more than our faces.

Our toilet facilities, however, were more than adequate. Tiring of the alternative – digging a hole and squatting – we had purchased the splendid Bio-Pot chemical toilet (although, curiously, it bore exactly the same name as our favourite yoghurt). This was a throne indeed, equipped as it was with a comfortable seat and efficient flushing action. We set the Bio-Pot in the open lean-to – formerly a hen hut – that nestled amongst the tall nettles at the back of the barn, where the user could appreciate a panoramic view of the land.

Our personal hygiene dilemma was rectified one day when we dropped by to pay our respects to our next-door neighbour. Madame Desveaux was in her mid-sixties, although life had been hard to her and she could have been mistaken for an older lady. Although not tall, she cut a matronly figure, with a pale, round face and limpid eyes that appeared to be tinged with a measure of sadness. She wore large, clear-framed spectacles, the lenses of which were tinted a kind of nicotine brown, and her grey hair was cut in a short, practical style, trimmed close at the nape of the neck, that is popular with French ladies of her age. She wore a blue-chequered housecoat over her dress and battered, fleece-lined carpet-slippers. Although Madame Desveaux looked after her senile father-in-law, the old man had been in hospital ever since our arrival. Her own health was poor and she was obliged to sleep each night connected to an oxygen supply. Bad circulation in her legs meant that she tended to walk with an awkward swaying motion, supporting herself on a stick that was almost her height.

Madame Desveaux spoke no English and conversed in a heavily accented form of French in which words such as *oui* were pronounced *vee*. We soon discovered that our neighbour loved to chat, and possessed a mischievous, yet always respectful, sense of humour. After that first meeting, we were invited into her warm, if rather spartan, kitchen each day to sit around her big table and sip bowls of hot, fresh black coffee and consume one after another *petits-gâteaux*. After several of these delicious butter biscuits, and despite our protestations – 'Oh, *non merci*, Madame. I've eaten enough!' – she would insist that we eat more until the packet was empty. Al became adroit at shoving her biscuits in front of my cup while Madame's back was turned, so that our host would think I was procrastinating and so would inveigle me to eat up by forcing yet another biscuit on to me: '*Prend le gâteau, Monsieur Richard!*' she would order.

'Oh, Madame, but I'm so full!' I would moan in my by now rudimentary French, rubbing my stomach for emphasis.

'Oh, *non, non, non*, Monsieur Richard. It's very small. *Mangez!*' The biscuit box would be held in front of me until my will was broken, and I would pluck another out with a polite '*D'accord*, perhaps just one more ...'

One afternoon, while we were taking caramel tea (and more biscuits) with our neighbour, she posed an offer, like music to our grimy ears, which we could hardly refuse. '*Voulez vous prener une douche?*' she asked. Would we like to take a shower? Would we ever! Perhaps the smell of baby wipes had proven too much for the dear lady but, from that day on, we would trek across from the barn after a hard day's work, clutching our towels and clean clothes, and bask in the piping hot water from Madame

Desveaux's shower. It was pure bliss to be able to wash our hair at last and for me to be able to wet shave in comfort, and we were eternally grateful for our neighbour's generosity.

After we had washed, we would linger to chat and learn more about this proud, self-sufficient lady for whom we developed a fond affection. After a few visits, she insisted that we call her by her *prénom*, Véronique, and chastised us with a wagging finger should we forget and call her Madame by mistake. In return, she used our first names, although I was always referred to by the title 'Monsieur Richard'. We were also considered worthy of partaking in the French custom of kissing whenever we met for the first time each day, and when saying *au revoir*: not one, not two, not three, but four kisses planted on alternate cheeks.

When Al and I weren't imagining the way we'd spend our days together in Mauvis, we explored the surrounding villages and towns that constituted the area of the Haute-Vienne known as the Pays de Basse-Marche, a grouping of twenty-nine neighbouring communes. At the very heart of the *pays*, the hamlet of Le Mas Mauvis lies in gently undulating farmland about two kilometres south-west of the village of St Léger-Magnazeix, an austere jumble of houses at a junction where several roads intersect and fan out from a central square. La Place itself, a treeless patch of nondescript concrete on which stands a sombre war memorial surrounded by an iron railing, is no longer the site of bustling markets. Numbering about five hundred, the population of the commune is less than a third of the size it was at the turn of the nineteenth century, when many of the menfolk – *maçon-paveurs*, pavers by trade – headed for Paris and other large cities to seek their fortunes, never to return. Old postcards dating from the 1800s show the square resplendent with avenues of juvenile oaks. Known as the Champ de Foire, the fairground, it would have doubtless been the site of carnivals and other visiting attractions. Occasionally, however, small fairgrounds operated by clans of swarthy Gypsies do still appear for the enjoyment of the village's children.

Near the centre of the village is the town hall, or Mairie, a grand, turreted, nineteenth-century *château* with a steeply pitched grey slate roof, its windows framed with white-painted louvre shutters. A high stone wall surrounds the building, which is accessed through ornate wrought-iron gates. Diagonally opposite lies the schoolhouse, the original Mairie. The octagonal bell tower of the twelfth-century Romanesque church, L'Eglise St Maximin, looms over the village, its daunting arched entrance on a sharp bend in the road that leads to the adjoining commune of Mailhac-sur-Benaize. While the body of the church is stone-built, its angular spire is clad with chestnut shingles.

A small *auberge* advertised as '*Nouvelle!*' on a peeling signpost displayed in the square, seems open to customers only infrequently. Apart from a dilapidated automobile service station, a post office and a purveyor of *produits du sol, volaille et vin* (products of the soil, poultry and wine), the village boasts a small grocery store with a spartan *bar-tabac* adjoining. It is in this bar that the neighbourhood menfolk gather to sit at barstools smoking cigarettes, drinking *pastis* and watching football on the huge television screen mounted high above their heads. Few such bars are welcoming to the outsider. Very much a male province, they are generally drab, smoky and bare, furnished with Formica-topped tables, plastic chairs, the walls and ceiling covered with a thick film of nicotine.

If one was brave enough to enter the grocer's – the lack of internal illumination makes it a darkly forbidding prospect – one would be advised to touch nothing without the express permission of the proprietor, a small, bespectacled woman with tiny, pallid features resembling those of a porcelain doll. Al once committed the cardinal sin of opening one of the chiller cabinets that line one wall, in order to take a wedge of cheese, and the door was slammed shut by the diminutive Madame with a terse:

'Do not open this door! You tell me what you want and I will get it for you!'

Al, after checking to see that all her fingernails were still intact, dissolved into grovelling apologies: 'Oh, Madame, *je suis désolé!*' The lady remained stony-faced. We were obliged to select our cheeses through the beads of moisture that coated the inner surface of the door, pointing out the portions we would like, making sure that we did not touch the glass for fear of unleashing her wrath again. The same is true of other provisions: one is not permitted to test the firmness of, say, an apple, pear or avocado but to point to likely looking specimens and hope that they are not hard and unripe. The stress of shopping at this little establishment, although the nearest shop to our hamlet, meant that we tended to drive in the opposite direction, to the larger market town of Magnac-Laval eight kilometres to the south, where we could obtain our provisions from the supermarket without risk of physical danger.

Many of the older residents of the commune still converse amongst each other in one of two ancient patois, or unwritten regional dialects. This is because St Léger-Magnazeix lies within a zone of contact between speakers of the *langue d'Oïl* and the *langue d'Oc* (also called Occitan). The words *Oïl* and *Oc* simply mean 'yes' in these local dialects, which are generally spoken in the northern and southern halves of France respectively. Our neighbour Véronique could be heard to chatter in this unfamiliar rustic speech – regarded as being substandard by language purists – whenever she met her cousin, our electrician-plumber Monsieur Laborde.

The term 'Le Mas' is the dialect name for a farmhouse or a collection of farm buildings, presumably stemming from the verb *masser*, to gather. So in our area alone there were several hamlets known as Le Mas, although we liked to think there was only one Le Mas Mauvis. The origin of the word Mauvis is harder to define, particularly since it is also spelt Mauvy, usually in official documents issued by the Mairie. The former spelling, though, is the French name for a bird, a species of thrush called the redwing (known by the unfortunate Latin name *Turdus iliacus*). As its common name implies, this small bird has reddish flanks, in addition to a bold eye-stripe. Perhaps in times past there was a profusion of these birds in the locale. Quite how this theory squares with our neighbouring hamlet, Le Poux, I do not know, for *poux* is the word for lice. I used to quicken my pace passing through this particular collection of cottages just in case, although the English families we knew of who owned holiday homes at its centre had not been caught surreptitiously scratching their scalps.

Al and I loved to explore the countryside *à pied*, walking for hours at a time along deserted lanes and down the grassy paths that criss-crossed the pastures and woodland. While many of these long-established pathways would peter out after a few kilometres, or were rendered impassable by years of neglect, turning back was no hardship in such pleasant surroundings. Many of the routes, however, are maintained by the local authority to encourage their use by tourists. Some have become trails for the hordes of off-road cyclists drawn to the area during the summer season. Prescribed circuits are marked by colour-coded, numbered signs. For the walker – whether out for an hour's casual stroll, an all-day hike, or a long-distance trek – France is served by an incredible network of 110,000 miles of paths, established and maintained by the *Féderation Française de la Randonnée Pédestre* (FFRP), or French Long Distance Walking Association based in Paris and comprising over 2,000 local clubs.

Most of the land that the paths cross is privately owned and can allow the walker to pass through vineyards, orchards, pastures and forests, and frequently through farmyards and gardens. But the walker will not find the 'Keep out! Trespassers will be prosecuted!' signs that proliferate throughout the English countryside, for there is generally no resistance by local landowners to people crossing their land without asking permission. Individuals, on the other hand, might put up their own signs to discourage others from accessing their property for hunting, for example, or to ensure their privacy or the containment of their livestock.

My favourite way of exploring the locale was to slip on a pair of trainers and go for a run. In England, as a keen club runner, I would regularly compete in road and cross-country races up to marathon distance but, when not racing, running was my personal time. I could be alone with my thoughts, yet able to savour the beauty of the countryside and absorb the details of my surroundings at a pace that varied from a shuffling jog, through loping strides, to brisk sprinting. In running circles this kind of free-form pacing was known by a sniggeringly amusing Swedish word, *fartlek*, meaning 'speedplay'. As cycling is a national pastime, rural French folk think nothing of seeing legions of cyclists clad in shiny, vibrantly coloured Lycra perched atop impossibly flimsy bikes, haring along the highways and byways, but they gawped with uncomprehending amazement at the sight of a sweaty man in his forties, dressed in a dayglo yellow vest and blue tights trotting through their villages. Occasionally, however, a farmer would look up from his work to wave a greeting, or else thump his chest with clenched fist and call out an encouraging '*Bonne course, Monsieur!*', good run! Motorists, too, would usually moderate their typically high-velocity trajectory down the straight roads to give me a wide and sedate berth. This kind of gentle consideration is a far cry from the usual taunts runners receive from passing motorists in England who, when not trying to force you into the verge, seem obliged to yell obscenities or gesticulate lewdly through the window.

Running during spring and summer had its pitfalls, nevertheless. There was an abundance of flying insects to avoid: whilst I could run through and usually outpace a cloud of midges, it was wise to keep my mouth shut while passing, to avoid gulping down several hundred of the insects as a whale will trawl through shoals of tiny fish. Whilst one can safely swallow whole the occasional fly or beetle, I have learned from bitter experience that it's best not to do so with wasps, bees and other stinging insects that might chance to fly straight into the mouth. Running after rainfall was like performing an assault course, with the need to avoid the multitude of orange slugs bent on crossing the road, which tended to explode into a slimy mess when crushed beneath the ergonomically-styled rubber sole of the modern running shoe. A real pain to clean out of the treads later, I can vouch.

Running also had its dangers. On one particularly memorable run I narrowly missed being savaged by overprotective farm dogs on three separate occasions; they ran down the lane after me, snapping at my heels. Not long after, gazing at the countryside unfolding around me rather than the road ahead, I tripped over a large, very dead white goat lying on the verge at the roadside. A few seconds later my nostrils were assaulted by a foul stench that made me want to gag. The disgusting smell became identifiable as that of an abattoir, as I trotted past a high-fenced compound containing a row of bleak byres and an ancient, derelict and ivy-covered building. A bold notice affixed to the heavily secured gates stated: '*INTERDICTION de déposer de cadavres sous peine de poursuites!*', which, as I upped my running pace, I was able to loosely translate as a ban on dumping corpses outside the property. Perhaps the owner of the deceased goat could not read.

The sight of creatures lying dead and rotting at the roadside – whether the result of a traffic accident or an encounter between rival predators – was one of the less wholesome aspects of running in France and I was soon able to distinguish the scent of death from a distance of several paces, and hold my breath as I loped past.

On the whole, running in the sunshine in this rural oasis on largely traffic- and corpse-free lanes was sheer joy. I could run for ten miles and encounter but a single vehicle, and scarcely see another human. My time. A chance for me to empty my head of niggling worries and woes. To focus on the beauty of the countryside. Passing a field of grazing Limousin cows with their frisky calves, the animals would be startled and shy away at first. But then one brave soul would start to canter alongside, peering at me over the hedge line, and was soon joined by the entire herd. I would stop and converse with these docile creatures, rather one-sidedly, before continuing on my way.

After exploring the locale, Al and I would turn our minds to more immediate, if less tasteful tasks, such as removing the assortment of junk and mounds of animal dung that filled areas of the barns we had free access to. It was while we were hauling an aged refrigerator, its top encrusted with chicken droppings, from one of the barns that we received unexpected visitors. Al was busy extricating the flattened, mummified corpse of a rat from where it had apparently lain for years beneath the appliance, while I had been tentatively examining the interior of the fridge, which seemed to contain the previously frozen internal organs of an unidentifiable animal. We were alerted by the sound of footsteps squelching through the mud behind us and turned around to be greeted by a jovial couple beaming at us.

'*Bonjour!*' boomed the man with gusto, beaming widely. He resembled Ronnie Corbett, the smaller of the Two Ronnies, both in features and in stature (although he lacked the trademark horn-rimmed spectacles). A smiling, kindly looking lady, some inches taller than he was, accompanied him. They held out their hands for us to shake.

'Hello. My name's Gordon Timpson,' said the man. 'This is my wife, Maureen. Welcome to Le Mas Mauvis!'

His wife spoke: 'We'd noticed someone camping in the field and were worried you might have been washed away in all this rain. It's been really terrible, hasn't it?' The lady had a soft, motherly face, and her greying hair flecked with highlights was trimmed short and neat. She stood, hands clasped to her chest as if to say: 'Now, what can I do to help you?'

Al and I introduced ourselves and thanked them for their concern.

'We thought you might appreciate a drink and a chance to dry out one evening,' said Gordon. 'We live in the house over there.' He gestured behind him. Although we were reticent about being drawn into the community of British ex-pats we knew to exist in the area and keen to mingle with the French inhabitants, we were thrilled with the opportunity to escape the confines of the tent for a brief respite and readily accepted the invitation.

Over drinks and nibbles we learned that Gordon and Maureen had bought the tall farmhouse and attendant buildings we could just see from our back field four months earlier and, freed from the ties of their grown-up family, had upped sticks and moved permanently from England for the benefit of Maureen's health. Maureen suffered from multiple sclerosis and they hoped that the kinder climate would benefit her (ironically, however, the weather had been unseasonably dreadful since their arrival). Such was the nature of Maureen's illness that she could awake on some mornings and be unable to move her arms or legs or to get out of bed, and had in the past even been confined to a wheelchair.

Gordon and Maureen's grand plan was to renovate the property (which they had also bought from our vendor, Monsieur Jérôme) and take in bed and breakfast guests. Maureen, by all accounts an accomplished cook, harboured a wish to start a vegetarian cookery school at the house: a bold, somewhat bizarre notion given that French cuisine generally pays only fleeting lip service to food *sans viande*. The effusive Monsieur Laborde and his stoic accomplice Monsieur Jean-Philippe had been given the task of rewiring the entire house and installing several bathrooms. After months of daily attendance, however, the project was still far from completion and Gordon and Maureen were worried that the central heating system would not be installed before the onset of winter.

The couple had brought their beloved pets with them from England: Jess, a kind of midget black and tan German Shepherd equipped with the diminutive legs of a Dachshund; Floss, reputedly a spaniel beneath the white candyfloss ball of hair that engulfed her;

and Marmalade, an obese and antisocial ginger tomcat. Jess had assumed for himself the role of guard dog and this cantankerous and intensely nosy individual would constantly burst in and out of the enormous dog flap in the kitchen door to check out every passing tractor and would totter, growling, towards anyone who dared pass along the lane at the front of the house. His shortness of leg, however, ensured that any potential interlopers were long gone by the time he reached the end of the driveway.

Aged Floss – deaf, blind and apparently without a sense of smell, or in fact any sense at all – wandered around her new home in a daze. Like a child's battery-run toy that will continue its forward motion no matter what obstruction lies ahead, Floss would frequently be found with her nose pressed against a wall, yet persisting with her forward momentum. Spun around by helping hands, the animal would continue on its way towards the next obstacle.

Another animal turned up that evening, in the form of Monsieur Jérôme's three-legged cow dog, who Al and I had named Tripod.

'The poor animal's always starving,' explained Maureen as she doled out a tin of dog food, which was bolted down ravenously by the dog. 'Jérôme only ever feeds his dogs bread and milk. It's disgusting. Animals can't survive on just that! Look how hungry the poor creature is.'

However, I suspected that Tripod – driven by greed or the need to store up fat for lean times ahead – was merely working a scam on his English benefactors. I had noticed a mound of chicken bones beneath his shelter back at the farm. The dog was often seen sloping off with one of the fast depleting brood of hens that occupied our barn clamped firmly between his jaws.

After a pleasant evening of convivial conversation, Al and I wished our hosts goodnight and, escorted off the premises by a dutiful Jess, wandered back along the lane to the barn by the dim light of our torch, reflecting that we were lucky to have such interesting and kindly neighbours.

The next morning, a Sunday, we awoke to the sound of the hounds barking loudly, and rushed downstairs in time to see the entire pack, released from their prison cell, excitedly milling around the legs of a group of about half a dozen men dressed more or less identically in waxed jackets, thick trousers, high boots and sporting caps. Each carried a shotgun and a canvas bag slung over their shoulders. Monsieur Jérôme waved his arm and the troupe set off down the communal track, the hounds racing before them, eager for the thrill of the hunt. Slouched on Véronique's doorstep, jaw resting on his single front paw, a bloated Tripod gazed after his master and the departing pack of hounds with a look of dejection in his expressive eyes. Once the coast was clear, however, he hobbled off to beg breakfast from Maureen. Soon we heard the sound of spasmodic gunfire, seemingly all around us, which continued for the entire day without respite.

The hunting season in France has the reputation, not entirely a misconception, that each year men and women take to the fields and the woods to pit their wits, stealth, and their tracking and shooting skills against virtually any hapless creature that dares to break cover. While the season is, in reality, closely regulated by the local *préfecture*, it is true that the hunters' choice of game is broad, whether it is the graceful skylark, the cute rabbit, the majestic deer, or the ferocious wild boar. I suspect, however, that the Frenchman's love of *la chasse* has less to do with gastronomy than target practice.

Due to European Union directives, in the late nineties the open season in hunting was reduced to between 1 September and 31 January. Violent protests were staged by militant hunters, who claimed that they had traditional rights to shoot migratory birds, including wild geese and ducks, egrets, herons and woodcocks, during the months of August and February. The conflict was even exploited by a new political movement – the *Chasse, Peche, Nature, Tradition*, or CPNT – some of whose leaders were previously connected with the French far right. This hunting, shooting and fishing party made inroads into the European elections in 1999, winning over some staunch hunting districts such as Normandy and the Somme.

The new hunting laws in France were difficult to police. Throughout the entire sprawling country there were only 1,400 gamekeepers and their jobs could be quite risky. Two gamekeepers were shot dead in 1997 and two years later another seventeen were kidnapped by militant hunting groups and threatened with death unless they resigned from their jobs.

While the strict new dates for the hunting season were set, local authorities were permitted to extend them from 10 August until 20 February – according to demand – for some unfortunate species of wading birds, and the snipe, woodcock, dove, quail and skylark. Wednesday, a day when French schoolchildren do not attend school, was sensibly made a non-hunting day.

Hunters marching across private property had long been a disturbance, intrusion and safety hazard to French landowners wishing to protect the natural environment or simply avoid being shot. However, thirty *départements* had subscribed to a restrictive law called the *Loi Verdeille*. Under this law a landowner did not have the right to refuse access to his property for hunting and could only protect certain animals therein if he owned a minimum of between twenty and sixty hectares. Backed by the French Animal Rights League, the law was overruled by the European Court of Human Rights in April 1999. However, with the French love of bureaucracy, the process would only be enforceable after five years, during which time the beleaguered landowner could be subject to hostile outside pressures and buckle.

In any event, barring the *chasse* from one's land was not regarded as being sportsmanlike by certain staunch members of the hunting fraternity. My brother, who had been disturbed by the sight of a terrified young deer being pursued across his land by hunters, had been warned against displaying notices such as '*Chasse interdit*' at the perimeter of his field by his concerned neighbour: '*Prudence,*

Phillippe! You may arrive *en vacances* to find gunshot holes in your windows.' This would be mild retribution indeed in the light of other shocking cases that have been recorded: one British farmer in France had his sheep slaughtered, while a lamb callously had its front feet cut off before being left to die; another ex-pat Brit based in the Dordogne received the threat that his woodland would be set ablaze unless he withdrew his application to ban hunters from his land.

While Monsieur Jérôme's hounds were away, Al and I took the opportunity to enter their lair for the first time and, carefully picking our way across the sea of stinking excrement, discovered a room at the back of the barn which we had not even known existed. The upper floor of the barn, gingerly accessed by a pair of stepladders, was covered in a mound of hay soaked by the rain that poured through the gaping hole in the tiled roof. We took copious measurements of this barn and transferred them to our plans for future reference.

When the hunters returned with spoils filling their shoulder bags and hanging from their belts, it was, however, without several of Monsieur Jérôme's hounds. Unimpressed with *la chasse*, they appeared to have taken their brief freedom as a chance to abscond. The remaining dogs were ushered back into the barn and the door secured. Over the next few days we would see the escapees slinking back to the farm to feed on what poor, defenceless chickens Tripod had spared. We witnessed Monsieur Jérôme tempting them back to the fold with tasty morsels or, when that failed, springing from a hiding spot in an attempt to apprehend the wily animals. But his efforts were to no avail. Eventually he gave up, granting the dogs their freedom.

By the end of our two-week holiday, contracts had still not been exchanged and we were beginning to feel distinctly uneasy. Monsieur Jérôme merely shrugged and claimed to know of no reason why the sale had not been completed, and the estate agent seemed similarly in the dark. Hero promised to speak to Madame Marsolet on our behalf and report back with news. We were assured that there was no problem: the delay was simply caused by the need to feed the ravenous and obese French bureaucracy with a veritable gourmet feast of paperwork in duplicate, triplicate and quadruplicate. The fact that many government and associated offices closed for the month of August – France's traditional summer holiday period – also contrived to hinder the smooth flow of documentation and responses to the *notaire*'s legal searches.

We decided to extend our holiday by another week and remain in France so that we could attend the completion of the sale, when the property would at last become ours. It was important to us to experience as much of the process of buying the farm as possible: the alternative being to assign Power of Attorney to another party, who could sign the necessary documents at completion.

The additional week gave us the opportunity to arrange for appointments with the water and electricity companies for the provision of water and power to the property: the existing systems, apart from the fact that they were connected to Véronique's own supply, were totally inadequate. For the former it would be necessary for a 25-metre-long trench to be dug along the track leading to the farm from the water main that served the hamlet: costly but necessary. For the latter, we had the choice between an overhead cable taken from the ugly *poteau* – a kind of miniature concrete pylon – situated on the common land, to the existing iron bracket that protruded obtrusively from the front wall of the barn, or an underground cable. There appeared to be little price difference, so we opted for the less visible method.

We were also paid a visit by an insurance broker recommended to us by Monsieur Jérôme, who gave us the happy news that our insurance premium would remain reasonably low until we had upgraded the property from agricultural building to habitation, while covering us for the usual risks. Messieurs Laborde and

Fugère returned brandishing their quotes for the electrical, plumbing and sanitation work, which we promised to study. After each tradesman had left, our vendor would conveniently and mysteriously appear in the barn to enquire as to the price we had been quoted. We tried to be vague.

'There are many English here, and they have a lot of money,' Monsieur Jérôme explained. '*L'Anglais* are like ducks ready for plucking!' He winked mischievously. Was he merely being helpful, warning us to be wary of loaded quotations from unscrupulous artisans, or was there another agenda?

At the end of that extra week, the situation regarding our purchase remained unchanged and we were obliged to pack up our tent and head back to England and our respective jobs. Investing Hero with the authority to sign the contract on our behalf, we left Le Mas Mauvis early on our last morning – after taking coffee with Véronique – thoroughly disheartened. As we drove that long route back, silent and insular, each kilometre seemed to wrench us further from the myriad dreams of the new life we so craved, and brought flooding back the problems that lay in wait for us in our other lives. We felt a sense of foreboding, nausea in the pit of our stomachs, that we would feel each time we were obliged to leave France. For a short while we had escaped the pressures of work, the tussles of divorce, the fragile health of Al's sister – and the taste of that escape was sublime. We arrived back in England exhausted and deflated.

Chapter Five

Mangers and Mushrooms

I returned to work the next day to discover that, during my absence, further internal restructuring had resulted in my old boss leaving to set up his own business, handing the reins over to his deputy, the capable Kenny. Sympathetic, supportive, and an ally with whom I had formed a close friendship since joining the company, Kenny broke the news that he was unable to offer me more than one week's work.

'I'm sorry, I can't promise you anything more just yet, Rick,' Kenny apologised to me in his soft Scottish lilt. 'My hands are tied. But maybe in two or three weeks' time, when the dust has settled …'

'Sure,' I said, from that all-too-familiar empty space that exists beyond disappointment. I seemed to be so used to setbacks that they scarcely fazed me any more.

On my return home that evening, Al was as upbeat as ever. 'Never mind, old fruit! Keep positive. There's always a Plan B,' she said with conviction, shaking me by the shoulders. I looked doubtful. 'And if that fails, there's a Plan C, and Plan D and so on.'

'So what's Plan B then?'

'I don't know yet. But I'm sure it'll turn up.'

Plan B came rapping its knuckles on our door later that same week, when we received a fax from Hero informing us that we were now the proud owners of the farm. It transpired that no sooner had we returned to England than the slumbering giant of French bureaucracy awoke from its vacation and the purchase was promptly completed. It came to light that the main hold-up had been the existence of several financial charges on the property, which had somehow become buried in paperwork and surfaced only at the last minute. Before the sale could be completed it was necessary for our vendor to pay his debts and have the charges lifted.

The statement of ownership – the *Attestation de Propriété* – became the subject of much celebration and consumption of champagne that evening, when we were joined for supper by our friends the ubiquitous Birdie and Doug, her partner. Now that we owned the farm, what was to be our next move? It was clear that we needed to put meat on the bones of Plan B.

'Look,' said Al, when we were alone. 'Kenny says he hopes to have work for you in two or three weeks. While that's by no means certain, the old goat wouldn't say it if he didn't think that there was a strong possibility, would he?'

'No.' The old goat was not one to beat about the bush.

'And it could take you a couple of weeks to find freelance work elsewhere.'

'I guess so.' I was beginning to see the direction in which Al's logic was leading me. It was not that I was entirely without earning capacity, for I still wrote occasional features for various magazines. In fact, I had been commissioned to write a series of articles on renovating houses in France for the English language magazine *Living France*, after I had approached the editor, Trevor Yorke, with the suggestion. The deadline for the first article was fast approaching, and I had yet to do the research.

'So let's turn these few weeks to our advantage, Rich,' Al continued. 'I've got work that'll pay the immediate bills. You take the opportunity to go back to Mauvis and start the renovation. That's Plan B!'

So, one week later, at the beginning of October, I found myself unexpectedly returning to France to take vacant possession of our farm at Le Mas Mauvis. Autumn had brought with it a bitter chill that precluded camping in the barn. A telephone call to Gordon and Maureen, however, had secured me a room in their home as a paying bed and breakfast guest. This was an ideal solution, for it meant that I would be virtually on site for the work I had planned to carry out over the following fortnight. By lucky coincidence, my brother was returning to his own house in France for a two-week period of renovation work and we agreed to assist each other with jobs requiring two pairs of hands. After spending the first evening with my brother, I left him to his work the next day and drove over to Le Mas Mauvis feeling apprehensive. It was a strange sensation to realise that the property actually belonged to us now.

First and foremost on my list of jobs to tackle was the need to clear up after the evacuation of the livestock from the premises. However, this was easier said than done. A clause had been inserted in the final contract by Madame Marsolet, which required our vendor to remove any possessions, including animals, still remaining on the property, but within what we thought was an overly generous period of two months. During our previous stay we had successfully confined to one barn most of the items Monsieur Jérôme regarded as valuable possessions (although to the untrained eye it was rubbish), and my joy at inspecting the property on this visit was tempered by the fact that much of the farm machinery and most of the isolated junk still remained. Although he had removed the herd of cows and their calves to his new farm, the pack of hunting dogs and the mangy cockerel were still ensconced in their respective hovels. In a field at the back of his aunt's property, Monsieur Jérôme and two of his nephews had begun to construct a wire-fenced compound, resembling a prisoner of war camp, to confine the dogs. The fate of the poor chickens, however, was unclear and frankly unpromising.

The slavering black beast that had been housed in the barn adjoining that of the hunting dogs had also been relocated to more salubrious quarters. He was now chained to a flea-infested kennel adjacent to Véronique's front door. His restraint was thankfully not long enough to permit him to savage visitors to the house, but not short enough to prevent him from lunging, growling and drooling from his dark pit whenever anyone approached, scaring the living daylights out of them. As a guard dog, Tom – as Véronique introduced me to him from a safe distance – was second to none, although he was unable to distinguish between friend and foe.

'Don't go near *le chien*, Monsieur Richard! He might bite,' said Véronique, wagging an admonishing finger at me when I arrived for coffee and biscuits one morning. The warning was unnecessary: I suspected Tom's propensity to bite first and ask questions later, and had no intention of getting any closer to this understudy to the Hound of the Baskervilles.

'Where's Tripod?' I enquired.

'Gone,' said Véronique bluntly, with a dismissive shrug. She lit the gas under the little pan of water she used to make coffee.

'Gone to Jérôme's new farm, eh?' I took my customary seat at the table.

'*Décédé*,' replied Véronique, scooping coffee grains into the filter.

'Dead? Oh, I am sorry, Véronique.'

'Why? He wasn't much help with *les vaches*. He became *obèse*. Too slow. I don't know, but I think he was scrounging food from someone.' She eyed me suspiciously. I blushed.

'Oh,' I said. 'That's terrible …'

Although Monsieur Jérôme had also intimated that he intended to muck out and pressure-clean the cattle pens and shovel out the mass of dog excrement from their quarters, I assumed that these tasks would be carried out in typical French fashion – that is, at some unspecified time in the future. Fired with enthusiasm, I was too impatient to wait. So, armed with shovel and wheelbarrow, and wearing overalls and wellingtons, I began to tackle this unsavoury task on my own. Digging out tons of deep litter from the cows' pen, I ferried it to a spot I had allotted as a temporary compost heap. Even wearing a facemask, the rancid stench of the dung made me want to retch: the deeper I dug, the fouler it became, assuming a thick, sludge-like consistency. After two days and countless barrowloads – and after I had dug down over half a metre – I finally reached the solid, roughly cobbled surface of the pen. From the doorway at the front of the building the floor sloped towards the back, its sides angled inwards to form a trench that led to a single drainage gully, long since clogged with straw and faeces; the pipe that was intended to drain excess slurry from the building was also blocked. Once this pen had been cleared, I started on the one on the opposite side of the barn, which thankfully contained less depth of litter, its gully clear enough to drain off most of the slurry.

At last I was able to survey the entire ground floor of the *grange* unencumbered. Al and I had decided that the central section, which contained the mangers, would become a spacious open hallway, with central corridors leading into the pens at each side of the slatted oak dividing walls. We wanted to retain the oak slats as surface features of the hall wall by fixing partition walls behind them. Another opening would be created to the right-hand side of the main barn entrance to access a staircase leading to the *grenier* floor. On one side, in the first pen I had cleared out, the space would be divided into two guest bedrooms separated by a small shower room and WC. On the other side we would create a storeroom and, off a dog-leg in the corridor, another shower room and WC – a room where a weary, grimy gardener could, after a hard day's weeding, enter from a back door, disrobe and bathe without having to traipse through the house. At a future stage, another entrance would also be created from this hallway to lead into the ground floor of the adjoining barn.

We considered the concrete mangers to be oppressively large, curving intrusively into the central hall. While friends who had seen the many photographs we had taken of the property suggested that the mangers could be retained and utilised as lidded storage containers, Al and I had become less sure as time went on. Apart from the fact that we had discovered families of rats inhabiting their core, we felt they were just too huge, standing a good metre high and half a metre wide. We decided to demolish them. In their place we would create concrete plinths from their bases that could double as seating and places on which to set items of furniture and indoor plants.

The floor in the central section of the barn was reasonably sound and damp-free, but the two former animal pens would require new concrete floors to be cast. I decided that I would be able to utilise the demolished mangers as hardcore to pack out the sub-floors in the outer sections, in preparation for the casting of the concrete. After breakfasting with Gordon and Maureen one morning, I slung my weighty sledgehammer over one shoulder and set off, whistling, to begin the task of smashing up the mangers. No sooner had I started than I realised that the job was going to be more problematic than I had thought.

Gripping the sledgehammer firmly by its shank in my gloved hands, I hefted it over my shoulder and swung it around in a graceful arc. The head of the tool made contact with the curved underside of the manger, which responded with the resonance of a huge church bell. Waves of vibrations shuddered through the shank of the sledgehammer, along my arms, up my neck and into my skull, leaving my ears ringing loudly. Every action has a reaction, and mine was that I was sent reeling backwards like a novice hammer-thrower. Disoriented, I dropped the sledgehammer and stood there twitching, teeth chattering, eyes rolling.

When I had recovered my composure, I inspected the mangers more carefully and determined that they were reinforced internally with a framework of metal rods. If I were to succeed with my demolition, it would be necessary to find and infiltrate a weak spot in their construction. I located a thin crack in one section and carefully began to chop into this with a bolster chisel and club hammer. When the crack had widened enough for me to insert the blade of a hacksaw, I cut through the reinforcing rod that ran within the manger's outer rim. To my delight, the next time I took a swing at the structure with my sledgehammer, the concrete shattered into hundreds of fragments. Monsieur Jérôme, passing by the front of the barn in his tractor, must have had his suspicions about my slender grasp on sanity confirmed, to see me jigging triumphantly amongst the ruin of the mangers, manic laughter issuing from my mouth.

To form the entrances to the proposed corridors, I needed to free a section of the oak beams from the slatted partition walls that divided the barn into thirds. Housed at the top in mortises cut in the massive oak ceiling beam, they were encased in mortar at their bases. Keen to salvage the timbers, I chiselled away the mortar to release them, then hauled them out of the way – I could barely lift one of the timbers on my own – before levering out the huge boulders that constituted the foundations of the mangers with a pickaxe. The room resembled the epicentre of a minor earthquake, with tons of rubble and ugly twists of metal littering the floor.

With the mangers finally reduced to chunks of concrete, I began to barrow this hardcore into the adjoining sections through my newly formed entrances, tipping it onto the cobbled floor. To my amazement, the demolished mangers, when firmly rammed down, barely filled one of the sections. In order to make my new concrete floor level, I would need to raise the surface substantially. Cannibalising the concrete breezeblock walls that divided the pigpens in the small cottage, I barrowed this rubble onto my foundations, but it was still not enough. Resorting to more drastic tactics, I borrowed Gordon's little trailer and trundled several loads of rough-hewn stone from the rocky area adjacent to our fish lake, the Ugly-Bugly; the spoil from Monsieur Jérôme's earthworks. Having raised the sub-floor level so that it was reasonably flat, I needed to add a layer of sand to fill the voids in the surface. Using my best sign language, I arranged for the delivery of a truckload of coarse sand from a local builders' merchant, and this was delivered the same day and dumped in the hangar. Barrowing loads of sand to the barn, I tipped it over the foundations and raked it out. A rudimentary system of datum pegs and planks determined the finished surface, minus a fifteen-centimetre allowance for the thickness of the concrete.

From time to time Monsieur Jérôme would appear in the cart entrance, gaze about him at the scene of devastation I had wreaked, scratch his head, sigh, then depart saying 'Bon courage, Richard. Bon courage.'

Each evening when it had become too dark for me to see to work – for there was now no electricity in the building, with the disconnection of Monsieur Jérôme's temporary supply – I would crawl back to the hospitality of Gordon and Maureen's house and, after a much needed shower, would slump into a chair at their kitchen table and chat to Gordon while Maureen busied herself preparing a meal. At that time, their gas Rayburn cooker, although fixed in position against the chimney breast, had yet to be connected up by Monsieur Laborde, and their only source of cooking was a small two-burner stove housed in the caravan parked on the driveway a few metres from the kitchen door. Wearing a thick winter coat, Maureen would scuttle in and out of the kitchen armed with bowls of prepared ingredients, returning some minutes later with steaming pans of delicious food. Gradually invigorated by a combination of nourishment and the restorative qualities of a bottle of Calissou Douze (at the equivalent of sixty pence a litre, exceedingly cheap but palatable *vin rouge de table*), I would wait for Al to telephone from England before retiring with the phone to the cosy *salon* just off the kitchen. During lengthy nightly conversations, we would each recount the events of the day and our plans for the next.

Each morning I would rise early and stagger back to the barn to find that the rats had burrowed into my carefully prepared foundations, leaving gaping holes.

One afternoon at Gordon and Maureen's house, the plumbing half of Monsieur Laborde's business, the stoic, droopy-moustachioed Jean-Philippe, knocked on the kitchen door and humbly offered a large plastic bag full of *champignons*, which he said he had gathered for our pleasure. The mushrooms, shaped like little trumpets, were small and jet black, with a strong earthy aroma.

'What are these called, Jean-Philippe?' asked Maureen, after thanking the plumber for his thoughtful gift.

'*Trompettes d'Amour*,' mumbled the Frenchman. '*Une spécialité*.'

'Oh, how lovely! Trumpets of love! How romantic!' sang Maureen, touched by the man's generosity. She gave him two smacking kisses on his cheeks, leaving him blushing. 'And how do you cook them, Jean-Philippe?'

'Heuh, *c'est facile*. You just *faire sauter* with a little butter and black pepper. *Et voilà*, you eat them with some bread.'

We ate the mushrooms that evening as a delicious starter on little squares of toast, reflecting upon how difficult it was to identify the edible mushrooms from the poisonous.

'Personally, I wouldn't risk it!' said Gordon, tucking into his portion of mushrooms. 'I just wouldn't trust my judgement. I mean, you could make yourself very ill, or even kill yourself if you picked the wrong variety.'

Maureen and I agreed with his wise words. It was good that Jean-Philippe seemed to be a skilled mushroom-gatherer. You could always trust the local people. That was the best guide. The following morning, however, Monsieur Laborde cast doubt on his accomplice's abilities and seemed to find the whole episode highly amusing.

'Purff! I wouldn't eat anything Jean-Philippe picked up in a wood,' he chuckled. 'I hope he was wearing his glasses at the time! Ha! Ha! Ha!'

Jean-Philippe shuffled into the room and handed Maureen a scrap of paper with a name written on it. 'I'm no expert, Madame,' he announced rather worryingly. 'But this is the name of the *champignons* I gave you yesterday, so you will remember them for the future.'

Maureen read the name and her eyes widened alarmingly. She swallowed hard. When the *plombier* had gone outside to pee on the drive, as was his frequent habit (despite the fact that he had just installed four toilets in the house), she handed me the paper.

'I'm not sure how to take this,' she said. It seemed that the mushrooms were not called *Trompettes d'Amour* after all. We must have misheard the plumber's mumbled words. Instead, they were known by the similar-sounding name *Trompettes de Mort*, or Trumpets of Death. Maybe Jean-Philippe's kind gift hid a more sinister undertone.

After my first week of strenuous manual labour, I felt in need of a more relaxing sojourn, and set off to visit my brother Phill. Since purchasing our respective properties in France, we had exchanged light-hearted if somewhat juvenile banter, which concerned the relative perceived merits of our *départements*. My brother, jokingly boasting that the Creuse was far superior to our own Haute-Vienne, had styled himself as Le Comte de Mandrezat, with Al and I as mere *paysans*, peasants who lived in a barn with the animals, fit only to toil on the land. Although he wasn't far off the mark, I was not to be outdone.

'Tell me, Count,' I asked one day. 'What does the word *Haute* mean, as in Haute-Vienne?'

'High, if I'm not mistaken.'

'That's right. High, as in superior, as in the opposite of low. And have you any idea what *Creuse* means?'

'I suppose you're going to tell me in any case ...'

'It means hollow, as in hole in the ground. I rest my case. Who's the peasant now?'

'*Touché,*' replied Phill.

'Welcome to my *région*, peasant,' he greeted me this time as I stepped from my lowly vehicle and, taking his hand, bowed humbly. 'Good job you've turned up, peasant,' he said flatly. 'You can help me fix my leaky roof.'

My brother baulked at the thought of scaling the alarmingly lofty height of his *grenier* roof, despite the fact that for many years he was apt to leap from clifftops dangling from a hang-glider, or take to the skies in a microlight aeroplane powered by little more than a souped-up lawnmower engine. However, a frightening incident while piloting a small plane, in which he fainted at an altitude of 3,000 feet, quashed his nerve for aviation to the extent that he would drive miles out of his way to avoid crossing a high bridge, and was intensely nervous of scaling ladders. Although I am a qualified balloon pilot, and supremely confident when suspended from a nylon bag of hot air in an oversized laundry basket, I also suffer from a mild form of vertigo, specifically when still connected to the ground. With me, it's a poor sense of balance rather than a fear of heights.

The usual method for accessing roofs is by a special ladder incorporating a big hook at the top to suspend over the ridge. Many French roofs are equipped with hooks secured to the rafters to which a normal ladder can be attached. But as we gazed up at the steep pitch of my brother's roof from ground level we both came to the same conclusion.

'There's absolutely no bloody way I'm going clambering about on *that* roof!' I announced, hands squarely on hips to indicate my steadfast resolve to stay firmly rooted to the ground.

'Me neither!' agreed the Count, paling visibly at the very thought. 'Maybe we can do it from inside …'

Repair a roof from inside? It was just crazy enough to work. And what brilliant research for the article I was about to write for *Living France* magazine, which, coincidentally, was on the subject of roof repairs in France! It would still mean working at height but, with an adequate system of scaffolding, would be safer than scrabbling about on the roof itself. We erected Phill's scaffold tower on the *grenier* floor to enable us to reach the underside of the roof, and drew straws for who would be the one to scale to the summit. I lost.

French roofs are broadly similar to English ones: the covering – of clay or concrete tiles – is attached to battens nailed across rafters. On some older properties, such as my brother's, the battens are short lengths spanning two rafters, fixed end-to-end across the roof (in the UK battens are long lengths providing a continuous fixing across the roof). This was fortuitous, enabling us to remove a small area for access to the roof surface from below.

The clay tiles overlapped and interlocked with their neighbours. The roof was not underfelted, so I pushed a tile up from the lower edge and, wiggling it free, pulled it between the battens. Removing a section of tiles and battens allowed me to squeeze between the rafters, emerging just below the ridge. It was disconcerting to have only the underside of the rafters to grip onto, which was all that prevented me from sliding down the slope towards the gutter and the four-metre drop from there to the ground. The mortar bedding the top row of half-round ridge tiles was cracked, allowing rain to leach in. I relaid the affected tiles on fresh mortar mixed by Phill from the safety of the *grenier* floor six metres below, hauled to my perch in a bucket on a rope.

After what seemed like an age, and with my nerves pretty frayed, I clambered down from the scaffold tower immensely self-satisfied. In celebration, we opened bottles of beer and clinked them together: '*Salut!*'

'Hungry?' asked the Count, rummaging in one of the kitchen cupboards. He produced a large clear glass jar containing what appeared to be laboratory specimens suspended in chemicals.

'Err, I was ...'

'Cassoulet. Delicious,' said Phill. I had seen these jars of animal parts in supermarkets before but had never been brave enough to try them.

'Yeah, sure,' I said. 'If this is what the locals eat, I'm game.'

The meal of cassoulet was indeed delicious and warming. We sat around the wood-burning *cuisinière* sipping wine; a satisfying end to a productive day. Phill and I drank and chatted until the wee hours about our plans for our respective French properties and reminiscing about our childhood.

As children Phill and I had waged continual warfare against each other. When I was a mere bald and toothless babe dribbling in my pram, my impish toddler brother – in the grip of the green-eyed monster of jealousy – could not resist a surreptitious nip as he passed, leaving me disfigured for life with cauliflower ears. In our youth, he would assail me with bow and arrow, air pistol or spear, while I would retaliate with catapult or well-aimed dart launched into the bone of his shin. Ensuing age and experience had mellowed our petty rivalries to the extent that in adulthood we were satisfied merely to exchange torrents of good-natured banter.

Phill and I were born in Newcastle upon Tyne, but our family had drifted southwards, settling first in a village on the outskirts of Kendal in the Lake District, then in suburban Manchester. On leaving school, I attended art college, being dissuaded from my dream of being a journalist by a dismissive and short-sighted careers master. Two years later, after completing a foundation course in fine art and design, I became disillusioned and dropped out. Dropping out from art college was, in the late sixties, quite unique, as dropouts populated most art establishments. In so doing, however, I found myself unemployable either as a budding fine artist or as a graphic designer in a commercial studio.

One morning, however, my eyes lit upon a classified advertisement in my father's *Daily Telegraph*, detailing the establishment of a one-year pre-entry course in periodical journalism at the London College of Printing, in the exotic-sounding locale of the Elephant & Castle. Seizing the opportunity to escape the depressing North, I fished out a garish, broad striped, bell-bottomed suit with enormous lapels and attended an interview at the college. Gaining entry to the course – one of only twenty-nine guinea pigs – I packed my bags and headed for London and a new life.

Circumstance and distance had separated my brother and me: some years later, he had divorced and remarried, while I had married a southern girl who attended the same journalism course as me. Work and love kept me in the south, while my brother had settled in Cheshire. We spoke with different accents. We lived very different lives. There was no love lost between Phill and my wife and although we kept in touch, we siblings, for a time, kept our distance. On separating from my wife, however, I was able to re-establish a relationship with Phill, who became my lifeline in those difficult months. Now here we were, having purchased properties only half an hour apart in the very heart of France. It was a happy circumstance that had resulted from an unpleasant period of my life.

The morning after I had helped the Count to repair the roof of his house, more than a little hungover from our alcohol-fuelled session of reminiscing, I waved goodbye and drove back to Le Mas Mauvis eager to progress with the next stage of my own renovations.

Chapter Six

Jean Le Grand

Demolishing the mangers and forming the entranceways had taken much longer than I had hoped, and as my brother was about to depart for England I realised that it would be impossible for me to cast the concrete floors in the former animal pens myself. It would be necessary for me to bring forward the heavy artillery. I thought immediately of my brawny friend, universally known as Big John the Builder.

I had known John for almost ten years. Originally employed to construct a Victorian-style porch at the Kentish cottage my wife and I owned at the time, he had somehow become a permanent fixture: there was always another job on the horizon to which his superb skills as bricklayer, plasterer or joiner could be applied. John, a self-confessed workaholic, was seldom happier than with a bricklayer's trowel in his hands. He had a quiet pride in his work and a gentleness that belied his appearance. Tall, powerfully built, with a closely shaven head of jet-black hair that looked and felt like Velcro, he was an ex-soldier who had, in his youth, lived life rather close to the edge, and who admitted to a wild, unruly past.

Now a hardworking civilian, a self-employed general builder with a wife and two young children, John had learned to curb his previous antisocial excesses and neither drank alcohol nor smoked, although he did have a penchant for eating the hottest of chilli peppers, whether incorporated in a powerful Indian jalfrezi dish, as the garnish on a doner kebab, or simply on their own as a snack with attitude. John channelled his abundant energy into his work or, when he permitted himself a rare day off, indulged in his fervent passion for firearms in the form of shooting clays.

When I started to learn to fly balloons John had been keen to participate. His stature and strength were invaluable when preparing the balloon for take-off for, although lighter than air when airborne, a balloon rig can weigh in excess of 500 kilograms when on the ground. Re-dubbed John the Retriever when wearing his ballooning hat, he would chase after the balloon by car and such were his tracking skills that he would invariably be parked at the side of the road, nonchalantly leaning against the trailer, as the balloon came in for a landing in an adjoining field. A daredevil at heart, he also loved to fly with me, particularly on the more hair-raising fast flights with firm landings. He was not even deterred when, during a heavy landing when I almost fell out of the basket, John hauled me back in and my skull collided with the bridge of his nose, breaking it.

A telephone call to John's mobile revealed that he would be ready, willing and able to join me in France the following month.

'Just name the date, matey, and I'll be there!' said the jolly giant. 'Organise your ready-mix – and make sure you've got a good pair of wellies and a rake handy!'

So, temporarily leaving my foundations to the mercy of the rodents, I locked up the barn the next morning and said *au revoir* to Véronique over coffee and an enormous chunk of the brioche she had bought from the mobile *boulangerie* as a farewell treat. Returning to my lodgings to collect my bags and wish a fond farewell to Gordon and Maureen, and to thank them for their kindness, I was obliged – but happy – to consume more coffee and a very large sticky wedge of Maureen's delicious chocolate fudge cake. Squeezing my bloated frame behind the wheel of my car, I waved from the window as I pulled out of their drive, out of the hamlet, and set off on the long journey home to Al to recharge my depleted batteries and place myself on a strict cake-free diet.

It was clear that my concentration was impaired, for, stopping near the end of my seven-hour journey back to Dieppe to purchase cheap wine and cheese from a supermarket in the town of Tôtes, I missed my ferry back to Newhaven and was forced to drive on to Calais in order to pick up another boat to Dover. Twit.

Undeniably a tough nut to crack, Big John was not, however, a good sailor. November heralded an atrocious weather front that formed a deep swell in the Channel, causing our ferry to pitch and yaw alarmingly as it headed out from Newhaven. I have never seen my friend as silent and pale as he was that morning. Rooted to a bench on the top deck of the boat, he kept close tabs on the constantly shifting horizon in an attempt to quell his nausea. Perversely amused by John's obvious discomfort – I had always felt inadequate next to a man who was fazed by nothing – I sat alongside him sipping my frothy coffee and munching on a bacon and egg sandwich, while he silently plotted the tortures he would inflict upon me in my forthcoming role as Building Labourer. For this part of the renovation at Le Mas Mauvis was to be very much *his* shooting match.

As we sped south in John's van, which was crammed to the gunnels with tools and equipment for our work, the weather deteriorated still further, and we passed through flurries of snow. Warm in the cab of the van, my eardrums assaulted by the heavy rock John loved to play at full volume, we furiously sucked the supply of fruit gums, humbugs and other boiled sweets my friend always stocked when travelling long distance, and discussed the beauty of the passing scenery over the raucous din. By the time we arrived at Gordon and Maureen's house (we had arranged to stay in their caravan for the next fortnight) my head was thumping, my voice was hoarse with shouting over the noise, and my tastebuds were in denial after an overdose of sugared fruit and mints. Outside, the temperature had dropped dramatically and a white frost had set in. Our hosts, wearing thick winter garments, greeted us warmly at the door. Strange that they were attired for arctic conditions while indoors, I thought. Modulating the tone of my voice to that of normal conversation, I introduced them to John and we followed them back indoors.

'You can't possibly stay in the caravan in this cold!' said Maureen. 'You can stay in the house, if you don't mind sharing a room.'

'Oh, that's no problem, Maureen!' bellowed Big John. 'I was in the army. I'm well used to sleeping with a lot of other men.' Tickled by his own humour, he guffawed and playfully slapped me on the back, knocking the breath out of me. 'You'll be all right, matey! Once I get my head down, nothing'll disturb me.'

I could believe this, for I recalled a particular ballooning weekend when John, tucked up in his ex-army tent adjacent to mine, could be heard snoring loudly throughout the night: of the team, he had been the only one who appeared to have achieved a peaceful night's sleep.

'I'm afraid even the house is chilly,' said Gordon apologetically, showing us up to our room. 'Monsieur Laborde still hasn't fired up the central heating.' He revealed that they possessed only a few electric radiators which, as they were also expecting their first 'real' bed and breakfast visitors later that evening, were employed in heating the guestrooms. No wonder he and Maureen were dressed for winter survival. It was only marginally warmer indoors than it was outdoors. We could hardly complain. At least we would have comfortable beds to sleep in.

When we returned to the kitchen, Maureen presented us with chunks of crusty white bread and a hearty stew prepared on her newly connected Rayburn, which helped to restore our circulation. After dinner, while Al and I spoke on the telephone and our hosts retired to bed, John lazily flicked through the satellite channels on television, which seemed to offer little choice other than seedy soft-porn gameshows and subtitled films.

Al informed me that her sister's health had taken a sudden turn for the worse, and that she had been rushed into hospital. 'She'll be all right,' said Al shakily. 'She's been here before. She'll be fine.'

'I hope so,' I said. 'When are you going to the hospital?'

'Mom and Dad are there now. I'm going in straight away.'

'What do the doctors say?'

'That Claire's very poorly. It's too early to say ...'

'OK, well you go and spend time with Claire and phone me here if there's any change. OK?'

'I will,' promised Al.

'Would you like me to come straight back?' I asked, thinking that Al might appreciate some support.

'No, darling. There's no need. Claire wouldn't want that. You stay and make Mauvis beautiful.'

'OK. If you're sure. But remember, we're only a few hours away.'

'I will.'

After we hung up, an overwhelming helplessness engulfed me. I became painfully aware of the huge distance that physically separated me from Al: a chasm across which I could not offer a comforting arm, a shoulder to cry on.

In view of the early start we were to have the next morning, John and I both decided to call it a day. I took a shower and emerged from the bathroom wearing a tracksuit, thick socks, a scarf and woollen gloves, ready for bed.

While John was showering, I selected what appeared to be the cosiest mattress and crept under the covers. By the time he returned I was snug and warm, yawning after our long journey. My room-mate inspected his bed, which appeared to be child-sized, climbed in and wriggled into various positions before settling down with his huge feet protruding from the bottom of the duvet, his head and shoulders sticking out at the top.

'I'm going to have to sleep in my gonk bag tomorrow night,' he announced, referring to his sleeping bag, which he had left in the van.

'Yeah. Put the light out, John, there's a good chap,' I said sleepily, in no mood for his pillow talk.

'You're nearest, mate,' he replied truculently.

'Aw, c'mon John, I've just got warm, and you've only just got into bed,' I protested.

'Yeah, but the difference is, I ain't getting out again,' he replied. 'Light don't bother me.'

'Selfish git!' I muttered, throwing back the covers, leaping from the bed and tiptoeing across the chilly room to the light switch. Clicking it off, I plunged the room into darkness and, shivering, stubbed my toe on a chair. 'Bollocks!' I groaned, nursing my throbbing foot as I fell back into bed.

'That'll teach you to take the piss out of me on the ferry!' said John, chortling. Shortly afterwards the deep rumble of snoring drifted across the room.

When the alarm clock woke us at seven o'clock the following morning, ice covering the inside of the bedroom window suggested that the temperature outside had plummeted to well below zero. We donned our thermal underwear, gloves, several layers of clothing, and woollen hats pulled down over our ears, and trotted downstairs. Starting up the van, we left it to heat up and defrost while we huddled around a tiny fan heater in the kitchen and consumed a breakfast of microwaved *pain au chocolat* and steaming mugs of strong, sweet coffee. Driving around to the *grange* before the sun had fully risen, John received his first view of the property Al and I had bought. He seemed impressed by the massive challenge we had undertaken.

'Got your work cut out for you there!' he commented, sliding open the side door of the van. 'You don't do things by halves, do you?'

'No. All or nothing, I guess.' I shivered in the cold.

After weeks of heavy rain the lane running in front of the *grange* had been churned to mud by the wheels of Monsieur Jérôme's tractor (in our absence he had come to collect his farm machinery) and heavy frost had solidified the tyre tracks into deep ruts filled with icy puddles. Our feet crunched on the hard ground as we opened the barn doors and set up the petrol generator that would not only provide light to work by during the dark mornings and afternoons, but also power for John's electric tools and equipment.

The silence that filled that crisp, cold morning as John and I set up our equipment told me that our canine lodgers had been removed from the adjoining barn. I looked beyond Véronique's house at the compound and could see several of the floppy-eared hounds gazing through the wire fence, their hot breath steaming in the chill air, their long tails wagging furiously. I was going to miss them. Examination of their previous cell revealed that, true to his word, Monsieur Jérôme had cleared the bulk of the excrement from the earth floor of the barn.

I thought it strange that we had managed to approach the property without being assailed by the attentions of Tom the guard dog and took a few tentative steps towards Véronique's front door. All of a sudden the snarling monster lunged from his kennel, his white fangs glistening in the dim light. I leaped backwards as the dog strained on its chain to reach me.

'Ooh, what a little pooch!' cooed John, a sucker for any dog, the fiercer the better. He himself owned a pair of man-eating German shepherds. 'Who's a good boy, then?' The idiot approached the foaming-mouthed creature, holding out a vulnerable hand.

'John,' I said in a serious tone. 'Back off, you fool. It only ever gets fed eggy bread. You don't know the lengths it will go to for the taste of flesh.'

Just then, Véronique's outside light clicked on and the door creaked open, the barking probably having roused her from her sleep, despite the noise from her oxygen machine. We two grown men then scarpered around the back of the van until Tom had been placated by his mistress with a sharp crack on the skull from her walking stick.

After my previous visit, I had furnished John with detailed photographs and relevant measurements of a potential problem I had found in the *grenier*: the two timber spreader plates that ran along the floor and connected the roof braces (preventing them from spreading apart) were badly rotten at one end, meaning that there was little to prevent the mighty weight of the roof from pushing the entire back wall of the barn out of alignment. Although the wall had not yet started to bulge unduly, it would be necessary to prevent future movement and structural damage by bolting metal straps to the floor plates, connected to threaded rods passing through the walls, to which X-shaped metal braces could be screwed to restore structural integrity. Armed with my specifications, which I prayed were accurate, John had organised the fabrication of the braces, and we decided that their installation would be our first major job.

'These should fit fine,' he said, testing the sturdy braces after we had coated them with red oxide primer to prevent them from rusting. 'But we'll have to chop out some of the stonework to fit them over the ends of the timbers.'

Armed with club hammers and cold chisels, we started to hack out the big stones from the wall around the ends of the rotten beams, setting them aside for re-laying once the braces had been attached. John went around the back of the barn and erected his three-section ladder so that he could complete the access holes. While we were working from each side of one of the holes, we were both startled when a long, wriggling rat's tail suddenly dangled down from the top of the hole. Then another appeared, accompanied by squeaking from within the wall.

'Ugh! Nasty bastards!' squirmed John. 'They're bloody nesting in the wall! Ugh! We'll have to get them out, mate! Fetch something long and hoick the buggers out. I can't reach from here.'

'Hang on a minute!' I said, grabbing a long metal wrecking bar. I started to prod inside the hole. The dry mud that held the masonry together was soft and crumbly and I had to crouch down at floor level in order to peer up into the top rim of the hole. I could see the entrances to a maze of tunnels carved by the rodents, and several pairs of beady eyes glaring at me. I prodded at the wall again. A large brown rat suddenly dropped from within, shot past my face and scurried away squealing. Alarmed, I fell over onto my back as another rat scampered past me. Clambering to my feet, I peered into the hole again. Several rats' tails dangled down. I prodded with my rod, inadvertently catching one of the creatures. Blood dripped from its tail. It scrabbled further into the wall.

'Ugh! Shit!' I recoiled, feeling nauseous. I might not like rats, but I was not keen on inflicting pain on them. Suddenly, deciding that it was time for them to desert this particular sinking ship, half a dozen of the creatures poured from their nest and scattered in all directions.

'What's going on in there?' called John, hearing the kerfuffle from his perch atop the ladder, some six metres above the ground. I saw his face squinting through the hole just as the rest of the rats decided to evacuate their nest, and was horrified to see two of the rodents launching themselves into mid-air straight towards him. John ducked, his feet clattering on the ladder rungs as he slipped and then regained his balance. The rats flew over his head and plunged to the ground, remarkably still alive after the drop. Not for long, however. Swiftly regaining his footing, John grabbed a hefty stone from the wall and lobbed it at one of the escapees with astonishingly accurate aim, crushing the rat into the ground at the foot of the ladder.

With the rodents cast out of their home, John and I were able to continue with our work: once the braces were bolted to the sides of the floor beams, the threaded rods were attached to their ends, protruding from the face of the wall. John scaled the ladder again and screwed on the large X-shaped brackets and tightened them against the stonework. Next, we mixed up some mortar and began the lengthy process of replacing the jigsaw of stones to fill the holes. Any rats left inside the wall had, as it were, missed the boat: there would be no way out now.

We had just finished cleaning up our tools when Véronique emerged on cue to offer us coffee, which we gratefully accepted. As we stepped past the gnashing chops of Tom into the smoky heat emitted from her *cuisinière*, we paused to remove our muddy boots. Véronique waved us in urgently.

'*Oh, non, non, non, Messieurs! Entrez, entrez!*' We entered. It was never necessary to remove one's footwear, no matter what noxious substance might be clinging to the treads: this was a working farmer's kitchen.

After the ritual of the four kisses, I introduced John. John, towering over Véronique, politely scraped the thick woollen hat from his bristly scalp and proffered a huge hand for the lady to shake. 'In England, we call him Big John,' I continued in ponderous French.

'Ah, *oui*! *C'est vrai*! He is big! Jean Le Grand!' grinned Véronique. 'Sit down, *Messieurs*. Sit down.' We sat. Out of the fridge came the inevitable packet of *petits-gâteaux*. Two huge black cups like soup bowls with handles were set before us, along with a teaspoon each, and strong, steaming black filter coffee poured from a glass jug. '*Voudriez-vous du sucre, Monsieur Jean?*' asked our hostess, sliding a Tupperware box containing sugar cubes towards John.

'*John, il ne parle aucun français*,' I said smugly. At last! Armed with my basic repertoire of phrases and the notebook of conjugated verbs I carried in my back pocket at all times, I was no longer He Who Speaks No French At All. It was payback time! I turned to Jean Le Grand and smirked.

'Mercy,' said John, helping himself to three lumps of sugar, dropping them into his coffee cup and stirring the liquid furiously.

'*Du lait?*' queried Véronique, offering a carton of skimmed UHT milk.

'No mercy, madam,' replied John.

'*Et Monsieur Richard?*'

'*Non, merci*,' I replied, mildly irritated that my burly companion managed to communicate quite successfully without even the faintest smattering of French, while I struggled to recall even the most basic phrases.

'*Prenez du gâteau*,' said Véronique. Those fateful words. There was to be no argument. We each took a biscuit. A lengthy silence followed, punctuated by slurps from our coffee cups and a gentle crunching of butter biscuits. While we were being force-fed biscuits, I pulled the tatty notebook from my pocket and started to leaf through, searching for the words with which I could initiate a meaningful sentence.

'And how is Al, Monsieur Richard?' asked Véronique, breaking the silence.

'Al?' I repeated. 'Al is very well.' Then I recalled that Al had previously told Véronique about her sister's ill health. 'But her sister,' I went on, 'she is not well. She is in hospital.'

'*Oh, c'est triste*,' said Véronique. 'How sad. How old is Al's sister?' My grasp of the ridiculously complex French numbering system was shoddy, and I had to resort to scribing on the table with my finger the numerals 38, inwardly reflecting how young Claire was to be so afflicted with ill health.

When John and I returned to Gordon and Maureen's later that evening, I telephoned Al at home and discovered the happy news that Claire had improved and was responding positively to treatment.

'She's just as lairy as ever,' laughed Al. 'Giving the nurses the run-around.' It seemed that the worst was over.

Since we bought the property at Le Mas Mauvis, I had been immersing myself in the *Breakthrough French* audio tape lessons, studiously using the two hours commuting time between London and Sussex to give me a jump start in making myself understood by our neighbours and in supermarkets and stores. But conversing in French over the telephone was far beyond my linguistic capabilities at that time. Gordon, who had a confident command of the language, volunteered to place the order for the ten cubic metres of ready-mixed concrete that we estimated would be necessary to fill the two former animal pens to a depth of fifteen centimetres.

He also ordered, by separate delivery, preservative-treated timber for constructing partition walls on the new floors; plasterboard sheets to clad the walls with; and a quantity of expanded polystyrene sheets that we would use to cover my foundations as an insulating layer beneath the concrete. I did not anticipate that we would experience a problem with dampness afflicting the new floor: the raised surface would be well above the level any moisture in the sub-floor would be likely to rise to. The metre-thick exterior walls of the building, although they had no foundations to speak of, were bone dry. I also have a theory that the installation of damp-proof courses in older buildings that were never intended to have such provisions can actually exacerbate a problem, shift it to another part of the structure, or cause other related problems.

The timber, plasterboard and polystyrene arrived promptly the next morning and John and I stacked it neatly in the central section of the barn. With the concrete due for delivery the following morning, we had a deadline to complete the preparation of the foundations, and started in earnest to lay the polystyrene sheets, working from the back of the building towards the doors at the front. The walls of the building would retain the wet concrete, while it was necessary for us to fit stout boards across the entrances to form a step down into the adjoining areas.

The following morning the largest ready-mix delivery truck I have ever seen rolled down the lane and pulled up outside the *grange*. Through a mix of rudimentary French phrases and sign language I indicated to the driver where we would like him to discharge the concrete, and left him connecting the extension chute that would reach deep into the first of the sections. John and I, wearing our wellington boots and armed with a rake and a shovel each, gingerly crept onto the polystyrene surface, taking care not to snap the fragile material.

'*D'accord?*' shouted the mixer operator from his control panel, out of our line of sight.

'OK!' yelled John. 'Let 'er go!'

'*Oui! D'accord, Monsieur!*' I hollered, staring at the chute. The mixer roared and the huge drum rotated faster as a sea of sloppy grey concrete spilled from its mouth, along the chute and onto the polystyrene. I staggered back as a mountain of concrete formed around my feet. John started to heft shovelfuls of the wet mix towards the back of the room.

'Come on, mate, get shovelling or you'll end up part of the floor!' he shouted. Still the concrete gushed from the chute, threatening to swamp the tops of my wellingtons. I dragged my feet up with a squelch and frantically began to toss shovelfuls of the concrete into the furthest reaches of the barn. Each shovelful seemed to weigh a ton. Suddenly John waved his arms at the operator.

'Hang on, mate! Stop a minute!' he cried. The operator held a hand to an ear, unable to hear over the din of the machinery. John made that universal gesture for 'Kill!' by slicing his hand across his throat. The mixer was immediately cranked down to a more sedate rotation and the chute became clear. 'It's not wet enough,' said John. 'We need more water added. What's the word for water?'

'*L'eau*,' I replied, impressed by my instant recall. I was just about to impress John and the mixer operator with my wonderful command of the language – I just needed time to construct a sentence – when John beat me to it.

'Low, me ol' mate!' he shouted, cupping his hands around his mouth. 'You add more low in the mix. OK?' He held up a big thumb, a gesture that was returned by the mixer operator.

'*Vous voulez encore de l'eau, Monsieur? Certainement!*' said the man, disappearing behind his truck, whereby he began to increase the water content of the concrete mix.

'Bloody doddle, this French malarkey, eh Rick?' laughed John, returning to the task of shovelling out the huge pile of concrete that encased our feet. A few minutes later the operator gave the signal that the mix was ready and we stood by the end of the chute as he adjusted his controls. This time the concrete, noticeably wetter, flooded from the drum, down the chute and onto the floor with such a force that it caught me off balance. I staggered backwards, losing my grip on the spade, which was sucked under the surface. John caught my elbow just before I fell flat on my back in the mix, but the momentum swung me around and my right leg kicked out as if my partner and I were performing a graceful balletic movement from a rather dubious modern interpretation of *Swan Lake*. My boot, however, was left behind in the concrete. Bent over backwards, inches from the surface, I swayed one-legged, while John adjusted his grip under both of my arms and hoisted me upright. Keeping my right leg extended behind me, I bent forward at the waist and reached down to pluck my boot out of the concrete. John effortlessly hefted me into the air and deposited me on dry land. I rammed by boot back on and slithered back into the lake of concrete while John, laughing uproariously, continued shovelling.

'Come on, stop buggering about, Rick. No time for dancing. We've got work to do.'

Once the final dregs of concrete had been coaxed from the mixer, and we had begun to spread it out roughly from the back of the barn to the front with our rakes, the operator – who had been highly amused by our antics – pointed to his wristwatch and indicated what time he would return with the second load, which was to fill the other bay. With that, he departed and left us to the task of smoothing out and levelling the concrete according to the guidelines we had previously notched around the walls. John, armed with a stout length of straight-edged timber, waded through the concrete to the back edge and began to tamp the concrete firmly to expel air, then drew the straight-edge from side to side in a sawing motion to level it off. In this way he worked his way back towards the front, leaving a relatively smooth, flat surface which, when set hard, would form our new floor.

By the time the mixer truck had returned with our second load of concrete and we had cast it in the other section of the barn, it was late in the afternoon and the autumn sky was rapidly darkening. My strength had been severely depleted by the physical toil of spreading out the concrete, and I was reduced to trailing behind John, panting, like an obedient puppy. He turned his boundless energy to creating a metre-wide pavement along the front of the barn – a constantly muddy area – using the several barrowloads of surplus ready-mix we had been left with.

Monsieur Jérôme trundled up on his tractor. Dismounting his steed, he strode over purposefully. I introduced Jean Le Grand.

'Bon jewer, mate,' said John breezily.

'*Bonjour Monsieur*,' replied the farmer, proffering the back of his wrist instead of his filthy hands. The two men shook awkwardly, eyeing each other shiftily: of comparable build, their body language revealed a kind of grudging admiration. They resembled a pair of junior league sumo wrestlers squaring up to each other. Monsieur Jérôme folded his brawny arms across his chest and studied our pavement.

'*Ça c'est communal*,' he said pointedly, nodding towards the wet concrete.

'Communal?' I repeated.

'*Ce chemin. C'est communal.* Where you're laying this concrete. This is the communal path. It's not your property. Your boundary is the front façade of the building.'

I looked up and down the line of the pavement. He was right, of course. But I was not intending to 'steal' part of the path, merely to make it less of a mud bath along the front of the barn, for our own comfort.

'Yes, but it's not a problem, though. Who's going to complain?' I said.

'Oh, *je ne sais pas ...*'

'So you think someone might object, then?'

'Heuh, *peut-être*. Someone might.'

'Well, if anyone complains, we can soon dig it up again, *pas de problème*,' I said. 'Meanwhile, it will keep the mud at bay.'

'*De toute façon*, it's your problem,' he shrugged in his familiar I'm-only-telling-you-for-your-own-good manner. Then, waving dismissively, he mounted his tractor again and rumbled off down the track.

'Nosy bugger,' remarked John. 'What's his gripe?' He returned to his concreting, muttering under his breath.

When the builder had completed the illegal pavement, we closed up the doors to the barn and covered the wet concrete with sacking to protect it from the expected heavy frost and retired for the evening, tired but satisfied that this major job was over. In a few days, when the concrete floors were sufficiently hard, we could commence erecting the timber stud partition walls that would divide up the three ground-floor sections of the barn into bedrooms, bathrooms and a storeroom.

When we returned to the barn to examine the concrete the next morning, John was livid that armies of rats had wreaked revenge by leaving their telltale footprints all over his beautifully finished mix.

'Urgh! Little sods!' he moaned. 'This means war! We've got to bung up their flippin' orifices. We've got to keep the evil bastards out!'

High on my list of priorities was not only to block up the rodents' orifices but also to cut off their food supply, and the sight of hundreds of tiny clawed footprints scattered across our fresh concrete strengthened my resolve. It was urgent, I decided, to dispose of the vast mountain of grain that still covered much of the *grenier* floor. In my basic French I announced to Monsieur Jérôme, who had come to inspect our new floors, that if he did not take the grain within the next few days, I would be forced to remove and burn it.

This mild threat seemed to have hit home, for the very next day, while John and I were starting to mark out the stud wall positions on the concrete floors, a tractor rumbled up outside. We were greeted by the sight of Monsieur André Thierry, a neighbouring farmer whom I had met briefly before. The farmer – a muscular man with a gravelly voice, small, intensely piercing eyes, quizzical eyebrows, receding, swept-back hair and a bristly goatee beard – wore a waxed jacket, jeans and wellington boots, with an ill-fitting chequered cloth cap perched on top of his head. He was covered from head to foot in what appeared to be mud but was probably cow dung. He offered the relatively clean back of his right wrist for us to shake, apparently apologising for his otherwise soiled demeanour in a rapid delivery that I just could not grasp in its entirety: '*Excusez-moi, Messieurs. Je suis ... sale ... j'ai poursuivi ... des cochons ...*'

'What'd he say?' asked John, as the farmer stood before us, with hands on hips and a toothy grin.

'I'm not sure, but I think he said he's a dirty pig,' I replied, convinced that my translation skills had severely let me down on this occasion. 'No, that can't be right, I must have misheard.'

'Don't be too sure,' said John, returning to his work. 'He sure does whiff a bit.'

'*Je suis venu ... prendre le grain ... Je l'ai acheté ... Monsieur L'Heureux ...*' Monsieur André rattled off like a machine-gun discharging. I looked at him blankly, unable to translate his speech, which seemed to omit huge chunks, leaving only fragments of the sentence that gave no clue to its meaning. '*La céréale!*' he repeated firmly, holding his forefinger and thumb together at his lips. Was he asking for breakfast cereal? Was this some ancient French custom I was unfamiliar with? '*Le grain, Monsieur. J'enlève le grain.*' He pointed to the floor above.

'*Ah! Le grain! Oui, Monsieur. Je comprends!*' Suddenly it all made sense. He had not come to join John and me for a spot of breakfast: he had come to take away the grain – although I could not figure out where the pigs came into it. Perhaps he was going to feed his animals with the grain. The grain was going and that was all that mattered! Scarcely bothered with the fine print, the whys and wherefores, I pointed to the ladder. '*S'il vous plaît, Monsieur.*'

'*Merci!*' growled Monsieur André, starting up the ladder. Pausing halfway up, he swiped the cap from his shiny head, scratched his scalp with a grimy hand and glared around the interior of the barn, as if he had just noticed the structural changes that had taken place.

'*Beaucoup de travail ici. Beaucoup, beaucoup de travail,*' he said, nodding.

'Yes!' I agreed, much work; much, much work.

'*Bon courage!*' he quipped, disappearing through the hatch.

While John and I carried on with our work, Monsieur André began to shovel the grain through the central loading door of the *grenier* into a box-like attachment at the back of his tractor. After several trips, the mountain of grain had virtually gone, although a choking cloud of dust had formed that filled the entire *grange*, forcing John and I to abandon work until it settled.

While the dust was settling, we decided to pay a visit to the rubbish tip Al and I had inherited along with the farm, situated adjacent to the Ugly-Bugly, in order to salvage any serviceable items before putting it to the torch and reducing it to ashes. The tip, we had learned, consisted of the unwanted contents of the barns attached to Gordon and Maureen's home. Frustrated that Monsieur Jérôme had not removed the items some six months after they had purchased their property from him, they had finally insisted that it be taken at once. No one was more surprised than they were when the procrastinating farmer had turned up one morning, cheerfully loaded up his big red trailer and, apologising profusely to the couple for the delay, had promptly driven it around the corner and dumped it on the land we were in the process of buying from him. No doubt he intended to bury it one day, as is the habit of farmers in this region, but events had overtaken him.

Although it was mainly junk, Al and I had already pulled a number of desirable *choses françaises* from the unkempt pile: rickety wooden stick-back chairs, some interesting ceramic vessels, a collection of coloured glass bottles, and a box full of metal signs that read *Réserve de Chasse*. We also rescued several rotten but salvageable oak window frames, which we were later to use as the model for the *grange* windows. Rummaging through the broken heap of old sofas, radios, rain-swollen books and magazines, John and I decided that there was really nothing else of any value.

'This is all rubbish, Rick. Let's burn it, eh?' said John, his eyes glinting at the thought of the conflagration to come.

'OK,' I agreed enthusiastically. We fetched some newspaper from John's van and a soupçon of petrol to start the fire off and soon found ourselves warming our hands on the licking yellow flames of a splendid bonfire.

'First time I've been warm all day,' I remarked, prodding the fire with a pitchfork. A column of grey smoke curled its way skywards. Several mice that had been nesting within the heap scuttled from the pyre and disappeared into the grass. 'God, it's so peaceful here, don't you think John?' I said, taking in the view the fields and trees spread out before us.

'It's bloody lovely, mate,' confirmed John. 'Bloody lovely.'

Suddenly, from the core of the bonfire, there came a series of loud cracks as projectiles whizzed past our ears.

'Jesus Christ! Hit the deck!' cried John, diving behind a nearby bush with the lightning reflexes he had learned during his military training, as we were assailed by what sounded like rapid gunfire. I flung myself to the ground as smoky trails exploded from the fire and more projectiles shot past us.

'There's live ammo in there!' called John. 'Let's get out of the bloody way, before we get shot!'

Keeping low, we half ran, half crept to a safe distance from the bonfire, which was still spewing forth bullets.

'Let's hope you live long enough to appreciate the place, me old mate!' laughed Jean Le Grand, slapping me across the back.

One evening, after we had dined, Maureen announced that there was expected to be a rare display of shooting stars in the night sky, in the form of a meteor shower. It was to be a once-in-a-lifetime chance to witness such an explosion of lights streaking across the horizon as the space debris burned up in the Earth's atmosphere. The gin-clear skies over that part of rural France, unpolluted by the orange glow of city streetlights, would surely provide a magnificent panorama.

At the hour recommended by the newspapers, while Gordon and John remained indoors and engaged in building talk, Maureen and I, hopeless romantics, donned thick jumpers, coats, hats, scarves and gloves and, armed with a hot drink and joined by faithful Jess, stood outside in the freezing cold, eyes fixed on the heavens. The Milky Way, a dense mass of stars, planets, dust and gas curving above our heads, was like a vibrant airbrushed streak across the enveloping blackness of the night sky. All around it we could make out distant galaxies and solitary bright, twinkling stars that formed the recognisable geometry of constellations such as the Plough and Orion's Belt.

As a young boy, I had been fascinated by astronomy and man's exploration of space, and was hooked on the unfolding drama of the Moon missions, brought to reality by the medium of television. I was intrigued by the promise of space flight, the colonisation of distant planets, and the search for extraterrestrial life evoked by science fiction writers. Somehow, over the years, that passion had been diluted by the pressures of adulthood: I had simply forgotten to look above my head. But on that evening in France, although Maureen and I did not see a single shooting star for reasons we never discovered, I realised what I had been missing.

Although I am not religious or given to pondering the meaning of life and death, that evening's star-gazing was a cathartic experience that put into perspective how incredibly tiny we are in the scheme of all things – tiny, yet not insignificant. In one memorable evening I felt tough protective layers peel from me, allowing me the freedom to dream again.

Chapter Seven

Cold Reality

The next morning at six o'clock, reality grabbed me by the scruff of the neck and booted me from my bed and into the ice-cold *grange*. I could not remember ever having felt as cold as I did that morning. Despite multiple layers of clothes, my teeth chattered uncontrollably, my shoulders shook, and I felt the tenseness at the base of my skull that would often precede an attack of wryneck. My joints felt delicate enough to snap if I should make a sudden move. Jean Le Grand, seemingly immune to intense cold after many years of working outdoors in all types of weather, whistled merrily as he unloaded his toolkit from the van. The mad fool wasn't even wearing gloves! Mind you, the stubborn ox probably would not have admitted to feeling even a mite chilly if frostbite was nipping at his toes.

'What's the matter with you? Too cold for you?' boomed John, sounding far too jovial for the time of the morning. I held up my hands, one of which had been stuffed inside my jacket in the vague warmth of my armpit, the other in my mouth. My shaking fingers glowed a ghostly white.

'Bloody hell! They look like shit, mate! Let me get the stove on.' John set up his portable gas stove and placed a big, soot-blackened kettle on the burner to brew tea. 'Stick your mitts over the heat; warm 'em up.' I did as I was told, wafting my hands over the rising warmth.

It is a bald fact that I simply do not function well in the cold. At the risk of revealing myself to be a hopeless hypochondriac or a wimp susceptible to all manner of ailments, I suffer from an unpleasant condition called Raynaud's Phenomenon, popularly known as 'white finger'. Like my father and brother before me, I am afflicted by this disorder of blood circulation, which mainly affects the fingers (although my toes are also prone to the symptoms). Aggravated by exposure to the cold, the condition has the effect of abnormally reducing blood circulation and causing the fingers to become pale, waxy-white or purple. Blanching is accompanied by a tingling sensation, loss of dexterity and numbness of the fingers.

'How's that feel, mate?' asked John, peering at my fingers, which were gradually becoming red and blotchy.

'It's bloody painful when the blood circulation comes back,' I said through gritted teeth. On some occasions it could take half an hour or more for my fingers to return to normal, and during that time I would be rendered helpless. Even household chores and some leisure activities were enough to drain the blood from my fingers: while this has long been my excuse for never having to wash the car (a job I despise), the condition also hampers my real enjoyment of gardening, winter ballooning and cycling (gripping cold handlebars will soon numb my digits).

'What causes that, then?' asked John, after my fingers had assumed a more healthy pink hue, aided by the warmth from grasping the steaming mug of tea he prepared for me.

'White finger? As well as cold conditions they reckon it can also be brought on by stress.'

'Hah! Well you've had your fair share of that lately, eh, me old mate?' he said, presumably referring to my protracted divorce proceedings.

'I guess so. What about you, though? Don't you ever get stressed out?'

'Me? No! I just keep busy, mate. Just keep working. Don't have time for stress. When I'm working I'm happy. I love it. That's why I work all the bloody time.' He handed me a saw. 'And talking of work, Mr Wiles … if you were to get moving about, you mightn't feel so flippin' cold!'

Now that the new concrete floors had hardened we set ourselves the task of constructing the partition walls to divide up the outer sections of the *grange*. I relished this stage of the renovations, when the former agricultural building would gradually start to assume the appearance of a home. We had a strict timetable in constructing the walls: we had less than a week left before we had to return to the UK, and live-wire Monsieur Laborde and his solemn assistant Jean-Philippe were expected to arrive the next week to commence the installation of electricity and plumbing.

It is commonplace in France to build lightweight internal walls using a metal frame partition: a series of galvanised aluminium rails screwed together to form a rigid frame that can be clad both sides with plasterboard. However, despite realising that we were flying in the face of modern French practice, John and I had decided to opt for a more traditional method of partitioning: the timber stud wall widely used in the UK. Whereas the metal frames doubtless produced sturdy walls, I felt that timber was more complementary to the structure of a barn that was built largely of wood and stone; the walls of older French properties, after all, were built using a variation of the studwork we were familiar with. To my traditionalist sensibilities, it seemed incongruous to add brash aluminium in a period renovation, despite the fact that it would be permanently sealed out of sight within the wall. Although the partitions would be non-load bearing – that is, they would not be supporting any part of the building's structure – they would contribute a certain measure of additional rigidity to the upper *grenier* floor. They would also be thick enough to take a layer of mineral fibre blanket insulation and conceal electrical cables and plumbing pipework.

The walls were to be assembled using the rough-sawn timber that had been delivered previously. John set himself the task of taking pertinent measurements, while I marked out and cut to size the ten-metre lengths of timber, which were stained a custard-yellow colour by the preservative treatment.

'Make sure you measure accurately, and cut them squarely on the waste side of the cutting line,' instructed John. 'We want a nice tight fit.'

John vociferously rejected several of my pieces: no matter how hard I tried, the saw blade was determined to follow its own course through the gaudy yellow timber rather than following my marked guidelines.

'Jesus, mate! Can't you bloody saw straight?' boomed John.

'It's my saw. I think the blade's bent,' I whinged unconvincingly.

'It's not the flippin' blade that's bent, mate! You're tickling the wood like a big girl! Saw from the shoulder, man, not the elbow. Trust me to get lumbered with a bloomin' do-it-yourselfer!'

Eventually, however, my technique apparently improved and John was able to nail a headplate along the underside of one of the huge oak joists that ran the width of the section. He then used a plumb line and bob to transfer its position to the floor, and a matching soleplate was aligned and nailed into the concrete.

Upright timber studs were cut to fit between the plates at each end of the proposed partition, tapped vertical and skew-fixed in place, with nails driven in at conflicting angles to resist pulling out. Intermediate studs were cut and skew-nailed in place between the plates, then short horizontal timbers known as noggins cut to fit in a row between the studs. These were positioned at a height at which they would support the abutting edges of the plasterboard sheets that would eventually clad the framework.

By midday we had constructed the framework for one of the hall walls, which also created our proposed storeroom.

'Come on,' said John. 'Drag some of those polystyrene sheets in and put them against the partition.'

'What for?' I asked.

'We'll make a nice little insulated den where we can have a bit of scoff.'

We fashioned a cosy hideaway from the surplus polystyrene sheets and soon we were sitting on warm cushions of polystyrene off-cuts, sipping mugfuls of piping hot *potage* – a delicious soup of leeks and potatoes – cooked on John's stove. After the soup we were still hungry from our physical exertions, and made sandwiches from chunks of fresh baguette purchased from the mobile *boulangerie*, filled with Cantal cheese and thick slices of beef tomatoes. Suitably refreshed, we continued with our work.

After a few days we had completed the framework that delineated the internal corridor and bathroom, and on the other side of the barn had formed the skeleton of the second guest bathroom, and the two spacious bedrooms it would separate. Over the next few days John and I panelled the newly constructed partition walls on one side with sheets of plasterboard, leaving the other side temporarily open so that pipes and electrical cables could be concealed within. The oak-slatted walls of the central hall required a different treatment, however. Because we wanted to retain the slats as a decorative feature on the hall side, we fixed panels of expanded polystyrene sandwiched between two sheets of plasterboard behind the oak slats, creating a thick, insulated layer. From the hall side, the walls resembled the exposed oak beams commonly found in medieval houses.

Monsieur Fugère arrived as arranged to install our septic tank. He sat proudly behind the wheel of an impressive shiny red machine. The vehicle, which had a large, green-tinted glass cab containing an array of levers, panels of buttons, driving wheels and other devices, sat on knobbly tractor tyres almost as tall as a man, and also boasted several extendable arms with various hooks, shovels, drills and other attachments. From a spindly crane arm dangled a weighty grey concrete container that resembled the sarcophagus of a particularly corpulent pharaoh. Monsieur Fugère clambered down from the cab and greeted me in his usual genteel manner, his warm handshake accompanied by a distinct waft of alcohol.

He indicated the septic tank swaying perilously above his head.

'That's your *fosse*, Monsieur Wheels,' he explained, somewhat unnecessarily. 'I've come to install it.'

Monsieur Fugère introduced his ever-smiling but dentally challenged assistant, Jean-Jacques, who appeared incongruously attired in a trilby hat and a rather unkempt green business suit, complete with orange shirt and brown tie (although he did pull on overalls before starting work). In return, I introduced Jean Le Grand to them and there was much shaking of hands. Returning to our work, we left the pair to lower the huge concrete tank to the ground and uncouple it. Then, driving around to the back of the barn in the impressive vehicle, Monsieur Fugère utilised its integral digging arm to gouge a huge hole in the earth. After about half an hour, the *fosse* was reconnected to the crane arm and lowered with precision into the pit, while I stood a safe distance away and took numerous photographs of this momentous occasion in our renovations.

The process had apparently been physically taxing on Monsieur Fugère, who found it necessary to make frequent trips to the cab of his van, which his assistant had driven. He emerged each time exuding his characteristic sangfroid.

Careful back-filling with earth around the *fosse* left only a small access pipe protruding from the ground. Monsieur Fugère then trundled his vehicle further down into the field and began to dig a network of narrow trenches fanning out from the tank in the shape of a giant fishbone. In these trenches he spread a layer of gravel and on this positioned lengths of perforated plastic pipe to channel the filtered waste water from the *fosse* harmlessly into the earth. The pipes were covered with fibrous blanket material, which prevented them from becoming silted up with soil, and the trenches were back-filled with earth.

The whole procedure of installing our sanitation system, including the fixing of a soil stack to the back wall of the barn and its connection to the *fosse* via an underground pipe, took the two men only half a day. All we needed now were the services of Monsieur Laborde to install the internal plumbing, and he had promised to commence his work any day now.

It was our last Friday, at the end of our second week at Le Mas Mauvis (we were due to depart for England on Sunday), and we were determined to complete as much as we could in the limited time left to us. We had planned to make good the demolished mangers by casting fresh concrete plinths as seating and surfaces for furniture. The concrete would also seal off the holes through which the rats entered the barn. This would require us to set up sturdy timber shuttering to mould the wet mix until hard. For this we would use the flooring-grade chipboard panels I had purchased on impulse from Mr Bricolage on a previous shopping trip to Limoges, sure that they would come in handy one day. Assisted by Gordon's mellifluous telephone manner, we ordered three cubic metres of sharp river sand, the same quantity of coarse gravel, and eight sacks of cement from a local builders' merchant. These were delivered and deposited in Bill the Ancillary Barn (or was it Ben?).

The day was colder than the previous one, if that was possible, and it was necessary for me to thaw out my bloodless fingers once again before I could be of any use to Big John. He, meanwhile, had already begun to erect the shuttering. Setting up vertical boards to retain the front edge of the manger-seats on each side of the broad central section of the barn, he braced them with long lengths of our stud work timber and a series of the adjustable Acrow props he had brought with him from England. The short ends of the manger-seats, where they were intersected by the internal corridors we had just constructed, were closed off with short lengths of chipboard and similarly propped. The difference in floor level between the two outer sections and the inner section was made up by the formation of shuttering for two steps.

Mixing the concrete was accomplished using John's electric mixing machine, which we set up outside the open doors of Bill and was powered by a long lead from the generator. As there was no longer running water laid on at the property, it was necessary for us to traipse twenty metres along the communal *chemin* to the outflow pipe discharging from the pond into the little *ruisseau*, or stream that intersected our land, to fill our buckets. We would then return to replenish the rusty metal oil drum that acted as a reservoir. On each visit, however, it was necessary to break the thick ice that was forming around the pipe outlet, in order to let the water flow again.

While I loaded the revolving mixer with John's recommended proportions of sand, cement and gravel, and added bucketfuls of water, John ferried barrowloads of the sloppy concrete into the barn and tipped it into the shuttering. I lost count of the number of trips to fetch water we made, the loads of concrete I mixed, and John's frequent return trips with his groaning barrow. But when the rain started to pelt down, I began to have serious doubts about the common sense of standing shovelling materials into an electrically powered machine and pouring in gallons of water.

'John?' I called out feebly. 'It's raining …'

He poked his head around the door and gazed up at the sky. 'Yes. And your point is?'

'Oh, nothing,' I said sheepishly, pouring another bucketful of water into the revolving drum of the mixer. John tutted and retreated into the barn. I was relieved when, as darkness began to fall, he emerged bleary-eyed from the depths of the *grange* to announce that he had completed the back-filling of the shutter work, and now just had to finish off the surface. By the flickering illumination of the generator-powered lamp we had rigged up, I watched with admiration as John worked the wet concrete with a steel trowel, drawing it across in broad sweeps of his arm to gradually smooth the surface. He completed the procedure by forming neat, decorative borders around the top.

Not long after we arrived back at Gordon and Maureen's house that evening, filthy, cold and weary, I received a telephone call from Al in a state of sadness and distress. Her sister Claire, having rallied over the last few days, had suffered a major setback and tragically – despite her fighting spirit – had failed to pull through.

Nevertheless, Al thought herself blessed to have been able to spend the last week at her sister's bedside in the intensive care unit of the hospital, snatching moments of sleep whenever she could, sharing the vigil with her father and mother. Claire had by no means given up the struggle without a fight: when the surgeon explained that it would be necessary for his patient to be transferred to another hospital, Al and her parents had feared the worst, but the very next morning Claire had awoken as bright as a new pin, cracking jokes with the nurses, eyeing up the tasty young doctors, and demanding a hearty breakfast followed by a cigarette. Her poor body, however, was unable to sustain her boundless enthusiasm for life, and preparations were made to take her by ambulance to a London hospital.

In a cruel twist of fate, whilst Al had returned home briefly to pick up her forgotten wallet and more overnight items so that she could trail the ambulance to London, Claire had slipped into a coma from which she never re-emerged. The two sisters had been robbed of a chance to say a final goodbye. It was the most poignant moment Al had ever experienced, and she loyally remained at her sister's bedside with only the life-support machines signalling her failing heartbeat. Eventually, however, even the machines were silent.

'She'll be happy now, Rich,' said Al over the telephone, stifling her tears. 'At peace. She won't be in pain any more. She's somewhere where there's laughter, fun and comfort.'

'Yes,' I said, respecting Al's belief in the existence of a God of sorts, an afterlife, although it was a difficult concept for me to concur with. In the reality of this situation, I was overwhelmed by the same numbness I had felt on the death of my dear mother: an inability to grieve openly. Perhaps, for me, it was a means of coping with the practicalities, of putting my feelings on the back burner. With this physical distance between Al and me, however, I felt unable to express words of sufficient comfort down the telephone line.

'She'll be up there to greet all the new arrivals, Rich, and all her horsey and moggy friends, showing them the ropes and having a laugh, eh?'

'Yes, you bet she will!' I smiled. I admired Al for her ability to see the humour in this sad event. Laughter was her survival kit, which buffered the tears and pain of her sister's sickness and now her death. But I just wanted to reach out and hug her, to allow her to cry.

'She'll be nipping outside the Pearly Gates for a quick fag when no one is watching, I expect!' Al laughed again.

'I'm sure she will, darling! Listen. I'm going to come straight back,' I said. I was absolutely no use to Al all those miles away when she needed support.

'No, Rich,' said Al bravely. 'You'll be leaving the day after tomorrow anyway. I'll be all right until then.'

'It's no problem to change the ferry; all it takes is a phone call. And old John here won't mind; we've done everything we'd planned to do at Mauvis. But mainly I want to come back to be with you, darling. Would you like me to come straight back?'

'Yes please,' she admitted wanly. 'I'd appreciate that.'

So it was that early the following morning, while it was still dark, John and I hurried around to the *grange* to dismantle the chipboard shuttering, hoping upon hope that the concrete was going to be hard enough, for ideally the mould should have remained in place for another day. Luck was with us and the shuttering came away, leaving perfectly moulded plinths. We tidied up the barn as best we could as the sun rose and, bidding *au revoir* to Véronique – with no time even to partake in a farewell coffee – we loaded our belongings into John's van and headed hell-for-leather for Dieppe.

Chapter Eight

Nature's Abundance

The balance of life is so critical that it often takes little to tip it one way or the other. If something new is placed on the scales, something of equal weight must be removed from the other side to restore the balance. Al felt that in meeting me she had been given a precious gift, only to have another one taken away. In bitter paradox, she had found the soulmate she had hoped would enter her life, yet she had lost a part of herself with Claire's death.

Claire's funeral, although undeniably a sad and sombre occasion, was also, conversely, a joyous one. Had she been able, Claire would doubtless have delivered a quick kick up the rump to anyone daring to feel sorry for her or themselves on this, her special day. The tiny village church was bedecked with masses of miniature roses in pots, an abundance of floral tributes, scores of gently flickering candles and numerous framed photographs of Claire with her horses, with her pals, with her family. The church was packed to overflowing with hundreds of friends, acquaintances and relations eager to pay their respects to the passing of this widely popular young lady.

'You know what's really upsetting?' sniffled Al in a quiet moment. 'Claire's going to be really ticked off that she never got to see our French château, as she called it.'

Following a ceremony at which friends of the family read moving eulogies, a cremation was carried out, after which people gathered at the home of the Doctor and his wife to reminisce about their eldest daughter. The following day a group of horseriders led by Al on Dickens, Claire's beloved steed, and carrying the urn containing her sister's ashes, headed for a windblown clump of trees in Ashdown Forest. They were joined by a small band of close friends and relatives trailing a motley assortment of dogs. Claire had loved to ride here and long insisted that she would like to be lain to rest at this spot after her death.

Whilst manoeuvring the horses into the tight circle of trees, the excitable dogs unsettled the horses and in the ensuing mêlée Al momentarily lost her grip on the urn. There was a general gasp of horror from the assembled group as we all imagined the vessel crashing to the ground, unceremoniously dumping the contents amidst the heather. As Al regained control of her mount and the urn, there was a simultaneous peal of laughter, which helped to break the ice on this solemn occasion. On that cold, windy day, we sipped coffee from thermos flasks and munched biscuits, and Al scattered her sister's ashes beneath the trees. The stump of a fallen tree was adorned with plants, posies and a plaque inscribed with a touching message.

Over the following months, Al and I were distracted from thoughts of our future life at Le Mas Mauvis as the aftermath of Claire's untimely death hit home. Feeling emotionally and physically weak, and a need to spend time with her grieving parents, Al was unable to work for some weeks, eventually returning to a temporary part-time position. When ready to resume a full five-day week, she found secretarial work at a local architect's office, where she remained for some months. I, meanwhile, returned to the London publisher and immersed myself in the launch of a magazine series called 'The Wonderful World of Teddy Bears' – a far cry from the subject of home renovation, yet suitably diverting.

Al and I returned to France for an all-too-brief week in spring that year to discover the property sinking beneath a sea of nettles and thistles. To our great dismay the electrical and plumbing systems, although fairly advanced, had yet to be completed – the winter storms had diverted Monsieur Laborde to more urgent repairs on other properties – and we were frustrated in our efforts to press on with the renovations. Pitching our trusty tent inside the *grenier*, we busied ourselves sweeping up the mass of dust that had fallen during the winter, ripping out the old electric cables and pipework, placing bowls under new leaks in the roof and, of course, taking coffee with Véronique.

We no longer had to run the gauntlet of avoiding the snarling teeth of Tom the guard dog for, like Tripod before him, he had thrown off his temporal coil and his chain lay vacant on the path in front of his kennel. Véronique seemed to be getting through dogs at a fair old rate, and she had decided not to replace the animal.

'He barked too much anyway,' she commented in a bleak eulogy.

Often during our coffee mornings we would be joined by another neighbour, Madame Jolanda Bussiere, who lived in the little prefabricated bungalow that was just visible from the top floor of our *grange*, nestling at the far side of the communal land. Jolanda was a tiny, frail lady in her late sixties, who walked with a shuffling, stooped gait. She possessed shoulder-length greying fair hair usually held in a girlish Alice band or tortoiseshell clip at the back of her head, and wore an enormous pair of horn-rimmed spectacles flecked with blue, which magnified her enquiring eyes disconcertingly while dwarfing the rest of her features.

Polish by birth, Jolanda had lived in France for over thirty years, after meeting her husband-to-be, the dashing Gendarme Bruno Bussiere, in Paris after the Second World War. She spoke fluent French, although her somewhat coarse accent was difficult to understand at the best of times, due to her habit of slurring some words while barking others: a difficult combination in any language. Until Al and I became attuned to Jolanda's guttural growl, we were prone to imagining that we were being scolded severely for some vile transgression of coffee morning etiquette (did we not slurp enough, perchance?), while she was probably merely commenting on the mild weather we were currently enjoying, or politely asking after our health. Weather was the usual line of conversation, however, because Madame Météo, as her husband playfully nicknamed her, was something of an expert on the climatic conditions of the region, indeed of the whole of France.

'Is it going to rain today?' I enquired one day, taking up my usual chair to the right of the little lady – there were strict, unwritten rules for where one should sit on these occasions – while Véronique poured us coffee. Madame Météo theatrically peered through the open window into the sky, a hand shading her squinting eyes. Scudding grey clouds suggested a touch of precipitation, I thought, although the seer thought otherwise: '*Non*, Monsieur Richard!' she growled, as if clearing her throat. She raised an arthritic finger. 'It will not rain this day!' And sure enough, despite all indications to the contrary, no rain fell on Le Mas Mauvis that day. Further consultations on subsequent days resulted in startlingly accurate forecasts: rain one day, high winds another, and even her pronouncements on the ambient temperature were amazingly accurate.

'How can you tell?' I dared to ask after several days of precision forecasting. She stabbed a finger at her eyes, then at the wall behind me. I looked around: was she pointing at the clock on the wall (which wasn't working)? What mysterious method did the lady use to forecast the weather?

'The clock?' I asked, puzzled by this conundrum. Madame Météo frowned at me as though she thought I was a lunatic.

'*L'horloge?* What are you talking about?' came the grating reply. '*La télé!*' I looked around again. No, she had not been pointing at the clock, but at the object sitting atop the sideboard. It appeared that Madame Météo's amazing powers were not gleaned from watching the formation of clouds, from studying the subtly changing nature of flora and fauna, or from some supernatural hypersensitivity to meteorological conditions: it was simply that Jolanda was known to be glued to every single weather report that was broadcast on television each day, to the extent that she had become a walking, or rather shuffling, database of climatic knowledge.

Jolanda would pay twice-, often thrice-daily visits to Véronique for a little conversation and a little coffee (a dainty cup – unlike the capacious bowls Al and I were presented with – laced with three huge chunks of sugar to form a thick, sweet syrup). Rarely did she miss a visit: once in the morning for elevenses; again just after lunch, when Monsieur Bruno liked nothing better than to flop onto the sofa for an hour or two's *sieste*; and again for a cup of tea at around four in the afternoon (which Véronique labelled '*un petit quatre*', a little four o'clock).

Véronique and Jolanda were in many ways an odd couple but the circumstances of their quiet life in this sleepy hamlet had the effect of throwing them together for much-needed company. Days could drag, particularly when, in Véronique's case, mobility was limited and there were few visitors. Their only communication with the outside world was during the daily deliveries of bread from the travelling *boulanger* (three separate bakers delivered on alternate days to the hamlet), a fleeting chat with one of the two postwomen who shared the round, or on Thursdays when the grocer's van lumbered up the lane and, like a blossoming flower, opened up to reveal its bounty within. The entire side of the vehicle unfolded to present a well-stocked food store, complete with smoked ham and dried sausage dangling from hooks, shelves crammed with tins and packets of produce, and racks containing fresh fruit and vegetables (although Véronique, suspicious of the widespread use of insecticides, did not trust any fresh vegetables other than those which she could pull from the furrows of her own plot). A glass-fronted chiller cabinet offered fresh meat, cheese and other dairy produce. The grocer, a kindly man with a thatch of iron-grey hair and a bushy black moustache, addressed Véronique informally by her *prénom*. He spent far longer than he needed to idly chatting and discussing his friend's grocery requirements. The grocer would then exit his vehicle and courteously carry Véronique's bulging wicker basket into the house for her before heading off for the next stage of his round.

'*Écoutez*,' Véronique said to us one day, with a tinge of sadness in her voice, when we were partaking in *un petit quatre*. 'Listen, without Madame Bussiere's little visits, I would see virtually no one. I would be all alone.' And of course, the same was true for her Polish friend.

Monsieur Bruno Bussiere, ex-Gendarme, ex-cook, skilled raconteur, was a gentle, humble, yet wickedly humorous man who spent his retirement pottering in his vegetable garden or tending his chickens and ducks. To my mind, he bore a strong physical resemblance to Sean Connery, had the 007 actor been considerably shorter, broader and a little more rumpled around the edges. I think the Frenchman's dark, quizzical eyebrows were the main feature that evoked in my befuddled mind a cloudy image of the handsome Scotsman, although few people other than Al seemed to share my opinion when I pointed out the similarities.

Bruno (we were instructed to drop the 'Monsieur' from his name) loved to chat and prided himself on being a little au fait with the English language. He would often turn up on a Sunday morning, dressed in his finest lumberjack shirt and baggy jeans, and wearing a tartan peaked cap with a pompon on the top (reinforcing my belief that he somehow had Scots roots), clutching a well-thumbed French-English dictionary to impress us with a new word he had added to his vocabulary. There would invariably be a crumpled cigarette clamped in the corner of his mouth, although he frequently attempted to give up smoking and used sticks of liquorice root as an alternative, chewing the twigs to extract the strong flavour. His nicotine-stained teeth suggested a lifetime of trying to give up. Bruno would start his English lesson by naming various objects around us: shovel, hammer, spectacles, grass and so on. However, the French inability to form the letter W created some comical interchanges.

'Curr-ohh,' he blurted out on one occasion, trying his best to manoeuvre his lips into the correct formation. 'Caa-ooh. Corr-ah.' The cartoonesque eyebrows gyrated on his brow like dancing caterpillars as he became increasingly frustrated.

I shook my head. '*Je ne comprends pas*,' I said.

'*Comment on dit ça? La vache?*' he asked, rubbing his chin with a grim look on his face.

'Cow?' I queried. He nodded furiously. 'Cowww,' I stressed carefully. But it was no use: this small word had defeated him.

'Pworr! No good, eh? I say, no good, eh?' He grasped his tongue and gave it a twist, making me wince. Frowning, he leafed through the book until he could find a less challenging word with which to impress us.

'Shit,' he said, knowing that the word was always a good standby. He beamed broadly. 'Shit, yes? *Merde*, shit!'

On another occasion, Bruno ambled past the *grange*, taking his daughter Claudine for a relaxing stroll in the cool afternoon. We knew that he often liked to follow the little *chemin* down to the communal pond, and perhaps to saunter down the leafy track that led through our woods and onto the Pentecostal way, but this time he returned and politely knocked on our door. When we greeted him, he scraped his tartan cap from his head and clutched it across his chest. He humbly proposed an offer, which, he said, would be beneficial to us and to him. There were a number of fallen trees on our land, he explained, the victims of recent storms. We would be shrewd to have these cut up into logs and stored before they succumbed to rot. If we would allow him, he would be pleased to chop up the trees, to prepare the logs and, in return for his labours, to take a fair share for his own use. The idea seemed like an ideal solution to our problem, as we had been only too aware that the wood needed to be cut up and correctly stored: there would come a time when we would need the logs for our own heating needs. But with so many other major jobs to complete, it was difficult to see when we would ever find the time to deal with the logs and it felt good to be helping our dear neighbours with their winter supplies.

'The idea sounds fine, Bruno, but what would you consider fair? It's going to be a lot of hard work for you,' said Al, worried that our neighbour, no spring chicken, might find the task too arduous.

'*Moitié-moitié*,' Bruno suggested, gesticulating with two fingers. 'Feefty-feefty. *Beaucoup de travail pour moi!* Much, much work. Pworr, but don't worry, I'm as strong as an ox!' He struck an exaggerated strongman pose, slapping his ample biceps. 'Gud deal, yes?'

'Yes! Great!' laughed Al and I, and we shook on the deal.

The following afternoon the budding lumberjack, dressed for the part in jeans and chequered shirt, traipsed past the *grange* pushing a wheelbarrow loaded with a chainsaw, long-handled axe and sledgehammer, plus a set of metal wedges to use for splitting the logs, and headed off to render his first tree into firewood.

Al and I felt we belonged in Le Mas Mauvis, and had gained the acceptance of our close neighbours. We longed to be there constantly but no longer suffered from the frustration we had felt earlier. Perhaps the *calme* of the hamlet had rubbed off on us. There was, too, a great joy in living amidst Mother Nature's glorious abundance – although at times it could be a little *over*abundant.

The sweet sound of birdsong filled the air from dawn until dusk, while the gentle lowing of cattle in verdant pastures soothed our nerves; the tinkling of their bells carried on the breeze in the late evening. A steady percussion of crickets in the long grass started up, setting the cadence to which other members of this eclectic orchestra played. Cicadas hummed in the trees to their own high-pitched throbbing rhythm, while a deep tenor rumble emanated from the colony of frogs that inhabited the brackish water of the communal pond.

As Al and I crept into our tent, exhausted after a day's physical toil, that creative improviser the nightingale began its mellifluous song. I yawned loudly and thrashed madly on the old mattress in a vain attempt to warm up the cold sheet. I yawned again, emitting a kind of throaty, Tarzan-like wail.

'Ssh, doll,' urged Al, already snug in bed. 'Just listen to the nightingale. Isn't it just beautiful?'

I fell back on my pillow, shivering, and listened. Sure enough, the night bird's song was a sweet, delicate warble, a glorious counterpoint to the distant tinny clang of the cow bells. After a few hours, however, the damned bird's croaking as it neared the crescendo of its song threatened to put the mockers on the early night we had hoped for, after an exhausting day of hard work. The nightingale fell silent, its place taken up by a barn owl, whose piercing screech told us he was using the ridge of our roof as a vantage point for spotting likely prey. When eventually we fell into a deep sleep it seemed like no time at all that we were roused by the call of a nearby cuckoo.

'Oh, listen, darling,' whispered Al dreamily. 'Isn't it wonderful to wake up to the sound of the cuckoo? It tells you spring is here.'

'Wh-whaat?' I slurred sleepily. 'Whassa matter?'

'The cuckoo, darling,' repeated Al. Now irreversibly roused, I cocked an ear and sure enough, the bird's distinctive call echoing across the fields conjured up thoughts of crisp, clear spring mornings. Yes, it was so good to be here, falling asleep and waking to the gentle sounds of wildlife all around us. I stretched lazily on the mattress and dozed. Side by side we lay catnapping in silence for what seemed like a few hours, listening to the cuckoo until its endlessly repetitive drone became intensely irritating. I stuck my fingers in my ears until I could no longer stand the thump of my own pulse amplified inside my head. The cuckoo was going for an endurance record. Was it the hunting season? Perhaps I could get myself a shotgun? But when the bird failed to hit the final note of its ubiquitous call, Al and I chuckled heartily. The repetitive call ceased. There was silence.

'That'll teach the bugger! I'll bet he's embarrassed after that!' I giggled.

The calm was suddenly shattered by the sound of the neighbourhood dogs and their various offspring barking – or rather, yelping – at the first signs of activity in the sleepy hamlet. Deafening for us in our remote spot away from the main cluster of cottages, we wondered just what technique our neighbours had for blanking out the constant din. A crow cawed as it flapped energetically over the roof of the *grange*. The dawn chorus began in earnest; the whistles, tweets and warbles of hundreds of sparrows, wrens, martins, thrushes, blackbirds, robins and assorted tits accentuated by the *cock-a-doodle-doo!* of distant cockerels. A woodpecker began to drum – *rat-a-tat-tat* – on a nearby tree, its cry a snide laugh at having disturbed us.

If that was not enough to rouse the sleepy, mumbling humans, the flocks of sheep in the surrounding fields clambered onto their stiff pins of legs and began to bleat mournfully. Finally, with the cuckoo's vocal chords apparently re-oiled and sounding in a distant tree, the cows started to moan and the occasional bull would bellow noisily.

'That's it! I can't sleep now!' I grumbled, sitting bolt upright. Al, who would find no trouble at all in sleeping on stage with a heavy-metal band in full swing, simply turned over and began to snore. I scrambled out of the tent, pulled on my shorts and moccasins and descended the ladder. Pushing open the barn doors, I stepped out into the glaring early morning light, momentarily blinded, only to be dive-bombed by the family of housemartins desperate to protect their twittering young who peered from the neat little mud nests that clung to the joists just inside. The air outside was fresh and cool and it promised to be a fine day: I had it on the good authority of Madame Météo, after all.

Strolling down the path towards the pond, grasshoppers leaping ahead of me, I stepped aside as an adder slithered past. Taking over the cuckoo's shift, I heard the distant cry of the hoopoe. This most monotonous of spring birdsongs – *hoop hoop hoop; hoop hoop hoop* – issues from the slender, downward-curving beak of a flamboyant character with black and white striped wings, pinkish plumage and a distinctive crest on its head, raised when startled or in danger. I stared into the trees but could not see the rarely spotted vocalist. I wished I'd remembered to bring my binoculars.

Down by the pond I caught sight of four baby coypu, each about the size of a full-grown otter, paddling across the water emitting a throaty hum. I stood for some minutes watching them cavort as they eyed me nervously from a distance. Turning away, I stood stock-still as, no more than two metres away sat the babies' parents. About the size of a badger, one of the coypu turned a blind eye to my presence, intent as it was on chewing vegetation at the edge of the *chemin*. Its mate, however, sat up on its webbed hind feet, nose twitching within a grey muzzle as it scrutinised me through its small eyes set high on its angular head. The rodent's arched body was covered with long, coarse guard hairs coloured a reddish brown, and a thick, scaly, rat-like tail curled around to one side.

Coypu have spread like wildfire since they were introduced to France from their native South America in the nineteenth century. Although originally bred in captivity for their soft, grey underfur, many French now regard these rodents – cousins of the beaver – as vermin, although they are sometimes hunted for their meat.

The 'hare of the marsh', it seems, makes a tasty stew! This aquatic vegetarian, colloquially known as *grosse-rat* (fat rat), is immensely destructive, decimating vegetation at pond and riverside and massacring garden planting, and its burrows are responsible for weakening riverbanks and dams. On one occasion I witnessed an adult coypu vandalising the bulrushes and pond reeds in our own Ugly-Bugly, grasping the stems in its front claws, chomping through them with its huge pair of broad orange incisors, then tossing them nonchalantly over its shoulder. But I had never managed to get this close to one of these fascinating, if incongruous creatures. The watching coypu waggled its frilly guinea-pig ears and continued to sniff the air while its mate turned away and lolloped along the path before scuttling off into the broom.

'Boo!' I said suddenly, testing how the remaining animal would react. The coypu just continued to stare, unruffled, twitching its long whiskers. Then, hearing the low *hmm hmm hmm* call of its young, the attentive parent turned away calmly and slipped into the undergrowth.

I returned to the barn just in time to hear the croaking, tinny voice of Cocky the cockerel-shaped alarm clock – somehow mysteriously activated – crowing insistently where I had carefully positioned it at the dozing Al's side before leaving the tent. When angrily switched off, the infuriating clock uttered a squeaky '*gurd-morneeng*' in American-Chinese. When shortly afterwards I heard that most familiar of bird calls – *Rich-Rich! Rich-Rich!* – I knew that it was time to put the kettle on and make coffee.

Later, while Al paid a visit to Véronique, I took the opportunity to go for a run in the spring sunshine, heading off on a ten-kilometre circuit that would take me through the nearby tiny hamlet of Les Herbets, onto a pretty track lined with oak trees that passed between fields in which newly sheared sheep and their lambs grazed, eventually rejoining the poker-straight tar road to St Léger-Magnazeix. Crunching across the gravel in front of the schoolhouse, I took a left turn onto an unusually winding lane that led me towards Le Poux and thence back to Le Mas Mauvis. While running, I emptied my mind so that I could absorb the beauty of the hedgerows, the trees and the lush fields beyond. It was mid-May and the purple spikes of wild orchids that grew in abundance on the verges had faded, replaced by flushes of dainty yellow buttercups and tall white daisies, clusters of white and mauve clover, and the lacy white heads of cow parsley. Strands of purple vetch climbed through the lush undergrowth, their tiny pinnate leaves borne on slender, twining stems. Elder trees heavy with white, fragrant blossom dangled over hawthorn hedges intermingled with the delicate yellow and white flowers of wild honeysuckle, which wafted their heady perfume into the warm air as I plodded past. Pure, unadulterated bliss.

Shadier spots beneath the avenues of oaks and chestnut trees that lined the lanes sprouted fronds of bracken slowly unfurling like pieces of broderie anglaise, while nettles tried their best to crowd out the other wild plants with their serrated, stinging leaves and juicy, bristly stems. With the plentiful spring rainfall there had come a determined vigour in growth and the verges were thick with lush green grasses, heralding the arrival of the municipal tractors and their cutters to trim the verges. Waving to the driver of a tractor I overtook on the final leg of my run, I inhaled the herbal aroma of freshly mown grass, so evocative of the onset of summer. This verge-cutting process would be repeated weekly throughout the season, not only on the major roads but also on the narrowest of lanes: an indication of the intense pride the French take in the appearance of their rural environment.

The farmers of the Limousin had little time to sit back and savour the beauty of their surroundings. Spring was a busy period in the agricultural calendar, with the need for the ploughed fields to be prepared for the sowing of the summer crops. Monsieur Jérôme had been arriving at Le Mas Mauvis at about six o'clock each morning, having already tended to the beasts on his home farm. The journey by tractor must have taken him some forty minutes each way to cover a distance of only a dozen kilometres, but the vehicle was needed at both locations and he could not afford to buy two. With the machine's throaty engine coughing away outside Véronique's house, the farmer would first connect the sowing attachment to its rear amidst much clattering, banging and cursing, then pour sackloads of seed into its hopper. Then, after clambering into the cab, he would trundle down the lane running along the side of our property and into the undulating fields beyond the line of oaks at the back of our *grange*. All day long we would see him rumbling back and forth across the fields, sowing the seeds in the furrows, returning only briefly to reload the hopper. Working by the yellow beams of his tractor lights until ten o'clock each night, he seemed tireless in his efforts to meet some looming deadline.

'Jérôme must have the seeds sown by a certain date,' explained Véronique, as we watched the big man, looking tired and drawn, wrestling with his machinery. 'He is part of a co-operative. It is *impératif* that all the farmers sow their crops at the same time. But the fine weather is threatening to break. He must hurry.'

Day after day Monsieur Jérôme returned to the hamlet to complete his task until the deadline was met. But there was no time to rest on his laurels, for the fields of his home farm beckoned – another crop, another deadline to meet, and with an ominous weather front approaching came the risk of failure. It was a thankless existence for farmers barely able to support themselves and their families through their back-breaking efforts: days off were scarce indeed and holidays were merely to be dreamt of, never experienced. Illness and injury were feared, for they could mean the difference between survival and bankruptcy. Nature's abundance, for some, was a curse.

The life of a farmer was, nevertheless, considerably better than it had been before the advent of the big agricultural co-operatives that were set up after the Second World War. An aim of the co-operatives was to cut out the middleman and sell produce direct to retailers. Loans from the government enabled members to share expensive equipment, to pool resources, and even to enter into joint ownership of land in order to create larger, more economical farms. Families sometimes combined adjoining properties for this reason: our own Monsieur Jérôme and his family once owned more than fifty per cent of the entire hamlet.

Land parcellisation carved up most of rural France into a complex patchwork of narrow, often misshapen strips. In some cases a farmer would own dozens of small fields, frequently scattered kilometres apart. Our own property was originally composed of some twenty-eight individual parcels – some little more than a few metres wide by several metres long – before sensible recoding during our purchase reduced the total to a still cumbersome thirteen. Government-aided regrouping of parcels had in the past attempted to rationalise the situation, and some landowners exchanged parcels. But in the main, sentimentality scuppered the plan: *paysan* families who might have owned the land for generations frequently clung on to even the smallest, least viable fields.

It was difficult to see how some farmers made enough to live on. The brothers Messieurs Cédric and Émile possessed only a dozen cows – a mix of Limousin and Friesian – which they would escort each morning after milking to the small, scrubby pasture they owned at the other side of the hamlet. You could set an alarm clock by them: at 8.45 a.m. the precursor to the procession was the eerie sound of Émile's high-pitched call '*Iieeer-r-r-r! Iieeer-r-r-r! Iieeer-r-r-r!*', a kind of banshee wail ending with a series of rolling 'r's at the end. The brothers did not own a cow dog. As the stooped, shorter brother paced out along the lane with his long walking cane, the swaying cows would merely follow obediently in strict single file. Any rebels that decided to linger over the sweet grass at the side of the lane would be rapped gently but firmly on the flank by brother Cédric bringing up the rear with his stick and stammering '*Allez! Allez l-a-a-a!*' At 5.45 p.m. the procession would return to the milking shed.

At this time, farmers were also making their first cuts of grass for silage, the juicy green blades swept up by machines that passed over the cut rows and jettisoned the grass via chutes into attendant trailers that were tugged alongside. Other fields were striped with neat rows of cut stalks drying in the sun to make hay, which, after being turned regularly, were gathered up and spun into the huge, bobbin-shaped bales that soon began to dot the landscape. Tractors with twin forks on their lifting arms would then stack the bales onto the backs of flat-bed trailers, which carted them away to barns for storage.

Véronique had her work cut out for her, too. During this busy farming period, which coincided with the school holidays, her nephew would deliver his two young children to her each morning and she would tend to their needs until the evening, playing with them, feeding them and trying (usually unsuccessfully) to get them to lie down for an afternoon *sieste*. Monsieur Jérôme's wife Clarisse, when not looking after her baby, worked as a district nurse, and when obliged to attend to her rounds, delivered the infant to Véronique as well. We knew that our neighbour found her role as childminder taxing but she considered it her family duty.

'*Au demeurant*, what can I do? I am needed,' she said one day, physically exhausted after the rumbustious children had departed. The children loved their Tata, as they affectionately called their great-aunt, and of course she loved them too.

Although the weather had been kind to us and our farmer neighbours, a break in the climate, as gloomily foretold by Madame Météo, occurred after a day that had become increasingly hot as evening approached. Sitting on a log seat outside the main *grange* door, sipping a beer, I received prior warning of the imminent storm from Monsieur Jérôme, who came haring from the fields in his tractor, which he parked awkwardly on the common land, leaping from the cab as if it were about to explode.

'*Fermez les volets! Le vent est arrivé!*' he called out, running past with a look of sheer horror on his face.

'*Comment?*' I said lazily from my seat. I was hot and sticky, and wearing nothing but shorts and a pair of moccasins. I took another sip of beer. The farmer glared at me, ashen-faced, and repeated his apparently dire warning, which I still did not catch. He always spoke too quickly for me. '*Lentement, lentement,*' I said, urging him to calm down and speak slowly. He had a look of abject panic on his face now. I detected a waft of cool air that made my skin bristle with goose pimples. The farmer gesticulated towards our upper floor shutters, which were folded back against the front wall of the building.

'Ven zere iz vind,' he enunciated in heavily accented English. Gosh! I thought, it was indeed a rare occasion for Monsieur Jérôme to speak in English. Must be something important. '*Fermez les volets!* Get inside! The *orage* approaches!' With that, he sprinted across the track, secured the shutters across Véronique's windows, then disappeared inside the house and slammed the door behind him.

I rose and strode around the barn to study the sky. Mountainous, anvil-shaped strato cumulus clouds tinged with grey had formed along the horizon and heralded the onset of a thunderstorm of somewhat mammoth proportions. Already a warm breeze had arisen as if from nowhere. I scuttled back around the building and, taking the long pole I used to reach the shutters, swung the two outer oak doors around and secured their bolts. I clambered up the ladder into the *grenier* to join Al, who had been lounging in the tent reading a book.

'Hey, you,' she murmured. 'What was old beefy so upset about?'

'Jérôme? Oh, he was telling me to go and hide from the storm that's brewing. But I like a nice thunderstorm, don't you?'

The central shutters opened inwards so, there being no danger that they would be ripped off their hinges by the wind, I positioned two chairs in the open window. Al joined me and, holding hands romantically, we watched as the storm rumbled directly overhead, delivering a magnificently fierce downpour, first of pea-sized hailstones which bounced high on touching the ground, then a deluge of big raindrops that poured from the sides of the gutter like a waterfall, forming a sheet across the window opening. We sat in wonder and witnessed the powerful force of the sheet lightning that flashed across the dark sky and jumped at the deafening cracks of thunder. Meanwhile Monsieur Jérôme, we learned later from his aunt, was cowering in the house opposite with the power turned off and the telephone disconnected. In his youth, so her story ran, he had been caught out in a field during a thunderstorm and had been in close proximity to a lightning strike. Although uninjured, the experience had been sufficiently frightening to make him severely nervous of storms.

His insistence on switching off the power and unplugging the telephone and all electrical devices – which I first considered a little excessive – had been a sensible precaution, too: lightning tends to have a destructive effect upon the electrical and telecommunication systems of France, and it is not uncommon for answering machines, water heaters and other unsuspecting household electrical gizmos to be rendered totally useless in the event of being zapped, even down the cables of a system isolated from the mains, as we were to discover after another storm. On that occasion the element of our water heater was destroyed by a strike.

When we left for the UK after our short break, our departure was not accompanied by the usual feelings of homesickness or loss, for we had become more relaxed in our approach to our future. Certainly, we wished to reside here in Le Mas Mauvis, but we had other responsibilities back in England which demanded our close attention. But we knew in our heart of hearts that our future lay here in this crumbling barn and its overgrown fields and we consoled ourselves with the fact that we were going to return the very next month for a two-week summer holiday, and this time my son was to accompany us.

Chapter Nine

Monsieur Moustache

'Come on Landy! Pedal faster; it's not much further!' I gasped, furiously pedalling my own bicycle up the final hill and onto the downward stretch of road that would lead us to the cool waters of Lac du Mondon, the swimming lake some ten kilometres from Le Mas Mauvis. My son had come to realise the bald fact that distances in France seem to be double those in England: he was puffing strenuously, still unused to the twenty-one gears of the bright yellow bike Al and I had bought him for Christmas, but too stubborn to admit it.

It was July, the last summer of the twentieth century, and we had brought Landy to France for a one-week holiday, the first time he had seen the farm other than in the hundreds of photographs we had taken during initial renovations. The weather was glorious, although intensely hot that day, probably a little too hot for cycling. But frequent stops to imbibe water along the way kept us going and the signpost at the last junction told us that our goal was very near.

As we freewheeled into the car park under an awning of shady trees we could see the welcoming waters of the pretty lake before us skirted by a closely mown area of grass that led down to the little sandy beach. Beyond, an area of water defined by a line of orange buoys was filled with cavorting children and their parents, some diving from the metal tower at its centre, or leaping from the floating pontoon to one side. The little café overlooking the lake was throbbing with the sound of pop music.

While I arranged our towels on a patch of grass beneath the shade of a little tree, Landy stripped down to his swimming shorts and ran exuberantly towards the water's edge, only to double-back as soon as his toes touched the water.

'Blimey, it's freezing, Dad!' he yelped, dancing on the spot, hugging himself and shivering.

'Go on! Get in!' I called. 'I'll be right behind you.'

Bravely, Landy turned back and launched himself into the water, taking high steps, arms aloft, until he was obliged to dive in completely. When he reappeared from beneath the surface some metres away, his expression was a mixture of pain and pleasure. Then he began to swim for the pontoon and soon I saw him clamber out, only to dive straight back in again. Now he swam with a confident racing crawl to the diving tower, hauled himself up the ladder to the top and plunged into the depths, feet first, one arm aloft, the other hand grasping his nose.

I stripped down to my swimming shorts and trotted to the water, dabbling my toes to test the temperature. Sure enough, it was freezing cold. But what the hell! I plunged forwards and soon was enveloped by the bracing yet welcome coldness. Opening my eyes while submerged I could see that the water was not absolutely clear: it possessed a greenish tinge in common with many of the freshwater lakes that dotted the landscape of the Limousin. A lifeguard constantly stationed on site to ensure that swimming was safe, however, strictly monitored the condition of the water. Frequent samples were taken and checks were made as to the algae content and, should the balance fall below specific levels, bathing would be banned – denoted by the raising of a red flag outside the lifeguard's little hut near the water's edge.

Landy and I frolicked in the water until it became too cold for me to continue – an attack of the dreaded white finger sent me scuttling back to our spot under the tree – while my son, completely at home in the water no matter what the temperature, continued to amuse himself by performing underwater handstands, or disconcertingly giving the appearance that he was drowning, the victim of a shark attack. A strange game, this, but one that he had perfected to the extent that it was necessary for me to restrain the lifeguard from launching himself into the water to perform his rescue skills. While Landy swam, I took advantage of the glorious weather to bask in the sun, a pleasure only slightly marred by the pesky flies that insisted upon biting my exposed flesh just as I was getting comfortable.

Al had been unable to join us on our expedition due to the need to unravel a knotty problem regarding our application for planning permission to install windows and doors in the *grange*. Not wanting to spoil Landy's holiday by being trailed around various dreary planning offices, it was agreed that Al, the confident French speaker, would tackle the situation while we boys headed for the lake.

Rather naively, some ten months previously we had submitted to the local turreted town hall a declaration of works exempt from planning permission, believing that merely installing windows in existing openings would not require further consent. We had also helpfully attached snapshots of the front and rear elevations of the *grange* with tracing overlays indicating our wish to install wooden casement windows and a large glazed door in the cart entrance, all painted white. Shortly after returning to the UK we had received in the post a rather blunt response from *le maire* himself: '*Dossier Irrecevable*.' Our application form and photographs were returned.

'What have we done wrong?' I sighed, scratching my head. 'The photograph and overlay system worked fine for my brother when he applied to put pivoting windows in his roof, and even Gordon – a building surveyor by trade, who's qualified to work in France – says the method's commonplace.'

I was aware that, officially, if one wants to change the external appearance of a property in France it is usually necessary to first obtain outline planning permission, the *Certificat d'Urbanisme Positif*, from the Mairie after your proposal has been considered by the mayor and the town or village council. The application can be submitted by a *notaire* or *geometre*, land surveyor. With the French love for bureaucratic complexities, applications are usually then forwarded to the Direction Departmentale de l'Equipment, or departmental planning office for approval, after which it wends its way back to the Mairie to issue a certificate. But we were not planning to alter the outward appearance of the *grange* unduly.

Al, having finished translating Monsieur Le Maire's missive, said, 'It's simple really. Because the barn is still classified as *un bâtiment agricole*, an agricultural building, it's necessary for us to apply for a change of use to transform it into a *habitation*.' Building works, explained the letter, must conform to the *Code de l'Urbanisme* and additionally because the surface area of the barn was greater than 170 square metres, we would be obliged to employ the services of an architect, or a registered professional such as a surveyor.

'That's me!' said the perennially confident Gordon when I telephoned him for his advice. 'I'm registered to submit this kind of application. I can prepare the drawings and I'll get hold of a *permis de construire* application form, fill it out and send it off on your behalf as your agent. Don't worry! *Pas de problème*!'

But worry we did. Not because we doubted Gordon's abilities, but rather we questioned his faith that our paperwork would find its way through the maze of divisions and subdivisions that existed at the heart of the overly-complex French bureaucracy. Our worries were not without foundation because, after months of silence from France, we made several telephone calls to the Mairie only to discover that the progress of our application had indeed inexplicably stalled.

Arriving in France with Orlando for our holiday during that hot, sunny July, we had made an appointment to attend a rendezvous with Monsieur Benoît Pépin, representative of the rather grandiose-sounding *Le Technicien Supérieur* at the subdivision of the planning authority. Monsieur Pépin explained that our *permis de construire* would need to be accompanied by proper architectural drawings.

It appeared that Gordon had not, as we believed, provided his own technical drawings but had instead resubmitted our original photograph-and-tracing overlays. Back to square one, I thought. We could scarcely afford such additional unexpected expenditure, but it seemed that if our project was to progress at all we would need to engage an architect.

Monsieur Pépin helpfully suggested that we would need to take advice on what type of development would be best for our property and which materials and styles were permissible. He advised us to pay a visit, preferably with our chosen architect, to the offices of the *Conseil d'architecture d'urbanisme et de l'environment de la Haute-Vienne* (shortened to the acronym CAUE). This public department of information, located in the city of Limoges, would be able to make recommendations that would help speed our application through the vagaries of the complex and strict planning process. Great, I thought, we're being shunted from one subdivision to another.

'How are we going to be able to find a reputable French architect?' Al asked me. 'We've only got three days of our holiday left!'

'I don't know,' I sighed, deflated. 'I just don't know ...'

'Can you recommend an architect, Monsieur Pépin?' Al inquired. A reasonable question, but one which caused the man to recoil in horror, hands raised aloft, as if he had been asked to divulge his innermost personal secrets.

'*Oh, non, Madame! Ce n'est pas possible!* We at this subdivision cannot be seen to recommend specific artisans! *Mais*, it would not be professional!'

Al and I lowered our heads guiltily. How could we have stooped so low as to suggest that he could pass on such sensitive information as the name of a good architect? Glancing about him suspiciously, Monsieur Pépin inched a large, rolled up document closer to him and deftly released the ribbon securing it. The paper flopped open, revealing technical scale drawings of the finest detail, with all measurements included in fine print.

Monsieur Pépin lowered his voice: 'These drawings are examples of the type you would need to submit. They were prepared by an architect in Limoges for another English client. *Mais*,' he winked, stabbing a perfectly manicured forefinger at the name of the architect printed in one corner of the plans. 'If you were to note down the name of the architect, I could not be held responsible, *n'est-ce pas?*'

Al, quick off the mark, was already scribbling the name and telephone number of the architect on her notepad, as though we were spies in a wartime melodrama being shown some top-secret information by a double agent. It must have felt good for Monsieur Pépin, bound by the strict procedures and regulations of the sprawling French system, to bend the rules slightly.

Al was able to make an appointment to meet the architect at the *Conseil's* Limoges offices the very next day. Whether he would turn out to be suitable (and affordable) for our particular project remained to be seen. In writing interiors features I had experienced the excesses unbridled architects bestowed upon unsuspecting householders and had a fear that any architect worth his salt, on seeing our barn – a blank canvas by any standards – would want to vent the full extent of his design prowess on its immense potential. But all we wanted was to bung in a few casement windows. And for this we needed an architect!

An hour or so after Landy and I arrived back at Le Mas Mauvis from the lake, Al returned exhausted after an intense afternoon conversing in French about a subject she knew only cursorily. But she was keen to tell us not so much about her meeting, but more specifically about the impressive facial adornment of the architect, Monsieur Jean-Luc Bordes.

'Oh, he has such a fine, splendid moustache!' she enthused, demonstrating twin twirls of facial hair being teased aloft at the corners of her own mouth and reaching – somewhat exaggeratedly, I assumed – to well above eye level.

'So this architect has a corker of a moustache,' I said, pouring a glass of wine for my intended. 'But what about the meeting? What about our planning permission?'

'Well, I parked the car and I got to the office in good time. I'm glad I set off that bit earlier –'

'Yes, yes,' I snapped. 'Get on with the story.' Al was always one to set the scene with detailed, if sometimes irrelevant facts.

'So I met Jean-Luc as arranged. And what a charming, charming man he is, and with this magnificent –'

'Yes, so he has a sodding moustache! What happened next?' I gasped, as Landy and I raised our eyes to the skies.

'Well, we went in and we met Monsieur Lacotte – another charming man – and, well, it was all very productive. I showed them the photos of Mauvis and Monsieur Lacotte explained what we could do and what we couldn't. He suggested that on the back of the barn we could install these big pointy windows in the roof –'

'*Lucarnes*,' I interrupted. These dormer windows with high-pitched tile or slate roofs are common on the grander houses where rooms have been created in the roof. Attractive, I thought, but not on a barn conversion.

'But Monsieur Bordes said he didn't think they would suit the style and age of the building,' continued Al. Good, I thought, perhaps there's hope for Monsieur Moustache after all! Al went on: 'He's got an affinity with old properties – I could tell that immediately – and he made some sensible suggestions. Upshot is, he's coming here tomorrow at eleven o'clock to look at the property, discuss it with us and –'

'– work out how he can sting us for an arm and a leg, no doubt,' I interrupted cynically.

'Not necessarily. Well, we'll just have to take it a step at a time, won't we?' continued Al. 'But, I must say, I've never seen such an impressive moustache!'

Monsieur Jean-Luc Bordes certainly did possess the most magnificent moustache I have ever seen. Stepping out of a battered old white Renault, a smouldering Gitanes hanging loosely from between his fingers, Monsieur Bordes was every centimetre the archetypal architect I had imagined. Aged in his late forties, he was what I would describe as well worn. He was casually but expensively dressed in baggy brown corduroy trousers, tan sandals, a matching leather belt at his trim waist, and a rumpled linen shirt, open at the neck. A cotton-knit beige sweater was draped over his shoulders. His dark hair – thinning yet rebelliously unkempt – was swept back from his face with the merest hint of wax holding it in place. His face, deeply ridged and tanned, showed the signs of a rumbustious youth, of a man who had lived life to the full. His lower eyelids were baggy, suggesting long hours under a desk lamp, poring over architectural drawings (or perhaps late nights in some smoky jazz club). And that moustache! Thick and full, carefully waxed, brushed to each side and twirled and tweaked into graceful curves, it rose away from his cheeks like a cat's whiskers. I found myself wondering whether the moustache was ever left to hang freely from his lip, or whether he wore the facial equivalent of a hairnet to hold it neatly in place while he slept.

Monsieur Bordes swapped his cigarette from his right to his left hand and shook our hands in greeting with a sideways nod of the head. His right hand slipped casually into his trouser pocket and began jingling his small change as he stood back and admired the *grange*, taking a long, deep drag of his Gitanes, allowing the smoke to curl around his face before flicking the butt into a patch of nettles behind him. And then he was off, trudging around the building, arms outstretched as if trying to hug this fine piece of architecture. Al and I trotted along behind him as he strode through the long grass, oblivious to the lingering dew soaking his fashionable sandals.

'*Magnifique!*' he uttered. '*Splendide!*' He turned to us. '*Et maintenant, si je peux, l'intérieur.*'

We led the way back to the entrance and showed him the divisions of the rooms downstairs. He seemed impressed, though curious about our choice of timber stud partition walls rather than the traditional French metal framework. Clambering up the ladder into the huge upper floor of the *grenier*, the architect gazed up into the lofty roof with a look of rapture on his face. I thought that he was about to grasp one of the huge oak beams in an embrace and smother it with kisses, but he merely sighed and allowed his arms to drop to his sides, bereft of words and actions to express his appreciation for the building.

'*Tenez!* You are right to want to retain this space as it is. The room will be so light and airy – *glorieux! Merveilleux!*' He turned to look at the back wall with its single small window at the centre, then spun on his heels to examine the front wall with its three openings. 'But it is *très, très simple*! You should simply mirror these three openings in the front façade with three matching openings in the back façade. This will retain the symmetry of the building.' Monsieur Bordes paused, smiling, as if expecting recognition of his brilliance. Al obliged with a little ripple of applause. We both nodded our agreement.

'*En bas,*' he said, indicating the cart entrance downstairs. 'Simply mirror this opening with a matching one at the back, giving you *un merveilleux* view of your garden,' he continued. It seemed that our architect shared our own thoughts for the minimal but sympathetic changes we needed to make to the building. Maybe I had been wrong to tar all architects with the same brush, for this man did not appear to feel the need to suggest avant-garde or outlandish proposals about the use of contrasting shape and form and the marriage of diverse materials.

We showed him the example of the traditional casement window we had rescued from Monsieur Jérôme's rubbish tip that we wanted to use as the template for our new windows: elegant outer stiles with moulded glazing bars dividing each casement into three panes. The windows would open inwards, folding back against the metre-thick reveals. In many ways this is a more sensible format than conventional outward-opening English windows, which can easily be caught by a gust of wind and dislodged or ripped off. Our windows would be operated by turning the simple centrally positioned handle: thin rods protruding from the top and bottom of the metal handle would be pushed into retainers fixed to the outer frame to lock the casements shut.

'*Parfait*,' enthused Monsieur Bordes. '*Très traditionnel! Très français! Mais oui*, it's perfect for you! *Ça suffit! C'est tout!*' he smiled, lighting up a decisive cigarette. Good heavens! I thought gleefully, he didn't even try to convince us to install hideous PVC windows or the varnished hardwood frames that were universally popular in France.

The architect promised to let us know the cost of his services, which he indicated would not be excessive. After shaking hands, he eased himself back into his car.

'*Bon courage, Madame et Monsieur!*' he quipped before driving off, a curl of cigarette smoke streaming from the open window.

The following morning Landy and I arose from our beds and, leaving Al sleeping, started construction of a boules pitch. Cutting away the turf, we dug down a few inches to fairly firm earth, then set timber boards around the perimeter nailed to pegs driven into the ground. We barrowed gravel to the site, tipped it into the excavation and levelled it off. Several barrowloads of sharp sand followed, which we raked level to form our playing surface. By the time Al rose from her slumbers, we had already completed several games, watched by a smiling Véronique from the doorway of her house.

The remainder of our holiday was spent visiting other lakes in the vicinity for swimming and picnics. The weather was consistently fine with blue, cloudless skies. At the Lac de Saint-Pardoux, one of the larger lakes dedicated to water sports, situated amongst the densely wooded foothills of the Mont d'Ambazac, Landy and I hired kayaks and paddled around the ragged shoreline. At another picturesque lake within the neighbouring Creuse region we met up with the Count and Countess and their daughter Hollie for more swimming, an impromptu picnic and a game of *pétanque* before heading to a pizza parlour.

On one particularly balmy evening the three of us attended the annual *son et lumière* production in Le Dorat. This year it was *D'Artagnan*. The open-air performance was held in a broad, open patch of land overlooked by a raised bank of seating with the belfry of the Collegiate and its fortified towers as a darkly sinister backdrop. The show attracted thousands of locals and tourists alike over its three nightly airings. Each year a different tale is told by a cast of over one hundred performers attired in exquisite period costumes, plus attendant horses, sheep, dogs and other extras who act out vignettes on various parts of the stage, which measures some one hundred metres wide by fifty metres deep. The unfolding action – a series of linked set pieces – takes place in marvellously detailed sets constructed at points across this diorama, and is illuminated by spotlights which lead the eye.

On other warm evenings during that precious holiday, after dining at our rickety camp table or cooking a barbecue in the lane outside the *grange* entrance, Al, Landy and I would spread a blanket out on the dusty upper floor and, by candlelight, make hand shadows on the walls and play charades until we were too tired to continue. Retiring to our separate tents – Landy's pitched alongside ours – Al would fall asleep instantly while my son would chat to me across the void to a light show provided by his waving torch, until sleep finally overtook us.

We left France after our all-too-short break with Orlando, disheartened that we were no further forward with our renovation of the *grange*, although pleased that we had been able to act as tourists for a while in a country that was still very new to us. Back in England we could do no more than sit and wait for the architectural drawings to be sent over from France for our inspection. Jean-Luc's meticulous work, when finally it arrived, required few amendments and we were pleased when he was at last able to submit them to the planning authority on our behalf. However, a few weeks later we received in the post another document from Monsieur Pépin's subdivision: '*Dossier Incomplet*' read the subject line.

'What now?' I moaned. 'Did Jean-Luc forget to send the form in bloody triplicate, quadruplicate or whatever these petty-minded bureaucrats demand?'

'It seems that they want some information about *l'assainissement*, whatever that is,' said Al, translating the formal letter as best she could. 'I'm not very good with this official gargoyle.'

'Jargon,' I corrected absently.

'Yes, whatever, Lol. But what does it mean?'

'Drainage,' I stated, recognising the word from my studies of the Tout-Faire catalogue of building materials, which had become my major source of reading matter since buying the farm. 'They'll be wanting to know where we dump our ... er ...'

'Waste.'

'Exactly.'

'Actually, they seem to want to know what type of *fosse septique* we plan to install,' said Al. 'And there's mention of the *perméabilité du sol*.'

'Permeability of the ground: how quickly water drains away and at what depths, I expect. But we've already installed the damn thing!' I was exasperated.

'Maybe we neglected to say so.' Al's prophetic statements were, of late, becoming all too commonplace. Sure enough, we had failed to specify the fact that Monsieur Fugère had already installed the septic tank and there followed a delay of two months while the permeability of our soil was duly tested by yet another subdivision of a subdivision.

We eventually received notification that Monsieur Marcel Fugère's septic tank was deemed to deal satisfactorily with our waste matter.

'We should be home and dry now,' I said confidently.

Chapter Ten

A Rock and a Hard Place

One month later yet another missive dropped onto our doormat from the increasingly irritating Monsieur Benoît Pépin: '*Dossier Incomplet*' ran the subject line once more.

'They're asking if we have authorisation to use parcel E910,' explained Al, plainly confused.

'E910? What's that then?' I asked, fishing out the bulky file on Le Mas Mauvis from my desk drawer. I found our copy of the *plan cadastral*, an entry in the register that shows details of ownership and boundaries, originally for taxation purposes. The date-stamped official plan clearly showed our property outlined in blue highlighter pen in relation to the surrounding properties.

The property itself was divided up into individual parcels of land of various shapes and sizes, each one labelled with its own code number. These numbers, along with an identifying prefix, were listed in the accompanying *Désignations des immeubles ruraux*, along with details of all previous ownership. I cast my eyes over the plan and located the quoted parcel number.

'That's the communal land!' I shrieked. 'It's not even part of our property. What the hell are they talking about?' Sure enough, the portion of land in question was indeed the 'village green' that stretched in front of and to the left of our property.

'Yes, but this seems to say that we need authorisation in order to *emprunter*, to borrow in other words, the parcel E910 in order to *accéder*, to reach our property,' said Al, translating more of the letter. This situation was getting more ridiculous by the day.

A call to Jean-Luc and his subsequent investigations revealed that we did indeed need to obtain permission from yet another department within the planning authority in order to reach our own property via the communal land at the centre of the hamlet. '*Une formalité*,' assured the architect. '*Pas de problème.*' Thankfully, Jean-Luc took the matter in hand and, no doubt with a twirl of his splendid moustache, convinced the relevant officials that the land referred to in the letter was indeed communal, as marked on the cadastral plan and that, as owners of the property, we had every right to '*emprunter la parcelle*'.

Nevertheless it was another month before Monsieur Pépin – now with apparent disregard for his personal safety – risked having parts of his anatomy torn violently from his trendy body and fed to him one by one, by sending us yet another letter with the maddening subject line: '*Notification du delai d'instruction.*'

'I recognise that word *delai* and I'm not at all a happy bunny,' I grumbled, fearing the worst.

'There will be a delay of three months while our case is put before *Monsieur l'Architecte des Bâtiments de France à Limoges*,' paraphrased Al, becoming quite adept at translating these officious proclamations.

'Who the hell's he, then?'

'Someone important,' replied Al, somewhat obviously.

'But three months? For God's sake! Three months? We only want to turn the barn into a house. We only have one near neighbour and she couldn't give a hoot about what we do. In fact, Véronique can't wait for us to turn the place into a house instead of the rat-infested muck heap it is now! So what's the delay for?' My usually normal blood pressure, I felt sure, was fit to blow a gasket.

Al read the punchline from Monsieur Pépin's letter: '*Votre projet est situé dans le champ de visibilité d'un édifice classé.*' Further telephone enquiries and liaison with the redoubtable Jean-Luc confirmed that our barn was, as Monsieur Pépin's letter stated, 'in the field of visibility of an *édifice classé* located on farmland adjoining ours, namely an ancient stone, Le Polissoir, known as *Le Poulvan de Sejotte.*' Unknown to us and not revealed in Madame Marsolet's searches, we had bought property that fell within an area of historic interest, which would require the special attention and judgement of another authority, the Architect of Buildings of France.

On one of our fleeting 'red-eye' three-day trips to Le Mas Mauvis (one long day to drive there; one too-short day there; one long day to drive back), Al and I stood at the corner of the hangar adjoining the *grange* and gazed at the distant treeline beyond, the farm we knew as Sejotte.

'So they're saying that if all the trees in our woodland weren't there, which they are, and if the ground was perfectly flat, which it isn't, and if we had a pair of super-powerful binoculars, which we don't, we might just be able to make out a skanky rock behind that herd of brown cows?' I said.

'Sacrificial stone,' stressed Al. 'It's supposed to be an ancient sacrificial stone, according to Jérôme. Remember, he pointed it out to us on the first day we came to see Mauvis? It's on the other side of the Pentecostal pathway.'

'Yeah, I remember. And I know exactly who I'd sacrifice on the sodding stone, too,' I said. 'Monsieur Benoît flippin' Pépin and all his subdivision cronies ... and Monsieur bleeding Architect des Bâtiments de France if he rejects our planning consent.'

'I think you're using poor Monsieur Pépin as an escape goat,' said Al. I let the Alism go rather than interrupt my theatrical dark mood. 'He's only doing his job, Rich.' She continued in an attempt to introduce the cool voice of reason to my ranting. 'You of all people can appreciate the importance of planning permission and the preservation of ancient buildings and such.'

'Yes, I know, I know,' I said, slinging an arm over Al's shoulder. 'But we only want to put windows in a barn on walls that don't even face this chunk of rock. And if we don't get planning permission, where does that leave us? It means we can't convert the barn into a house. It means we'll never be able to live here. Remember how long this place had been on the market? Three years or more! They couldn't find a buyer for it.'

'Do you think the rock was the reason the place didn't sell, then?'

'I don't know, Al. But it's possible we've been sold a pig in a poke by Monsieur Smiling Jérôme ...'

Prevented from carrying on with our major renovation work on the *grange* – we were also legally unable to complete the electrical installation and plumbing work until formal permission had been received – we spent a late autumn visit to Le Mas Mauvis tinkering with those small, less important jobs we would ordinarily rather leave until later. It was on one such occasion, while I was tending a huge, smoky bonfire we had created from the useless, dusty hay that had been stored in one of the ancillary barns, that I heard a voice calling out in the distance.

'Oi! Buggerlugs!'

I looked up from my work at the high-pitched call. Did I mishear something? Perhaps it was simply the dulcet tones of Monsieur André summoning his cows for milking, or calling to his favourite porker.

'Oi! Baldy!' There it was again. I looked around but could see no one. 'Oi! You deaf old git!' No, this was definitely not the sound of genteel country folk going about their rural tasks. I straightened up and discerned a blotchy pink object waving from a distant rooftop, leaning on the chimney stack. One of Monsieur André's *cochons*, perhaps, escaped from its pen and marooned on the ridge of the roof? No, pigs might fly! This was a semi-naked man, wearing a large Australian bushman's hat and a pair of disreputable tracksuit bottoms, perched on the roof of one of the little cottages Gordon was planning to convert into holiday accommodation. The man waved a bricklayer's trowel. 'Rick, you old tart! Cooee!'

Now I recognised the figure. Jean Le Grand! Whatever was he doing here? And what was he doing on Gordon's roof? Rounding the bend that led to the cottage, I saw my builder friend hard at work rebuilding part of the gable wall of the house. There, too, was Gordon, also semi-clad in true English builder fashion (but, a blessing, without the bum cleavage), drafted in as labourer, mixing mortar in John's mixer.

'Hello, me ol' fruit!' greeted John from the rooftop, obviously in his element: the phrase 'a pig in shit' sprang to mind.

'Hope you don't mind,' said Gordon, wiping perspiration from his brow. 'I pinched your builder.'

'You're welcome to him!' I said. 'How's the great lug working out? I didn't think they'd let him back in the country, actually.'

'He's fine, but I didn't realise he talked so much drivel,' replied Gordon, grinning.

'He never stops, Gordon. He never stops.'

'And I didn't realise you were such a slacker, Gordon!' hollered John. 'How long's that pug going to take to mix? All bloody morning?' He indicated his empty mortar bucket.

'OK, OK,' grunted Gordon.

'Anyway, Gordon, I was intending to come around to see you. Would you and Maureen care to attend our first dinner party tomorrow evening in the *grange*?'

'Love to,' said the reluctant navvy. 'What time?'

'Seven-thirty suit you? Véronique's coming and she doesn't do late evenings.'

'Fine. I'll be exhausted after all this physical labour and the constant jabbering from John up there!'

'What about me?' wailed a dejected John.

'OK, you can come too. But put some flipping clothes on!'

Our first dinner party at Le Mas Mauvis was more of a glorified picnic because of our limited facilities, but nonetheless an auspicious occasion. The lack of a staircase meant that we would be obliged to hold the party in the central ground floor hall: it would be impossible for Véronique to clamber up the ladder, and Maureen would find the task difficult. We cleared the hall of junk and swept down the concrete plinths that had been created from the mangers. On one of the plinths we laid out the banquet: a spit-roasted chicken; beef tomato and basil salad drizzled with olive oil; a fresh herb salad; pasta with tuna, onions, peppers and mushrooms; a rice salad; and a *couronne*, a circular bread loaf. On the opposite side we positioned director's chairs and laid out rugs on the other concrete plinth, and placed a long wooden bench between as a narrow table. Candles in terracotta pots of sand illuminated the room.

Some time after John, Maureen and Gordon had arrived, there was still no sign of our guest of honour, Véronique. Al went in search of her, only to return some minutes later with sad news. Our neighbour's father-in-law, who had been briefly returned from confinement in hospital, had suffered a relapse and, rushed back to hospital, had died. Naturally Véronique, being consoled by her nephew Jérôme and other relations, was not in the mood to party and sent her apologies.

Our gathering was somewhat muted after learning of our neighbour's loss, and we were mindful to modify our raucous gabbling to a more sensitive level, even managing to muffle the normally ebullient Jean Le Grand.

We suspected that Monsieur Jérôme had waxed a little overly lyrical about the purpose of Le Polissoir, the ancient stone whose presence on the adjoining farmland threatened to hinder our conversion of the *grange*. Intrigued, I carried out a little research on the history of this edifice and discovered that, rather than being a sacrificial stone it was, as the name translates, a 'polisher'. Such stones are found in many places around the world, many in parts of Europe, notably Luxembourg, France, Sweden, Ireland and Wales, where they have been the subject of lively debate by archaeologists and historians alike. *Polissoirs*, also known as arrow stones, are reputed to have been employed by our Iron Age ancestors to sharpen their early metal tools and arrowheads. They are identified by the glyphs, carved channels or grooves, which mark their surface. Some sources argue that the glyphs are merely rock art, while others lean towards the somewhat bizarre notion that the channels were created during an inner visual experience by some latter-day acidhead experimenting with hallucinogenic substances, or during incantations. Experts cast doubt on the sharpening purpose of the *polissoirs* by claiming that the action needed to produce v-shaped grooves would actually blunt the blade. There are other ways in which the *polissoirs* might have been employed. Similar grooves found on stones in Southern Africa have been attributed to Iron Age farmers grinding grain. Different types of glyphs have been identified. Lenticular grooves were used to grind millet, whereas flat and bowl shaped ones were used for maize: the glume or membranous bract of the grain leaving behind a residue, or polish.

'C'mon, Al,' I said one morning. 'We might as well go and see this polishing stone. Might as well know what we're up against, eh?'

We sauntered down the path and through the long grass of the back field, clambering over the wire fence that separated our property from the Pentecostal way. A little stile allowed access to our neighbour's field, in which the *polissoir* languished, along with its attendant smaller stones. The stone – a large dome-shaped boulder about two metres high – dominated a small valley, where legend has it there exists an ancient tomb, which gave rise to the belief that *Le Poulvan de Sejotte* might once have been a site of human sacrifice. Nestling amidst the long grass and bracken in the shade of a line of leafy trees, our foe the stone had an unnatural appearance rather like plaster of Paris poured over fabric and set in broad folds. Patches of green and yellow lichen clung to the pitted surface of the sand-coloured edifice. The domed top of the stone was deeply ridged with vertical glyphs, which were clearly artificially formed. Whilst fascinated to see this undoubted cultural treasure, the damn thing was nevertheless holding up our project!

'Wait here a minute,' I said suddenly. 'I'll go and fetch a crowbar to use as a lever.' Suppressing a laugh, I set off across the field with Al trotting behind, unsure if I was serious.

Al need not have worried. Although peeved that its presence was causing us serious delays, I could not help being fascinated by the infernal rock and had determined to find out more about its chequered history. Our commune, I learned, was rich in edifices such as the *polissoir* – several ancient rocks could be seen protruding from the surrounding fields, carefully mowed or ploughed around by the farmers – although not all were *classé*, officially listed as being of archaeological merit. I wondered whether the bramble-choked mounds that we had discovered dotted around our own back field and near the Ugly-Bugly also concealed similar remnants from man's ancient past, and could not wait to attack the rampant growth to find out what lay beneath.

It transpired that this part of the Limousin was abundant in signs of prehistory, which literally poked out of the soil. In the neighbouring commune of Mailhac-sur-Benaize, for example, was the site of Le Dolmen de Bouéry, and a few kilometres distant near the town of St Sulpice-les-Feuilles, Le Dolmen de Bras, both said to date from around 2,000 BC. The Breton word 'dolmen' means 'stone table' and these structures, thought to be megalithic tombs, consist of a single chamber formed by three or more upright stones roofed by a single capstone. There are, in fact, reckoned to be over four thousand dolmen in France. In other parts of the locale there were examples of individual standing stones – menhirs, from the Breton word meaning 'long stones' – in addition to other *polissoirs* such as the one that was causing us our current grief.

Back in the UK once again in the closing stages of the twentieth century, and still without word from France as to the status of our planning application, Al and I consoled ourselves with the happy news that my divorce had finally been declared absolute and that we could at last plot our own wedding the following summer.

We received a wonderfully kitsch *Joyeux Noël* card from the Bussieres, in which a little note from Bruno explained, most humbly and apologetically, that he was finding his efforts as lumberjack somewhat arduous, largely due to his bad back: therefore, would we consider revising our agreement from *moitié-moitié* status to two-thirds of the resultant logs to him (reflecting his physical input) and one-third to us (as owners of the property)? Al telephoned and wished the couple a happy Christmas and said that, of course, the suggested new division of logs was fine by us for the remaining fallen trees. We noted, however, that I would soon have to assume the role of lumberjack, for we would need all the wood we could get for our own heating requirements.

We spent an enjoyable few days during the New Year 2000 celebrations at the Count and Countess's Cheshire home, watching the clear night skies above the flat plains explode with light as hundreds of firework displays and bonfires were ignited at midnight. A banquet, copious amounts of champagne and convivial company made both couples think of their French homes and the fine times we could spend there. But what if our planning permission was refused or severe restrictions were placed upon us for the conversion work?

It was with trepidation, then, that we opened the next correspondence that we received from France, in April 2000, some five months after Jean-Luc Bordes submitted our *Demande de Permis de Construire*. The document was from the *Service Départmental de l'Architecture et du Patrimonie de la Haute-Vienne* – seemingly yet another office in the maze of divisions and subdivisions that proliferate throughout the country. Signed and dated at the end of January by Monsieur Poncet, *L'Architecte des Bâtiments de France*, it had been duly passed back to Monsieur Pépin's subdivision for rubber-stamping (literally) in February, then onward to *Le Préfet de la Haute-Vienne* for his approval some two months later, at the end of April. And the upshot? Our planning consent was approved on condition that we conserve the existing wooden shutters on the top floor of the barn (which we were going to do anyway); the new window openings were to be the same as the originals (which they were); and finally that the walls supporting the terrace planned for the rear of the grange (and indicated on the plans by Jean-Luc) be given a coating of mortar in the specified regional colour. We had not planned to reach the stage of building the terrace just yet, but the condition posed no problem.

Amazed but relieved that so few restrictions had been applied to our project, we felt that we were back on track at last. We spared no time in instructing Monsieur Laborde to recommence his electrical and plumbing work with as much haste as he could muster, while thanking the moustachioed Jean-Luc Bordes for his sterling efforts on our behalf. Our joy was only marginally blunted by a telephone call from Gordon with news that a particularly ferocious storm had ripped a sizeable part of the roof from the *grange*, allowing the rain to pour in. As temporary keyholder, he had done as much as he could to minimise the damage, but our presence was required in France *tout de suite*.

The storm had brought down a mass of slates from the front pitch of the roof, which now lay in razor-sharp shards on the floorboards, along with the metal clips that had held them to the rafters. There were gaping holes along the ridge, and in other places two or three slates had slipped out of place or had disappeared altogether. While the storm damage was not extensive, the sight of piles of slates and accumulated dirt littering the floor, plus the puddles of rainwater that soaked the boards, was severe enough to dampen our spirits when first we emerged through the trapdoor a week or so after Gordon's telephone call. We had managed to snatch a few days' holiday from work and had brought with us our friend Kenny – my future best man – who had been keen to see the property we had talked about for so long.

He was shocked, I think, not only by the devastation wreaked by the storm but also by the rather primitive conditions we lived in when at Le Mas Mauvis. Now, Kenny is a man who appreciates the good things in life: he has a plush bachelor pad in the heart of London and spends his evenings dining out in fashionable restaurants or attending the theatre. Always immaculately dressed in chinos and smart but casual shirts, with trendily styled hair, the nearest he comes to roughing it is taking the Tube rather than travelling by taxi – and that is only very rarely. Despite our warnings of the basic conditions at the barn, he had nevertheless seemed keen to join us for a four-day red-eye trip. Faced with grim reality, however, he was shocked by our lack of plumbing and functional sanitation.

'My God, man! There's no loo, never mind a shower! Where on earth do you wash?' I handed him a tub of baby wipes. 'What about the loo then?' I pointed through the large gap in the floorboards to the ground-floor room below, where the Bio-Pot was just visible. 'Oh, that's sure to bring on a wee bout of constipation!' he moaned. And sure enough, it did.

These factors, combined with the absence of electricity, must have made the sophisticated Scotsman think he had been transported to the Dark Ages. 'How do you manage at night, when it gets dark?' he enquired, flicking the non-functioning light switches. I handed him a candle, the likes of which he had only ever seen as the centrepiece to a romantic restaurant table.

A priority on arrival was to brew up a pot of tea. Tea calms frayed nerves and makes one feel at home. I unwrapped the little methylated spirit camping set we used and pulled out the tiny kettle. Once water was set to boil on the camping gas stove I laid out the aluminium saucepans on the camping table.

'We didn't do a very good job of cleaning this last time,' I announced, examining the brown granules in the bottom of the frying pan. Al peered over my shoulder.

'What is it?'

'Looks like instant coffee,' I said, sniffing the contents. 'Doesn't smell like coffee, though.'

'Oh, for heaven's sake, you two are hopeless!' said Kenny, for some inexplicable reason licking a forefinger, dipping it into the brown granules, then shoving the finger into his mouth. He immediately screwed up his face and began spitting frantically. 'My God! What was that?'

'I don't know, but it's not coffee,' I confirmed, indicating the fact that the granules were now on the move, scuttling around the perimeter of the pan on tiny sets of legs. 'Bugs!' I said. Kenny's face turned white. He started wiping his mouth furiously and making choking noises.

'Water! Water!' he shrieked, just as Al came to the rescue with a bottle of Evian. Kenny slurped down the liquid, slooshing his mouth. 'Bloody hell! What sort of place have you brought me to? It's freezing cold, pouring with rain, there are holes in the roof, you sleep indoors in a tent, the place is infested with rats – and you've given me bloody beetles to eat!'

Cursing loudly, he headed off down the ladder and out of the *grange*, presumably to throw up in some private place. Al and I looked at each other blankly, wondering why on earth our friend – normally very particular about what he ate – should decide to perform his taste test on our pan of bugs.

'Just think, Kenny,' I consoled him later, as he brushed his teeth for the umpteenth time. 'You were lucky. It could have been mouse droppings.' Judging by the scowl on his face, my friend did not necessarily agree.

To his credit, Wee Kenny, as we affectionately called him, adapted well to our 'ethnic' conditions after he had sufficiently recovered from the bug episode (although he suspiciously scrutinised any cup of coffee that was offered to him thereafter). Donning a pair of wellingtons, a plastic mackintosh and a pair of gardening gloves, he threw himself into the task of clearing up the interior of the *grenier* and dismantling the wreckage of Al's favourite shed, a little corrugated tin-roofed lean-to in which cut logs were stored. Robinson Crusoe – as Al had obscurely named it – had succumbed to the effects of the storm and lay in a crumpled heap in the lane.

The weather was appalling but the constant heavy rain, which soaked the two tents pitched beneath the gaping holes in the *grange* roof, did not dampen our resolve to enjoy our stay. After our insurance agent had visited the property with the promise to do what he could to claim for our roof repairs, Al and I took Kenny on a tour of the neighbourhood. Visiting Le Dorat for lunch, our guest was enthralled by the sight of the lofty Collegiate de St Pierre. After lunch we strolled in the rain through the maze of sixteenth- and seventeenth-century alleys and squares, passing the nineteenth-century fountain and terraced gardens that run along the ramparts with splendid views over the valley of the Courtoison.

In the 1400s Le Dorat was surrounded by some twenty fortification towers and some of the connecting ramparts are still visible in the town, particularly around the Porte Bergère, the only fortified gate remaining in the Haute-Vienne. The original eleventh-century church was equipped with its own defensive tower, which rises from the *chevet*, the semicircular east end of the building. The rounded wall of the tower is pierced with arrow slits, and three small corbelled turrets, the bartizans, protrude just beneath the conical roof, complementing the original Romanesque cornice of the church. The octagonal belfry recedes in diameter with each of its three floors, culminating in a 30-metre stone spire capped by a thirteenth-century gilded copper angel standing a metre and a half in height.

We entered the church through the imposing Moorish mosaic doorway, set at higher ground level than the opposite east elevation. From the top of a broad, steep stone staircase, the stones damp and worn irregularly by hundreds of years of use, the view is breathtaking. The church is laid out in a classic Latin cross plan some eighty metres long, with narrow side aisles and a central nave with five bays. As we walked down the flight of steps and towards the nave, we stared up into one of the two domed ceilings high above our heads. This cupola was supported on *pendentifs*, triangular sections of vaulting positioned at each corner of the space from which the dome rose. Apart from the faint glow that filtered through the eight stained glass windows within the octagonal belfry, illuminating one of the cupolae, the choir stalls and the entrance to the crypt, the light within this vast church was gloomy and its atmosphere was damp and musty.

After examining the capacious granite Carolingian baptismal font, we noticed that we were not the only occupants of the church: a lone figure dressed entirely in black sat hunched on a pew near the altar, praying. Not wishing to disturb the lady in her solemn prayers, we returned to the opposite end of the church and climbed the steps to the door. Al sauntered through the door and put up her umbrella. Just as Kenny and I were about to leave, my friend noticed an incongruous object situated to one side in a dark corner.

'What d'you reckon this wee thing is?' he whispered in his soft Scottish lilt, examining what appeared to be a dusty television screen set within a walnut veneer case. There were knobs on the front of this curious device and instructions too complicated to read.

'No idea,' I said absently. 'Look, there's a slot for money.'

Kenny immediately rifled through his pockets, produced a ten-franc coin and proceeded to insert it into the slot. Nothing happened until Kenny randomly pressed the little buttons located beneath the screen, which suddenly glowed eerily in the gloom. Whereupon the blessed calm of this holy place was shattered by a booming, deity-like pronouncement echoing from the depths of the cavernous building. Accompanied by concealed spotlights, which suddenly flared into dazzling life, casting all shadows from every nook and cranny, the guttural voice began to dictate the colourful history of the Collegiate in unintelligible French. The praying lady at the front of the church must have suffered a severe shock, wrenched as no doubt she was from her silent communion with God.

'Bollocks!' I said, diving for the open door, leaving a stunned Kenny to suffer the consequences of his foolhardy action.

'You bastard, leaving me alone in there like that!' said Kenny, catching us up around the corner. Light now glared from previously blank windows and the thick stone walls vibrated to the sound of organ music emanating through the open door.

'Pathetic!' sighed Al at the sight of two grown men scarpering like naughty schoolboys from the scene of a prank. Having disturbed the quiet gentility of Le Dorat with our sacrilegious behaviour, we returned to our car and headed back to Le Mas Mauvis.

Our insurance company very fairly agreed to pay out for the storm damage, which meant that we could instruct Monsieur Fugère to carry out repairs to the roof of the grange. He duly arrived on our last day to receive instructions, appearing at first uncustomarily sluggish when ascending the ladder we still used in order to reach the *grenier* floor.

'How's he going to make it onto the roof if he can't even get up to first-floor level?' whispered Kenny, while the artisan took measurements. It was a fair comment. However, after a timely rummage in his van's glove compartment, with the pretence of fetching a tile brochure for us to inspect (which, strangely, he failed to locate), Monsieur Fugère's movements appeared somewhat more lubricated.

Al and I had decided to replace the flimsy slates on the front pitch of the roof with terracotta tiles to match those on the back pitch, taking advantage of the opportunity – once the roof was stripped to the rafters – to fit an under-tile screen made of a tough plastic material, which serves a similar purpose as the bitumen underfelt widely used in the UK. Bituminous products were not generally used in the hot climate supposedly enjoyed in this part of France, as they tended to melt.

'Do you think he'll be all right, then, tottering about on the roof when he's had a few?' asked Al, waving farewell to Monsieur Fugère as his van sped out of the hamlet. 'His wife must worry.'

'He seems capable,' I replied.

'Maybe he needs a few nips to pluck up the courage to go on the roof in the first place,' suggested Kenny.

Chapter Eleven

The Grass Rustler

Despite George W. Bush's apparent observation that the problem with the French is that they don't have a word for entrepreneur, the French have a term for most things. It often seems that the longer the word, the better (although their widespread use of acronyms suggests that even they get tongue-tied or tired of pronouncing the abnormally long names of the various service industries that proliferate in their society). It appeared to us foreigners in their midst that this trait went hand in hand with the French penchant for drawing out occasions beyond the limits normally accepted or expected in other countries – the two-and-a-half-hour lunch break being a prime example; the multiple-course *dîner* being another.

They also seem to have the ability to make any job stretch to three times the duration it should realistically take.

While Gordon and Maureen had discovered that the rewiring and replumbing of their house – expected to take a matter of weeks – was still unfinished a year after Monsieur Laborde first turned up with his glum sidekick Jean-Philippe, reels of cable and lengths of copper tubing, Al and I were also frustrated by our incomplete systems, despite the assurance of the effervescent electrician-plumber that the task would be simple and speedy. After all, the barn had no existing system to remove (I had already ripped out Monsieur Jérôme's dangerously rudimentary circuits); there were no floors to lift up, as access was easy from the exposed joists below; while cables and pipes could either be buried in our stud walls or chased into grooves cut in the stonework. However, when Monsieur Laborde was not being called out to tackle urgent winter repairs on burst water pipes in other clients' houses, he was awaiting the arrival of an official inspection on his meticulous work by jobsworths from the electricity company or the water board. We were fearful that soon our project would be hit by that other long-winded French institution, the summer holiday, which writes off the entire month of August as companies shut down and much of the population heads off *en vacances*. Everything is put on hold.

Monsieur Jérôme was a procrastinator *par excellence*. It was not that he was lazy. Far from it: with his farm at Arnac-le-Poste ten kilometres away and the spread he still retained at Le Mas Mauvis, the farmer was constantly busy. This was in addition to the duties he shared with his wife Clarisse in caring for their young children. Yet time and again he would turn up with one helpful suggestion or another, which never saw fruition.

'I can pull that out with my tractor,' he helpfully offered one day, seeing Al and I struggling to uproot a tangle of wire fencing from where it had become buried in the ground.

'Can you, Jérôme? *Très gentil de vous*,' said Al.

'*Oui,*' he went on, shrugging. '*C'est facile. Pas de problème.*'
Waving, he turned back to his tractor, climbed aboard, and with
a guttural roar of its powerful engine, turned it around and drove
off, leaving us standing knee-high in rampant grass like a pair of
lemons. When two weeks had passed, Al and I returned to digging
the fence out by hand.

Maureen had waged a personal war against the surly farmer
ever since he had failed to remove a collection of *cuisinières*,
woodburning range cookers he'd obviously been stockpiling, from
the barn adjoining her and Gordon's house, a year after they had
bought the property from him. The war of nerves deteriorated into
a war of words, however, after an unfortunate incident regarding
a cow. Monsieur Jérôme still owned a barn and several fields
adjoining Gordon and Maureen's property and our own farm, and
kept several cows therein. Now Maureen, a committed vegetarian,
turned a blind eye to most of the dubious (to English sensibilities)
agricultural practices she knew to be rife in France. But when
one of the farmer's Limousin cows developed a fatal condition
and promptly expired, he lost no time in removing the corpse
from the barn (where its presence was obviously a hindrance to
the other occupants). But rather than summoning the veterinarian
and arranging for the poor animal's removal, he dumped the
cadaver, stiff with rigor mortis, in the yard just outside Maureen
and Gordon's house, in full view of their kitchen. The couple's
paying guests, on descending in the morning to partake of a spot
of breakfast, were treated to the unwholesome sight of Monsieur
Jérôme's hunting dogs – still running wild months after escaping
their cell on our property – plus other motley neighbourhood
mutts, savagely tearing the hapless cow to shreds.

Maureen herself went in for the kill when the farmer finally
appeared and nonchalantly shooed the dogs away from the
scene of carnage. Being physically unable to floor the hulking
farmer, however, she released such a torrent of verbal abuse that
the surprised monsieur – even if his knowledge of English was

as scant as he professed – got the gist of the tirade. He slunk off, metaphorical tail between his legs, and promptly had the cow removed. From that day on the big man kept a respectable distance from the ferocious vegetarian, who herself could be heard mumbling in a most unladylike fashion whenever he passed within a few metres of her.

Not long after the incident with the cow, Monsieur Jérôme sold the barn to his neighbouring farmer, the gravel-voiced Monsieur André, who promptly moved several pigs into the squalid premises. The cows had been relatively quiet compared with the porkers who, not unnaturally, put up a piercingly loud vocal protest when certain of their number were loaded into the clanking truck that Monsieur André drove, and ferried away to the slaughterhouse at five o'clock in the morning. The crafty pigs would frequently escape the poorly secured barn and run squealing through Gordon and Maureen's garden and, with Monsieur André typically occupied on another part of his spread, I would often be called in to help corral the escapees. Round and round the barn Gordon and I would chase the pigs until they surrendered and trotted back indoors, leaving behind them a trail of destruction that was once a vegetable patch, and two breathless blokes, humiliated at having been outrun and outsmarted by bacon.

Maureen found that living in a French farming community – particularly when one was a vegetarian – had its penalties.

If Monsieur Jérôme was genial, procrastinating, a little franc-obsessed, but basically kind-hearted, Monsieur Thierry André was quite another *bouilloire de poisson*, as Al and I found out to our cost. Apart from when the farmer had come to remove the grain from our *grenier*, I had only really encountered him on one other occasion, and had little means to measure his character. The fact was that I found him incomprehensible at the best of times. If it was true that he spoke French, then I was prepared to give up learning and stick to sign language. On our second unfortunate encounter, he had rumbled up on his tractor – dressed in baggy shorts, a filthy string vest and a pair of green wellingtons – dismounted and strode up to where I was mowing the scruffy patch of grass and clover in front of our barns using my father's old hover mower.

'You twat!' he said. Or at least it sounded like that. Admittedly the mower was designed for urban pocket handkerchief lawns rather than the gravel strewn sods I was attempting to trim. But I thought that his reaction to my efforts was a little excessive.

'*Pardonnez moi?*' I said, quite taken aback.

'*Toiture!*' he repeated, pointing skywards. I looked up. Then I realised that he had been pointing at the roof of our *grange* – the *toiture* – which had recently been re-covered with tiles by Monsieur Fugère after our insurance pay-out.

'Oh, you mean the roof,' I said, the light dawning on me. 'What about it?'

'*Où sont les ardoises?*' Monsieur André demanded, his voice hoarse and strained. Why did he want to know where the slates were? 'I eat *ardoises* for breakfast!' he elucidated, and made a gesture to his lips with his filthy fingers, as if demonstrating his unusual dietary habit. Consumption of roofing slates would surely explain his gravely voice. But no, I thought. There must be something seriously amiss with my understanding of even basic French.

'*Je ne comprends pas, Monsieur. Vous mangez les ardoises?*' I queried.

'*Comment? Mangez les ardoises?*' He looked at me as if I was crazy, then, without a by-your-leave, stomped over to the little rickety access door that lead into Bill the ancillary barn, almost ripping it from its hinges, and ducked inside under the lintel. I followed him.

'Ah! *Les ardoises!*' he said, pointing at the neat stack of slates which Monsieur Fugère had arranged after removing the old roof covering from the *grange*. 'Pah! *Pas beaucoup!*' he snapped, turning abruptly and stomping out of the barn. Mounting his tractor, he coaxed the machine into life, turned it around and sped off without even an '*au revoir*'.

I was none the wiser until, the next day, Al and I were woken from our slumbers by a deafening din. Crawling from our tent and peering through the little window in the back wall of the *grenier* towards Monsieur André's pig barn, we could see that the roof, which had lost many of its slates during the storm, was being shoddily patched by the farmer and a team of workers using sheets of rusty corrugated iron.

'So he was trying to cadge our slates to patch his own roof, eh?' I said in realisation. 'But we didn't have enough.' To this day I have no idea what the man was actually saying regarding the edibility of slates. Amused, I continued to watch the amateur roofers' progress as they nailed the iron sheets to the exposed rafters in an unusual manner: starting at the ridge at the top of the roof and working down, overlapping the lower sheets onto the upper ones, they guaranteed that any subsequent rainwater would simply pour between the joins and into the barn.

The slate-eating farmer had next clattered up in front of the *grange* in his pig wagon and clambered out of the cab looking as if he had just returned from wallowing with his porcine charges. Wearing a filthy, once-white baggy string vest, torn denim trousers and a pair of green wellingtons, the farmer's exposed skin was slick with sweat and spattered with dirt. His arms resembled the muscle-bound legs of a bodybuilder, his huge hands like baseball mitts. The ever-present grubby flat cap was wedged crookedly on his balding pate. He proffered the back of his right wrist for us to shake, apologising for his disreputable state: '*Pardon ... sale ... tout sale.*' Dirty. All dirty. We silently agreed, gingerly pressing the extended flesh and making a mental note to wash our hands thoroughly at the earliest opportunity.

Monsieur André pulled a huge stained handkerchief from his trouser pocket, blew his nose loudly and swiped the disgusting rag across the beads of sweat that trickled down his forehead, dislodging the cap so that it perched jauntily on the back of his head. After a few minutes' polite small talk about the weather and compliments on the fine work we had done on the *grange*, the farmer mooted a suggestion that at first sounded most appealing.

Pointing to our fields and the shoulder-high patches of nettles and thistles that covered much of the surface, he croaked: '*J'enlèverai les orties … et nettoierai les champs pour vous … si vous voulez*,' then pointed at his own chest. As usual, I hadn't a clue what he was talking about, and a glance in Al's direction told me she had only managed to catch part of the man's words. After a few minutes of miming from Al and more croaking from the farmer, we established that he was offering to get rid of the nettles and clean up the fields for us. We were puzzled by this strangely unprecedented offer. There must be a catch. There was. He qualified the statement: 'Let me graze my cows on your land. I clean the fields in return. It is good for both of us. We both win. It is a good deal.' He placed his hands on his hips and awaited our response, grinning broadly and nodding.

How timely, we thought. Because we were not on site permanently, the land was becoming unkempt and out of control. When Monsieur Jérôme was in residence, his cattle would graze the fields and twice a year he would cut the grass. But we were discovering how rapidly the nettles and thistles engulfed the property, despite our best efforts to keep them at bay with sickle and scythe. Because of the future presence of llamas on the land, we had chosen not to use chemicals to rid ourselves of the weeds, while realising that they would always regrow unless we killed off their roots. Monsieur André's offer, then, sounded like the ideal solution to our problem, while doing him a good turn in providing extra summer grazing for his animals.

We discussed terms: he would graze the fields only during summer, because his cattle would be confined to their byre in winter when the ground was too wet; he would erect his own electric fences to contain the beasts; he would, in return for the grazing, remove and burn the nettles and keep the perimeter of the buildings clear; he would also remove the remaining junk – an old rusty moped and the remnants of a dilapidated chicken shed we had half-demolished, amongst other things – from where it had become buried in the long grass.

Gratefully accepting the farmer's offer, we were impressed when he left no time in returning with his tractor and grass-cutter and conscientiously topped the rampant growth.

'This is such a good idea,' said Al confidently, as we watched him cutting swathes through the long grass. 'It'll be fantastic not to have to worry about clearing up the nettles each time we come to Mauvis, won't it? And when we want to start to create the garden, we can simply confine the cows to a smaller area.'

'Yeah,' I agreed, not for one moment considering that perhaps this helpful farmer might have his own hidden agenda. When next we visited Mauvis some months later, the fields had been efficiently grazed by the herd of cattle, yet islands of nettles and thistles still remained, the perimeter of the buildings was still engulfed, the moped still lay half-buried, and the broken wire fence that Monsieur André had promised to pull out with his tractor as part of his clean-up procedure still stood defiantly. It was, however, some months before we began to suspect that the wily farmer's motives were more selfish than they were neighbourly.

Al and I married in June 2000 amidst the medieval splendour of the Baronial Hall at Groombridge Place in East Sussex, the picturesque location of the enigmatic Peter Greenaway film *The Draughtsman's Contract*. The hall was decorated with wall hangings and wrought-iron candelabra, and rows of chairs had been positioned to face a broad stone fireplace beneath the minstrel's gallery, in front of which the ceremony was to be performed. A group of some sixty relations and close friends filed into the hall as I paced nervously, awaiting the arrival of my bride-to-be and her father. Wee Kenny, my best man, had done little to quell my bout of nerves, preoccupied as he was with his own fearful thoughts of the speech he was obliged to give at the reception. He and Landy, acting as usher, had also been at pains to convince me that I would rue the day I decried the styling properties of gel to tame my somewhat flyaway forelock for the forthcoming wedding photographs.

'Mark my words, it'll take the merest puff of wind to make you look more like Daffy Duck than the bridegroom!' warned Kenny darkly.

My nerves subsided, however, when I turned to see Al walking up the aisle on her father's arm to meet me, for she was the image of loveliness, wearing an unadorned ivory dress – the first girly clothes I had ever seen her in – with her dark hair down, as she knew I liked it best. At the sight of her broad smile my fears dissolved. The ceremony went without a hitch until it came to placing the ring on her finger, for it would not budge beyond her first knuckle. We fumbled. Behind us, our guests must have wondered what the delay was. I pushed. And then Al snorted. A loud, nasal, porcine and quite unladylike snort that reverberated around the hallowed hall. The registrar, a prim and proper middle-aged lady, frowned. Had we no sense of decorum? Obviously not, for Al snorted again. Those on the front line, who had witnessed our fumbling, looked down at their feet lest they lose their cool. Amidst more pig-grunts and a wave of giggles from the congregation the ring finally slipped over Al's knuckle and at last we were pronounced husband and wife.

The reception was held at Al's parents' nearby home, a lavish yet comfortably informal affair which was attended by another hundred or so guests. The day was terrifically hot and, in addition to the marquee that had been erected in the garden, we had placed intimate little seating arrangements under the shade of the trees and beneath pergolas erected on the lawn, where people could gather and dine on the fine buffet provided by local caterers. Claire's beloved horse Dickens and my mother-in-law's steed Thunder lapped up the attention lavished upon them at the fence that separated their paddock from the garden, and everyone agreed what a fine wedding it had been. Slipping away from the celebrations in the late afternoon, Al and I shared a romantic seafood dinner on board a floating restaurant in Little Venice and stayed overnight in Kenny's London flat.

I had managed to keep our honeymoon destination from Al until the last possible minute, and the following day we flew to Milan, picked up a hire car and headed north to spend a week in the village of Bellagio. Fittingly described as the Pearl of Lario, this charming village is located on a promontory that divides Lake Como in two: west towards the bustling town of Como, east towards Lecco.

The airline's loss of Al's luggage meant that after a few days of sharing my clothes, which swamped her slender frame, she was obliged to purchase an entire new wardrobe. We spent lazy days swimming in the cool, clear waters of Lake Como, sunbathing on the shingle beaches, or else rising early, pulling on our walking boots and setting off on lengthy hikes to explore the ruggedly beautiful terrain. The scenery was spectacular: a panorama with the snow-clad peaks of the Swiss Alps as a backdrop. On one memorable occasion we headed out of Bellagio and followed a steep and well maintained trail that led up the wooded slopes of Monte San Primo. After an enervating two-hour climb, passing through high meadows lush with wild flowers, we found ourselves overlooking the breathtaking view from a little restaurant that was doing a roaring lunchtime trade near the summit. We settled on the grass and marvelled at the sight of the gleaming waters of the lake and the terracotta-coloured buildings of the villages nestling around its shoreline some 1,600 feet below. Although it was nothing remotely like our little part of France, that awe-inspiring vista made us hungry to advance the plans for our future life together. It is at times like this – far from the pressures of everyday life – that one is able to see and think clearly.

So even as that mountainous beauty surrounded us, our farm at Le Mas Mauvis was never far from our thoughts. The idyll of our honeymoon served only to strengthen our resolve to relocate to France as soon as conditions would allow. During a romantic lakeside dinner one night we made the momentous decision that I should take a six-month sabbatical from work, initially to write the novel I had been planning for many years, and secondarily to plug on with the restoration work on the *grange* at Le Mas Mauvis. Finances would be tight, but Al felt sufficiently recuperated after the death of her sister to take on full-time employment. On our return to the UK she lost no time in finding a job back in the music industry.

When we returned to France with Orlando later that same summer we were thrilled to find that our electrical, plumbing and sanitation systems were fully functioning. The faithful Bio-Pot was summarily dismantled and put into retirement, replaced by a shiny new plumbed-in WC (which nevertheless had an unstable wooden seat that would pitch the hapless user disconcertingly onto the floor after any false move). The shower provided a magnificently powerful head of water at the rose and, rigging up a curtain around the tray, we basked in the novelty of cleansing ourselves in piping hot water rather than making do with baby wipes. Al and I were not at all disconcerted by the fact that the bathroom possessed no door, and that naked bathers could easily be glimpsed from the *grenier* due to a lack of floorboards directly above the shower. Landy, on the other hand, would sing loudly whenever bathing or using the loo, as a means of warning others of his ablutions.

Now that our modern facilities had projected us into the twenty-first century, Véronique voiced her sorrow that we would no longer need to shower at her house, and instead offered us the use of her washing machine, which we gratefully accepted.

Although the *grenier* was now equipped with numerous electrical sockets and dimmable bulbs concealed within the roof beams (we had yet to buy the spotlight fittings), we did not entirely forsake the use of candles at night, which provided an altogether more romantic ambience when dining, playing charades, or creating finger shadows on the massive backdrop of the stone walls.

The rolling fields at the back of our property were resplendent with the swaying heads of sunflowers held aloft on slender stems; a rich splash of gold against the intense blue of the summer sky softened only by the fine green textures of the surrounding trees. As the sun set each evening the sunflowers seemed to absorb and reflect its radiation so that the horizon glowed warmly, even as the first stars began to pierce the darkening sky.

Surrounded by such unadulterated beauty, we were rather embarrassed about the appalling state of our fields. We were becoming increasingly concerned about our grazing arrangement with Monsieur André. The fields at the back of the *grange* were in a sorry state. They had been over-grazed to the extent that the grass was reduced to an exhausted, pale yellowish-green stubble sapped of goodness, and the ground was pitted with deep hoof prints and spattered with cowpats. Our fields appeared to have been the epicentre of a bovine diarrhoea epidemic. No attempt seemed to have been made to care for the land or to rotate the grazing, and the nettles, thistles and brambles had been allowed to grow rampant. Landy was distraught that our boules pitch had been swallowed up by the exuberant growth. Monsieur André, who would ordinarily make an effort to come and greet us on our arrival in the hamlet – as was the polite convention with other neighbours – instead made himself conspicuous by his absence.

'The bugger's deliberately trying to avoid us,' I remarked to Al one afternoon, after we had just raced out of Véronique's kitchen during *un petit quatre* on hearing the unmistakable sound of the farmer's pig wagon clattering up the lane.

'I think you're right, Bertie!' agreed Al, using another of my inexplicable nicknames, as we watched the vehicle roar away in a cloud of dust and a screech of tyres, its tin siding banging noisily.

'*Il est malpoli!*' commented Véronique from the doorway. Calling Monsieur André rude was a strong comment from a woman who preferred to keep her opinions of her neighbours guarded.

When finally we collared the elusive Monsieur André one morning as he attempted to tiptoe past the *grange* at the rear of his herd of cows, he was evasive about the lack of his cleaning up operations, and tried to fob us off with one lame excuse after another as to why he had not kept to his side of the bargain.

'The ground is too wet for the cutter,' he rasped, visibly rattled at having been apprehended. We pointed out that apparently the ground had not been too wet for the cows, which had badly churned up the ground. He tried another tack, shrugging, palms up. '*Mais*, it's necessary to catch *les orties* just before they set seed,' was his next excuse. But surely the nettles had already cast their seeds to the wind weeks ago? We folded our arms and assumed stoical expressions. 'I've been laid up! I have *un mal au dos*,' he offered, rubbing the small of his reportedly troublesome back with a pained expression on his sweaty face. We continued to stare at him blankly. He wriggled some more. 'And my tractor, it is badly broken.' None of his excuses seemed convincing. And he knew it.

'Perhaps you were kidnapped by aliens as well?' I muttered under my breath in English.

'*Comment?*' he said, screwing up his porcine eyes. The farmer had dug himself into a deep hole and stood peering out of it with a decidedly sheepish look. Shuffling uneasily, he saw his chance to escape: since we had been grilling him his cows had made for the lush green of the communal land and were now beginning to wander onto the tar road. The sly farmer suddenly cried, '*Ah, les vaches!* I must go! *À plus tard, eh?* We talk later?' He slithered off, tail between his legs. But Al and I had already decided that the time for talk had passed. It appeared that our good nature was being abused.

I followed Al back into the barn where she took solace in a packet of rice cakes. Eating was sometimes a comfort to Al in times of stress, and at least rice cakes were a healthy and non-fattening option. The fact that they were tasteless and unsatisfying seemed irrelevant to my new wife. Frizzy-haired Monsieur Cyrille

Laborde, who had arrived that same morning to tweak parts of his electrical installation (and also to give us our bill), looked concerned when Al grumpily explained our plight to him. His eyes widened in an exaggerated expression of shock and rolled around manically in their sockets. He slapped a hand across his forehead with his usual verve.

'*Faites attention!*' he wheezed, drawing us aside, while stabbing a warning finger aloft in dramatic emphasis. 'It is *très, très important* that you are clear about such arrangements with farmers. I do not know this man, but here in France you must be *très, très attentive!*'

'What's the problem?' asked Al, nibbling on a rice cake like a distressed hamster, suddenly very worried.

'*Mais*, it is the law here in France, Al! If a farmer is given permission to graze the land, and the agreement exists uninterrupted for two years ... *alors*, then the man will have the right to do this ... *toujours!*'

'Always?' The hamster furiously demolished a second rice cake, little white flakes descending and adhering to the front of her T-shirt.

'*Certainement!* You must be *très, très* wary, or you will be stuck with this man and his cows for good! I know this to be true. A no-good relation of mine did this very thing to me! This farmer, I take it he does not pay you for the grazing?'

'No,' said Al, and we both shook our heads mournfully. 'We didn't want to make it a really formal agreement because eventually we want to create a garden at the back – and eventually we'll have the llamas to help us to keep the fields in good condition.'

'*Lamas?*' he shrieked loudly, looking mystified.

'Do you know what they are? Llamas?' asked Al, thinking perhaps there was another French word for the animals.

'*Oui, naturellement*, of course I do!' snapped the electrician, as if piqued that the extent of his general knowledge might be called into question. '*Mais*, I have never seen any around here. Only on *le télé* ...'

Al scoffed a third rice cake, trying in the name of expediency to ignore the electrician's divergent query about our llama plans.

She didn't want to complicate matters any further. 'Monsieur André's supposed to clear the nettles and brambles away in return for the grazing.'

'But this arrangement is not written down?'

'No.'

'Then you have no proof, and still he continues to graze the land.' Monsieur Laborde massaged his ruddy cheeks thoughtfully and shook his head. '*Oh, non, non, non, non, non! Faites attention*, my friends! *Faites attention!* If you take my advice, you will pay a visit to the *notaire*.'

Al offered the little electrician a rice cake, noticing how the morsels had intrigued him. 'What are these things?' he asked, curiously examining one of the circular slabs of compressed rice.

'*Riz ... galettes de riz ...*'

Monsieur Laborde nervously bit into a rice cake, his teeth squeaking on its spongy texture. Then he began to chew frantically with a look of utter disgust on his face. '*Mon dieu!*' he spluttered. '*C'est polystyrène!* Urgh! You're trying to poison me! *Sacré bleu*, this is disgusting! Is this the sort of thing you *Anglais* eat?' We both chuckled as the effervescent Monsieur Laborde recovered his composure, wiping his mouth with the back of his shirt sleeve. Al wandered off, clutching her rice cakes. The electrician continued stripping a length of cable of its insulation with a pensive expression on his face, while I rummaged around in my toolbox for a tape measure.

'*Alors!*' said the electrician, after an awkward silence. 'So tell me about these *lamas*. Do you pay them for this work?'

'Pardon?'

'Do you pay these *lamas* for the work they do on your land?'

'Pay them?' I trilled. What was the man on about? 'Well, no, Monsieur Laborde. You just have to feed them ... *c'est tout*.' The electrician scratched his head in incomprehension. I was saved from further explanation, however, by the timely arrival of the man's son who had come to collect his father.

A few days later, I realised that Monsieur Laborde might have been labouring under a false and somewhat ridiculous misconception. This notion occurred to me after a conversation I had with Bruno Bussiere, after I had helped him to transport his share of a load of logs from our woodland to his house. We had spent over an hour in the hot sun stacking the cord and I was grateful to be invited into the tiny kitchen for a refreshing glass of beer. After our ritual greeting, Jolanda ushered me to a seat and sat down opposite me, smiling across the table in between concentrated drags on a long menthol cigarette. She sipped her syrupy coffee from a minuscule cup. The lumberjack flopped down next to her, his tatty mauve vest drenched in perspiration.

We began a faltering conversation. So what exactly were we going to do with all that land we'd bought? Were we going to keep animals? Cows? Sheep? Were we going to grow vegetables? I brought up the subject of llamas, which seemed to tickle Bruno's sense of humour. I suspected that Madame Météo's attention, however, was more drawn to the images on the screen of the portable television set that flickered silently on the dresser just behind my head, rather than my admission. Bruno, always a man keen to expand his horizons, excused himself and wandered off, returning after a few minutes with an old, moth-eaten illustrated encyclopaedia, which he plonked on the table. Snatching his wife's spectacles from the bridge of her nose, which left her gazing about her in apparent near-blindness, he held the lenses in front of his own eyes and began to leaf through the pages of the book as if searching for information that would be proof positive of his English neighbours' suspected lunacy.

'Voilà, Richard!' he said, handing the spectacles back to his wife, who repositioned them on her face and continued to stare past my right ear at the television screen. Bruno spun the book around to show me, stabbing a grubby gardener's finger on the page.

'*C'est ça!*' I said, pointing to the picture of a particularly woolly llama, with its French spelling of the word, *lama*, written in bold type underneath.

'So this is *le lama*!' rasped Madame Météo, the smouldering cigarette dangling from her pursed lips, her attention momentarily diverted from the television. 'I have not seen a creature like that before. *Jamais!* It's like a sheep with a long neck, and a very ugly beast in my opinion!' She coughed heartily, drew on the cigarette and returned her gaze to the television.

'Pworr! Don't be ridiculous, woman. It looks nothing like a sheep,' mumbled Bruno. 'It is a type of camel. See, it is written here.'

'Pah!' said his dismissive wife, ash falling from the cigarette end into her coffee cup.

Bruno stroked his chin in contemplation of the curious creature in the photograph. 'Thees *lamas*,' he continued, now testing out his pigeon English. 'Thees *lamas* … iz gud eat, yes? Gud *manger*?' He proceeded to mime the action of chomping on a tasty cut of meat, then licked his lips.

'No! You don't eat them, Bruno!' I protested. 'In the past maybe, but not nowadays.' The man's smiling eyes told me he was teasing me.

'*Non? D'accord*. So what you do wiz thees *lamas*?'

I raised my eyes aloft. This was going to sound stupid. 'You take them for walks,' I revealed.

'Pworr!' uttered Bruno, shaking his head, his Connery-esque eyebrows cavorting like caterpillars on his forehead. He ran his stubby fingers through his sparse grey hair. He was clearly baffled. My eye was caught, however, by the alternative meaning of the word, which was illustrated by photograph of a bald-headed man of Eastern persuasion wearing a vivid orange robe, his hands clasped in prayer as he bowed towards the camera. It was then that an amusing thought suddenly occurred to me: could Monsieur Laborde possibly have assumed that we crazy *Anglais* were intending to have our farm maintained not by a herd of long-necked, domesticated, cud-chewing mammals, but by a gang of itinerant Buddhist monks from far-off

Tibet, willing to barter their agricultural skills in return for food and lodgings? The mind boggled.

Bruno was just about to further our discussion on the merits of llamas as walking companions as opposed to their potential use as a culinary ingredient when he was silenced abruptly by his wife, who brandished the television remote control at the flickering, silent screen. The volume suddenly boomed behind me, rattling the sides of the set and almost piercing my eardrums.

'Sshh!' hissed Madame Météo, and Bruno and I clammed up instantly. We both knew that it was time for the midday weather forecast, during which all conversation must cease.

The *notaire*, Madame Marsolet, leaned forward and placed her elbows daintily on her pristine desk blotter, interweaving her slender fingers with their perfectly manicured nails. Resting her chin lightly on her thumbs, she scrutinised us over her spectacles. We felt rather scruffy in the presence of this doyenne of the notarial profession, having not come to France equipped for socialising with the pillars of society.

'So, Monsieur and Madame Wiles! You are now married. You have bought your house in France. You have experienced a few legal, shall we say, *hoquet*, the hiccups. Ahem! Your renovations are progressing well.' She spoke in perfect English; a series of statements rather than questions. We couldn't disagree with her prognosis.

'Yes, Madame,' we chimed in unison, sitting stiffly on our chintz-cushioned chairs, our hands resting politely on our laps.

'But you have – what shall we call it? – a *désaccord*, a disagreement, with a neighbour.'

'Well, not so much a disagreement, Madame,' I said. 'We allowed this farmer to graze his cattle on our fields in return for him clearing up the nettles, brambles and so on. It was his suggestion –'

'Of course it was,' Madame Marsolet interrupted plainly but politely, with a pert smile.

'But, although he's grazed the fields heavily – in fact, he's stripped them bare! – he hasn't done a thing about clearing up.'

'No,' she said, as if that, too, was only to be expected. Gullible *Anglais*, she was probably thinking. 'Free food for his cows.'

'Yes, Madame. And we understand that if he is able to use the land for two years without, as it were, paying for it, he will have the right to do so forever.' Al delivered the punchline.

'Ah! *Vraiment!* This is quite so!' Madame Marsolet leaned against her high-backed chair and folded her hands across her slender waist. 'And you want to stop this from happening, of course. This would be most, shall we say, *non pratique.*' Again the little smile.

'Yes, Madame,' we echoed.

'You want to rescind this verbal arrangement.'

'Yes, Madame.'

'You want this *temporisateur* – this procrastinating *vacher* – to get off your land!' She raised her neatly plucked eyebrows. Madame Marsolet had the bit between her teeth now, apparently warming to her role of champion of the oppressed. The *notaire* suddenly spun around on her chair to face the computer on the desk behind her, and tapped a key to wake the screen from its state of slumber. '*Alors*, Monsieur and Madame Wiles, I shall write this lazy man a letter this instant! What is his surname please?'

'André,' said Al.

'And his *prénom*, please?'

'Thierry.'

Her fingers began clattering wildly on the keyboard as lines of text scrolled down the screen. After a few minutes, punctuated by brief pauses to ask us pertinent details about the farmer, a letter slid out of the printer, was deftly plucked from its tray and onto Madame's blotter, whence she signed her name with a flourish. '*Voilà!* It is done!'

Madame Marsolet read out the letter in French, paraphrasing its content in English for our benefit: in it she suggested that we, her English clients, requested that our previous verbal arrangement with Monsieur André be terminated at the beginning of the next October – some three months hence – because of the need to rest the land after a heavy summer's grazing and to allow us to arrange for the establishment of our garden (premature, but not untruthful). In the letter, the tactful Madame explained that we had been concerned that language difficulties might create a misunderstanding between Monsieur André and ourselves, and that the purpose of the letter was formally to record the situation and our wishes.

'I think that this will suffice,' said the *notaire*, sealing the letter in an envelope and tossing it into her out-tray. 'And now, if you will forgive me, I believe I have others waiting.' She rose and ushered us towards the door. When Al raised the delicate subject of our bill, Madame Marsolet was adamant that there would be no charge. '*Oh, non, Madame et Monsieur*. I am only pleased that I could be of assistance. There is no charge for this letter. No charge.'

If we left that office confident that an official missive from one of the most respected and – we understood – feared *notaire*s in the region would stop Monsieur André's nefarious plans for back-door domination of our fields, we would be proved totally wrong, as the events of the following months would show. No sooner had we left France after that summer visit than Monsieur André, who had remained scarce after delivery of Madame Marsolet's letter, blatantly moved his animals back into our already worn out fields, where they remained entrenched, not just until the October deadline, but throughout the winter and well into the following spring. Apparently gifted with precognition, the wily cattleman had the mysterious ability to remove the animals from the fields the day before we arrived, unannounced, in an attempt to catch the grass rustler red-handed.

Chapter Twelve

What Goes Around

An area of our renovations that we had been keen to proceed with was the installation of windows in the *grange*. This, we felt, would help to invest the building with its new identity as a human habitation rather than its previous outward appearance as a working barn, while sealing it for security and warmth. In a novel alternative to the traditional wedding list, we had instead asked friends and relatives to contribute to the French Window Fund. Such was the success of the fund that we were able to commission an English carpenter acquaintance (whose surname, coincidentally, was Carpenter) to construct the casements for Mauvis using as a template the old frame we had rescued from the rubbish tip, which the architect Jean-Luc had waxed so lyrically about. Simon the Carpenter had never before constructed window frames that opened inwards, and had been intrigued by the ancient example we had brought him.

'It's a bit arse-about-face really,' he had announced after close inspection of the window. 'But I'll give it a whirl.'

'*Llamas are good companions*' stated the little advertisement I discovered tucked away in the classified pages at the back of a dog-eared copy of *Living France* magazine. During a mild dose of writer's block I had been idly leafing through the journal, imagining I was back in France. Intrigued by the photograph of the cute little cria, or baby llama that accompanied the text, I read on:

For helping you clear your property
For trekking along French country lanes
Or just for pleasure
Call me for further info
Les Lamas de Briance-Ligoure

There was, in addition to a French telephone number, a website address. I soon found myself reading about the herd of llamas owned by Monsieur Bernard Morestin, based only eighty kilometres from Le Mas Mauvis, south of Limoges. I sent an email to Monsieur Morestin with a list of questions about llama-keeping. The next day I received an enthusiastic reply suggesting that I visit his farm on my next trip to France, when he would be able to answer all my questions in detail. He preferred the informal approach, he explained, and would have pleasure in devoting as much time to me as I needed.

As Al and I were travelling to France in a few weeks, I emailed Monsieur Morestin once more and promised to telephone him on our arrival in order to arrange a visit during our stay. Somehow, putting our plans for a future at Mauvis into action, even though it might have been a little premature, seemed to bring us closer to the day when we would finally relocate there.

Once I had completed a substantial wedge of my novel and the manuscript was touring literary agents and publishers, amassing a collection of rejection slips, but not without some favourable comments, Al, Landy and I temporarily evicted my hot-air balloon from the trailer in which it resided, loaded up our completed window frames plus sixty panes of glass (substantially cheaper in England than they were in France) and hauled the load down to Mauvis.

Work and family commitments had meant that this was our first visit since the previous summer and, although we expected to be faced with the jungle of weeds and brambles that choked the perimeter of the buildings, we were horrified to discover that the fields at the back of the *grange* had been turned into a sea of rock-hard ruts. The winter and spring had been particularly wet and it was obvious that a considerable number of cows had been ensconced on our land for some time: a fact confirmed by our spy in the camp, Véronique. The current dry weather had dried out the quagmire, leaving a dangerously uneven surface that could easily twist an ankle. It is normal farming practice for animals to be overwintered in byres during the wet months, but it seemed that our sneaky neighbour – despite the official letter from the *notaire* – had been availing himself of the free grazing our fields offered. After all, how could he prevent his animals from wandering onto our fenceless land? And anyway, what did it matter if *les Anglais'* fields were reduced to a mire? What did they want all that land for anyway? No, it was no skin off *his* grimy nose.

'What goes around goes around,' remarked Al sagaciously, if inaccurately.

'Comes around,' I corrected. 'It comes around. First it goes around. And then it comes around.'

'Yeah, whatever, Rich. He'll get what's coming to him one day.'

Little did we know how true those words would turn out to be.

Although we did not approve of the cattleman's underhand grass-rustling activities, we certainly would not have wished such a dramatic comeuppance upon him. His prize Limousin bull, fed up with his master's bullying tactics or annoyed at having been separated from his wives, turned on the farmer while he was cajoling the animal from one field into another and severely gored him. The incident was witnessed only by the diminutive Gordon who, descending his staircase one morning, chanced to peer from the landing window at the precise moment the huge animal attacked Monsieur André in the field beyond his garden.

'He was tossed in the air like a rag doll,' reported Gordon when we paid him and Maureen a visit the day after our arrival in France. 'I thought at first it was just a pile of old rags!' An easy assumption to make, I reflected; the farmer's general appearance was less than pristine at the best of times. 'Then, while poor André was splayed on the ground, the bloody animal gored away at him and then proceeded to trample all over him. He was in a terrible state! The poor devil didn't stand a chance of defending himself!'

'My God! What happened next?' asked Al, as shocked as I was that her dire prediction about Monsieur André getting his just retribution seemed to have come to fruition.

'Well, I didn't stop to think,' said Gordon. 'I just found myself running to help him, snatching the first item of defence I could see: a white plastic garden chair, if you can believe it! I really didn't think of the consequences; I just dived between this raging bull and poor stricken André, brandishing a plastic chair like a matador with a red cape and a sword.'

Quite how Gordon thought the flimsy chair would be adequate defence against 1,300 kilograms of rippling muscle is open to conjecture, but the plucky little man's intervention enabled the injured farmer to roll under a fence and into a ditch on the other side where the bull could not reach him. As soon as Monsieur André was safe from continued attack, Gordon beat a hasty retreat and joined the farmer on the other side of the fence. After making the man as comfortable as possible – he had suffered deep lacerations to his back, stomach and arms – Gordon telephoned for assistance. Airlifted by helicopter to hospital in Limoges, Monsieur André lay in intensive care for three weeks and was lucky to survive the ordeal, which left him severely scarred and vowing never to keep a bull again. His rescuer, although modest about his intervention, was highly praised for his bravery and even received an official commendation from *le maire* himself.

By the time we arrived at Le Mas Mauvis, Monsieur André had been discharged from hospital and, after a lengthy convalescence, had returned to working his land. He had, however, become a much more subdued individual since the goring incident and, true to his vow, never again owned a bull.

He did, however, retain his noisy coterie of pigs – much to Maureen's chagrin – and a modest herd of high-yielding black and white Friesian milking cows. These animals, a somewhat unfamiliar sight in this part of France, would, we discovered, still avail themselves of the free grazing our fields offered, whenever we were not around.

After a short five-day sojourn at Le Mas Mauvis, Al and Landy had to head back to the UK, my son to prepare for his first term at boarding school, my new wife – at that time the only breadwinner in our family – to return to work. I was to remain in France in order to commence the installation of the first of our windows and, when I had time, to continue writing my book. It was an odd feeling waving goodbye to them at La Souterraine railway station and even odder driving back to Le Mas Mauvis alone. When I drew up outside the *grange*, I was heartened to find a carrier bag deposited by the doors, which contained a slug-infested lettuce, a few juicy red tomatoes, a dozen freshly dug potatoes and a long, pale green vegetable that resembled a marrow. I was touched by the generosity of my mysterious benefactor. Hearing the car draw up, Véronique poked her head out of her back door and waved.

'I thought you might like *un petit peu de salade*, Monsieur Richard,' the dear lady called out.

'*Mais oui*, Véronique!' I replied, peering into the bag again. '*Vous êtes très gentille.*'

'*C'est rien! C'est normale!* I said to Al that I would look after you, Monsieur Richard. It's only a little salad.'

I pulled the marrow-like vegetable from the bag and held it up. '*C'est merveilleux*, Véronique. But what exactly is this vegetable?' My neighbour looked at me quizzically, as if my question was ridiculous.

'It's a courgette, Monsieur Richard,' she announced simply. 'Do you not have courgettes in England?'

'*Oui*, Véronique. We do. Of course. A courgette!' I called out. Big courgette, I thought to myself. Enormous courgette. Wrong colour courgette. Wrong shape as well. Thanking my neighbour once more, I promised to visit for coffee the next day, then retreated indoors with my spoils.

Back in the *grange*, I wrote down a plan of action for the coming fortnight, after which Al would return by train to spend another week with me. First on the list was to pay a visit to Bellac and the offices of France Télécom to arrange for the installation of a telephone at the *grange*. Although I was happy to forgo many of the trappings of modern technology, and at ease being with my own company, I drew the line at not being able to communicate with the outside world should I so choose. The ability to use my mobile phone in the hamlet was marginal and depended upon me locking onto a sufficiently strong signal, which seemed to drift from point to point by the hour. At times Véronique would peer from her windows puzzled to see me squatting just outside the hangar with the phone clamped to my ear, or else on a muddy patch in the lane at the edge of the common land, or next to a particular tree down the path, but never in the barn itself. I would be obliged to shout to make myself heard. No, clearly this was unsatisfactory. I left France Télécom's efficient office clutching my new state-of-the-art telephone, a thick tome describing its many miraculous functions, a telephone directory, a signed contract and our designated telephone number, plus a promise from the helpful sales lady that an engineer would arrive in two days' time to make the necessary connection.

'*Excusez moi, Monsieur*, but where exactly is the telephone to go?' asked the spotty youth who came to make the installation, as arranged. 'Where's the *maison*?' He was an odd-looking character indeed, wearing his hair cropped to within a few millimetres of his scalp except for a fluffy wisp at the front. The Tintin look was, I had noticed, a style popular with many a French youth, who for some inexplicable reason seemed to find the style attractive. Some got it completely wrong, however, by having the wispy fringe at the nape of the neck.

'Up there,' I said, indicating the *grenier*.

'*La grange? Dans la grange?*' The Tintin clone looked bemused. He scratched his bristly head. 'You want a telephone in your *grange*?'

'Don't laugh, but although it might look like a *grange*, it actually is my *maison*,' I corrected the young engineer in a friendly yet perhaps somewhat defensive manner. He merely pouted and shrugged his bony shoulders.

'So you live in a *grange*. So OK, Monsieur. It's up to you. You want a telephone in your *grange*. *Pas de problème pour moi!* It's your choice.'

While Tintin busied himself with running a lengthy new cable from the far side of the common via various telegraph poles to the concrete pylon outside Véronique's house, I began to prepare the window frames for installation.

They comprised stout, jointed outer frames made by Simon the Carpenter to precisely fit the existing openings in the front façade of the building, as decreed by the measurements I had furnished him with. Pairs of side-hinged casements, each with three panes separated by ornately moulded glazing bars, fitted within the frames, with ingenious interlocking mouldings on the meeting and hinge edges that would prevent rainwater from seeping through.

I was just in the process of test-fitting the first outer frame in one of the openings when Monsieur Jérôme ambled over. He was no doubt intrigued by our comings and goings and ever eager to monitor our progress with a contrived air of detachment. Swaggering over John Wayne-style, he wore an oil-smeared denim shirt open to the belly button and a pair of equally grubby jeans hanging from a belt at his broad hips. He squinted up at me for a few moments, then, receiving my invitation '*Montez! Montez!*', ascended the ladder. I shook the back of his proffered wrist and we exchanged brief pleasantries before he began to examine the wooden frames, pursing his lips thoughtfully and shaking his head. His oily hands left greasy fingerprints on the wood. The little telephone engineer appeared at the window like a glove puppet in a seaside Punch and Judy show, perched atop his long ladder and grinning inanely. He noisily proceeded to drill a hole through the metre-thick wall just below eaves level.

'*Alors*, Richard. Who made these *fenêtres?*' asked Monsieur Jérôme, curiosity finally getting the better of him.

'A friend in England, a carpenter, made them to our design,' I explained.

'Why did you not have them made *en France*? A French *menuisier* could have done these just as well. And from the right sort of wood.' The man winked wickedly at the grinning Tintin, who had now clambered through the window opening and was drawing a length of cable through the hole he had just drilled. What was this, a new game? Bait the gullible Englishman?

'Well, Jérôme, I know you have excellent carpenters here in France, but as we're here only now and then, we didn't have the time to search out someone suitable who could make them precisely the way we wanted them. Anyway, I happen to think the carpentry is *très bien*,' I said in stiff-lipped defence of Simon's craftsmanship.

'Heuh!' sneered the big farmer dismissively, leaving more grubby streaks on one of the frames. Tintin strode up and shook the farmer's hand and they mumbled something indecipherable, nodding and smiling wryly. The youth then cheekily wiggled one of the frames and the pair of them chuckled at some private joke.

'What do you mean, Jérôme, the right sort of wood?' I continued. What was wrong with the wood after all? Tintin began to staple the length of cable to the top of the nearest beam, but his attention was on Monsieur Jérôme and me.

'*Le bois? Écoutez*, Richard!' he said, grabbing my arm and drawing me aside. 'This is fir. It's soft,' he said, driving a chunky fingernail into the wood to demonstrate just how yielding it was. 'The termites will make a meal out of this in no time at all!'

'It's been treated against infestation,' I snapped in response, my guard well and truly up. I had spent hours with my in-laws daubing on successive coats of the colourless preservative and insecticide back in their garage in England, where the frames had been stored.

'Heuh!' countered Monsieur Jérôme. 'Against your little *termites Anglaise, sans doute!* But in France we have termites this big,' he boasted, indicating a gap of about five centimetres between his enormous forefinger and thumb, a somewhat exaggerated measurement I felt. Tintin spluttered. I sent him a stern look, as if to say 'Get on with your work, boy!' However, I must confess to having scant knowledge of the size to which local wood-boring beetles could grow. The farmer hadn't finished making me squirm yet, though. 'Just look at the damage they do to a hard wood like oak! Just look at the timbers in this *grange*! Heuh! This stuff won't last a season! Why did you not use *bois exotique*?'

'*Oui, bois exotique!* Or why not even PVC?' chipped in Tintin, unwrapping my telephone and connecting its various flexes. I shot the youth another stern look for even suggesting the abomination of plastic windows. Even Monsieur Jérôme gave the lad a frown. The engineer rolled his eyes like an adolescent scolded by his parents and, head down, continued with his work, whistling nonchalantly.

It was true that the majority of windows – in fact any form of joinery – we had seen in and around the neighbourhood were fashioned from reddish-brown hardwood, gaudily daubed with shiny varnish. Any softwood that was employed in the construction of windows, doors and shutters was commonly treated with a subtle sheen of lacquer in a diverse range of natural wood tones, or varnish in tones not only to imitate various ages of oak, mahogany and other hardwoods, but also in appalling vibrant greens, reds and yellows. However, it was *bois exotique* that was widely touted in do-it-yourself stores and joineries alike. I had assumed it was just dubious French taste rather than the practicality of defence against voracious insect attack. Al and I had been unified in our loathing for this look, however, and had opted for the classical elegance of white-painted exterior joinery which, we felt, beautifully complemented the honey tone and coarse texture of the stonework façade. We had even been able to obtain a satin sheen paint rather than the usual shiny gloss we both hated.

'We're going to paint the wood,' I announced to my visitor.

'*Pourquoi?*' asked Monsieur Jérôme, as if the mere suggestion of painting wood was anathema.

'Because we prefer it that way and also it looks good,' I opined decisively. 'And anyway, termites don't eat painted wood.'

'Heuh! Don't be too sure!' said my foe, and then continued in his petulant, I-was-only-trying-to-help manner: 'Oh, well. It's your house. You do as you please. It's nothing to do with me.'

Then he shrugged, smeared the frame with oil once more and hit me with his typical end-game: '*Et la prix?* How much did this English *charpentier* charge you?' And as usual, my typical response was to feign non-comprehension.

That evening, after Tintin had installed my telephone, I was able to converse with Al in England via this technological miracle. As I sat in my camping chair, sipping a glass of red wine and gazing out at Véronique tending her vegetable patch across the lane, I could picture my wife flopped on the sofa in our little Sussex house, with the television flickering in the background. So taken were we with the novelty of this method of communication that we telephoned each other several times that first evening, no doubt running up a considerable bill. Yet the phone helped to reduce the physical distance between us newlyweds and I was able to report fully on my endeavours at Le Mas Mauvis so that Al would 'have a visual', as she called it.

'Tomorrow,' I announced, 'I'm going to start to fit the frames.'

Although the window frames had been skilfully constructed to our precise measurements, the reality of the situation was that they simply did not fit. It was necessary for me to shave several centimetres off their width and height with my powerful planer. This fine tuning was needed not because Simon had erred too much on the side of caution in their manufacture, or that my skill with a tape measure was suspect, but because the openings were totally skew-whiff. Nevertheless, once the outer frames were trimmed to size and screwed within the reveals – a job which took me a full and labour-intensive three days – I was able to mark out and cut the hinge recesses, screw them in place and finally to hang the casements. With the addition of windows, even though the frames had yet to be glazed and painted, the barn was suddenly transformed into a house, and I stood back in the lane to admire my handiwork.

'Gud verk!' said Bruno Bussiere in his gruff, experimental English. He had been pushing a wheelbarrow loaded with tree-cutting accoutrements, and stopped to shake hands, then to light up the tiny, soggy roll-up that was stuck to his bottom lip. He gazed up at the façade of the grange, thumbs in his trouser belt, sway-backed like a jovial and portly garden gnome, and nodded his appreciation. 'Gud vindos, Richard. Very attractif.'

'*Merci*, Bruno,' I said, rather pleased with myself and grateful for our neighbour's kindly comment.

'*Toutefois*,' he said, reverting to his native French. 'I'd get them varnished quickly, if I were you, before the termites get to them. That's fir you've got there. The wrong sort of wood for these parts. You're sure to have *beaucoup, beaucoup* trouble. It's this unseasonable weather we've been having. They say on *la télé* that there's a devastating plague of termites sweeping up from the south.' Bruno drew long and hard on the roll-up and struck a contemplative pose, one Connery-esque eyebrow raised, furrowing his forehead.

Inwardly I began to panic. In fact, in the short space of time since having the telephone installed, I had received a cold-call from a man I could barely understand, who appeared to be trying to sell me not double glazing, as I first thought, but rather a government-approved preventative treatment against woodworm attack – and at a knock-down price to boot! – citing the nationwide epidemic that had befallen the country. It was all very worrying indeed, and me with the wrong sort of wood.

That night I awoke in a cold sweat, my mind sorely troubled by dreams of locust-like clouds of woodworm beetles sweeping across the countryside, devouring all in their path: I imagined entire houses crumbling as the insects made short work of their structural timbers and ploughed on. Crawling from the tent, I flicked on the torch to check the condition of my newly installed window frames and was relieved to see them still intact, rather than the piles of brown dust on the sills I had expected. Nevertheless, I made a detailed examination, looking for bore holes in the pristine wood. Happily there were none. Surely these tales of monster termites were just scaremongering? I was not about to take the risk. The sooner I was able to slap a protective coat of paint on my precious window frames the better!

On returning from a run one balmy evening I flopped down on the upended log which Bruno had thoughtfully fashioned as a kind of garden seat and placed next to our barn doors. Whilst I was regaining my breath I discovered another of Véronique's generous food parcels left by the jamb. Examining the contents of the carrier bag, I found, amongst a tangle of succulent *haricots verts* and more ripe tomatoes, another pale green vegetable of dubious genus. Although its tough skin was the same colour and texture as the courgette-marrow (which had formed the basis of a hearty soup I had prepared a few evenings ago) this specimen was large and round, like a melon.

Over coffee and *petits-gateaux* with my neighbour the next morning, I enquired as to the identity of the strange vegetable. Véronique screwed up her eyes and rubbed her chin thoughtfully. Obviously she wondered about my grasp of reality.

'It is a courgette, Monsieur Richard,' she pronounced slowly and deliberately, in case I should misunderstand.

'A courgette, Véronique?' I queried.

'Yes, a courgette.' I let the matter drop and turned the conversation to the weather: always a good gambit. Later that day, however, on visiting the supermarket, I made a point of wheeling my trolley past the vegetable counter. Sure enough, as I suspected, there lay rows of the familiar, long, shiny, dark green specimens I knew and loved as courgettes, and these were clearly labelled 'courgettes'. Proof positive. Surely these were not remotely related to the insipidly coloured courgette-marrow and courgette-melon my neighbour had kindly donated (as scrumptious as they were)? I determined to be ready for her next time, and bought a couple of these courgettes-*authentique* to use as evidence in my case against the courgettes-*faux*.

During one of our lengthy telephone conversations in the long, somewhat lonely evenings that stretched before me, Al confirmed what we had both feared: that our financial security was threatening to become a serious issue. Although her job ensured that we had sufficient funds to pay the rent on our Sussex home and to keep us fed and watered, our meagre savings were being whittled away by the escalating cost of renovations in France. It became clear to us that we would soon have no money to throw at the ravenous plans we had for the *grange* and its attendant buildings, and it was urgent that we find additional means of financing further works.

Our ambition to move to Mauvis seemed to fade before my eyes. Even if I returned to a full-time publishing job, I reasoned, it would take a great deal of time to amass enough spare cash: we were locked into the costly trap of renting property without the means to climb onto the ladder of house purchase in the UK.

'What can we do to raise some capital? Sell my balloon maybe?' I asked over the phone.

'No, Lol. You trained hard over the years to get your licence and buy the balloon, and selling it probably wouldn't give us sufficient funds anyway. But what about selling part of Mauvis?'

'Selling part of Mauvis?' I echoed down the already echoey line, momentarily stunned. However, I had to admit that the very thought had occurred to me on several previous occasions. But the notion had never been confirmed before. The concept had also been mooted by several of our friends, who could not for the life of them understand what we intended to do with not only the *grange* and its attendant barns, but also the little detached cottage with its pig pens, and the larger house containing the bread oven, and its huge barn. We had named these *maison de cochons* (house of pigs) and *maison du pain* (house of bread) respectively, in an attempt to readily identify them. Al, however, constantly referred to them as 'Piggy' and 'Bread Bin', nicknames which I tried in vain to discourage.

'Practically speaking, it's going to be years before we can restore the other buildings,' continued Al. 'And we're never going to actually live in them, are we? So what if we were to sell Bread Bin and a parcel of land behind and in front of it? It would be totally separate from the rest of the property and we wouldn't be overlooked by anyone.'

I mulled over my wife's words. The idea made sense. Although we had toyed with the possibility that we might one day convert both of our 'surplus' houses into *gîtes* for holidaymakers, we had soon talked ourselves out of the plan: we did not want to run a business from our future home. Part of the appeal of the remote and rustic hamlet was the fact that we would be escaping such responsibilities, where we could achieve a state of partial self-sufficiency. But the option of selling part of our property would simply give us the presence of neighbours, as well as boosting our funds.

'How much do you think we could ask for the house?' I asked tentatively.

'I haven't a clue, but property prices seem to be rising considerably. Why don't we test the water? Get in an estate agent and value the place?'

'OK,' I agreed. 'I'll make some enquiries. Nothing more at this stage, though, eh? We'll reserve judgement.'

The following day I telephoned the English agent through whom we had bought the farm and arranged for a representative to pay a visit with the intention of determining the value of the *maison du pain* and its barn.

While awaiting a visit from the agent, I began the long process of puttying and glazing my newly installed windows. It was a job that I had quite enjoyed in the past, but twenty-four panes and several tubs of linseed oil putty later, I was thoroughly disillusioned with the process. The results, however, were gratifying and at the end of my two weeks alone I had not only completed the glazing but also had applied two coats of white paint to all the windows. I was satisfied that no wood-boring insect would breach these defences.

Additionally, I had managed to mow the turf that fronted the grange and had planted a red grapevine at each corner of the building and a wisteria flanking each side of the cart entrance, which I hoped would one day create a green canopy resplendent with white trailing honey-scented racemes. In just two weeks of gloriously sunny weather all the plants seemed to have settled in and had responded by sending forth green tendrils, which I secured to a system of support wires.

Finally the estate agent managed to fit me in and an eager young lady arrived one day armed with a digital camera and a clipboard. Like her predecessor, the flame-haired Hero, this mini-skirted, high-heeled young lady was also inappropriately attired for scrambling about in bramble-choked gardens and clambering up ladders into dingy lofts. But she lost no time in taking pertinent measurements of the property, and was able to give me, in her professional opinion, the bottom-line figure we could ask for the house and a portion of land. It was considerably less than Al and I had expected and I explained that, in the circumstances, I would have to discuss the matter with my wife before we progressed any further with the sale.

'OK, Mr Wiles,' said the agent brightly. 'But I may as well take a few pictures while I'm here, if you don't mind – it will save another visit – and if you decide not to proceed with the sale, it's no problem just to erase the images from the disk.'

When she had finished taking her snapshots she said: 'It's just occurred to me, Mr Wiles, do you know your English neighbours across the way?'

'Gordon and Maureen?' I asked. 'Yes, I do.'

'No, not them. Your other English neighbours, over there.' She pointed across the common land towards the house that we had noticed undergoing substantial conversion over the three years we had owned our farm.

'No,' I said. 'Never met them. I've been told the place was owned by an Englishman who lives in Greece most of the time. But we've never seen a soul there.'

'Ah! Well, you're partly right. The place is owned by an English guy who lives in Greece – he's involved in building the Athens metro, I believe – but he and his wife rarely visit. The house is actually being renovated by the guy's brother, a charming man called David. Thing is, I know for a fact that he's looking for a property of his own close to his brother's place. Maybe he'd be interested in your house.'

'Well,' I said. 'Perhaps I'll pay him a visit.'

When the estate agent left, I strolled around the common and entered the property of our neighbour through a gate that opened onto a gravelled area in front of the house, which was set at a right-angle to the road. The façade was shrouded in a lush Russian vine, and its windows peeked out onto a spacious and well-maintained garden, which was contained and concealed from the road by a long-established hedge line. Broad areas of neatly trimmed lawn were interspersed with shapely and well-stocked herbaceous borders, divided by rustic wooden pergolas and iron rose arches. I noticed the remnants of an elderly orchard of apple and pear trees. A garden table and chairs languished under the shady and spreading canopy of a linden tree.

I tentatively rapped on the glazed door and it was swung open by a young girl dressed in shorts and T-shirt. Beyond her, the kitchen was filled with a gaggle of bikini-clad young ladies chattering animatedly around a large farmhouse table.

'*Bonjour*,' said the girl who had opened the door, smiling.

'Hello, I'm looking for David,' I explained.

'Oh, you're English! David? He's round the back somewhere. David! Visitor!' she called out, then retreated back to the kitchen table.

'Aye, lass! I'm here!' came a voice from beyond the large glazed conservatory that was attached to the far end of the broad house. 'I'm coming. Who is it?'

The man rounded the corner and approached me, wiping his right hand on the leg of his khaki utility trousers, then extending it. We shook. '*Bonjour*,' he said. Aged in his early fifties, he wore a chequered, open-necked shirt and over it a workman's waistcoat with numerous pockets out of which protruded pencils, screwdrivers and a tape measure. A cigarette was stuck behind his right ear and a lit one protruded from his lips. His face was slim and tanned, his complexion smooth; his mid-brown hair was swept back over his head, neatly styled. He was a man who obviously prided himself on his appearance: 'well scrubbed up' would be his own apt description, I later learned.

'Hi. I'm Richard. I have the place over there,' I said, indicating the roof of the *grange* and its attendant barns, which were just visible in the dip beyond the somewhat unruly common land.

'Hello Richard!' he said warmly. 'I'm David. Pleased to meet you. So you're t'journalist, eh?' His accent was, I thought, distinctly north of England, probably Yorkshire, with an underlying softness.

'How did you know that, then?'

'It's small village. People talk,' he laughed. 'Actually, Bruno and Jolanda – next-door neighbours – mentioned an English journalist with a place over there. 'Ow long have you had it?'

'About three years.'

'In't it strange! My brother and his wife have had this house the same length of time. I've been here working on the place all this time and we've never met till now.'

'Yeah, it's strange our paths have never crossed in such a small hamlet.'

We chatted for some minutes and I explained that the estate agent had suggested he might be looking for a property close at hand, and that, coincidentally, Al and I were reluctantly thinking about selling one of our houses. It might not be what he was looking for, but would he be interested in taking a look?

'Aye,' said David. 'I'd love to see it. But I've got these girls' lunches to sort out first – one of my daughters and her friends are staying with me. I've had ten young lasses staying here for the last fortnight, and they're all off home tomorrow – but maybe I could come over a bit later and take a look?'

'And perhaps we could have a beer and a chat?'

'Aye, that'd be grand!' he replied, eyes lighting up at the suggestion.

Later, David made a thorough examination of the *maison du pain* and, while he clearly appreciated its potential – he was obviously a man with boundless enthusiasm – he considered that taking on such a major renovation job was far beyond his means.

'No, it's a great house, Richard. Don't get me wrong,' he explained, almost apologetically, lighting up a cigarette after his investigations. 'It'd make a really super property, and so near Vic and Anne's place at that. But it's a major restoration job. I mean, there's nowt there really, except for the walls and roof, and that's pretty shot, in't it? And after three years living in the turmoil of Vic's place, I don't know if I could face it again.' He drew heavily on his cigarette.

'I see your point, David,' I agreed. 'It does need a complete overhaul. But never mind. To tell you the truth, I don't want to sell it anyway. How about that beer?'

'Aye! Now that'd be grand!'

We clambered up the ladder into the *grenier* and I explained our renovation plans to my guest, who seemed suitably impressed. Entering the vast space of the upper floor of the *grange* always seemed to take visitors by surprise, for the building, like Dr Who's time-travelling Tardis, appears to be smaller outside than it actually is inside. While we sat around the little camping table quaffing beers, David gave me a summary of his life and how he came to be renovating his brother's house in the middle of France.

Hailing from Sheffield, he had been a well-positioned and long-term employee in a respected company in the shopfitting trade. His job security and his personal confidence had taken a severe knock, however, with an unexpected redundancy. He was left, at fifty years old, quite at sea. Having divorced his wife many years before, David had brought up their two young children entirely on his own. Immensely proud of his girls, he had developed an extremely close relationship with them. 'They're my girls, but they're also my friends,' he explained. In their twenties, however, they had both flown the nest and David was left wondering where his own future lay.

As a stop-gap between the loss of his job and a decision about which direction he wanted to strike off in, David's elder brother Victor suggested that he come to France as his employee to supervise the renovation of the house he had recently bought in Le Mas Mauvis. Vic considered the project so complex that it needed someone permanently on site to ensure that the activities of electricians, plumbers, builders and other tradesmen dovetailed together. A widely experienced engineer in the field of tunnelling, Vic was involved with the digging of the underground network that would form the basis of a metro system for the Greek capital, Athens. Such was the nature of his work that he and his wife Anne found little time to make the trip to France to spend time in what was to be their dream home, where they would eventually retire. But this kind of project planning and management was right up his brother's street. It seemed an ideal solution and David readily accepted the offer.

At the same time that Al and I had been slowly transforming our barn into a house, David had been but a stone's throw away converting the row of three small cottages into what was to become a substantial home. Using a digital camera and the magic of email, David had been able to keep his brother up to date with the day-to-day developments of the house and the garden that was being created from the unkempt and waterlogged field surrounding the building. After nearly four years, the house was virtually complete, with a supremely comfortable and stylish interior. The garden was also firmly established.

'I'd only meant to stay here for a couple of months,' David explained to me. 'But here I am four years down the line. Now Vic's house is just about there, I feel like I need t'move on. I've decided I like it in France so much I'm going to stay. I'm selling the house in Sheffield, so I need to find a place of my own.'

David and I chatted for some time and promised one another that we would get together when Al arrived back in France in a few days' time. In just that short time I felt that I had met someone who would become a long-term friend.

'You come up to me Saturday night and we'll have barbecue, how's that sound, kid?'

'Great!' I agreed. And, shaking on the deal, my new friend plucked the perennial cigarette from behind his ear, descended the ladder and wove his tipsy way back along the lane, a wisp of smoke trailing behind him.

David had cast doubt in my mind about the amount of money we had hoped to ask for the *maison du pain*, believing the estate agent's lower figure to be more the mark. So the next day I strolled around to seek the professional opinion of Gordon, a qualified building surveyor. Surely he would be able to give a realistic opinion of the amount we had considered fair? I was gratified when he independently confirmed the very figure Al and I had discussed, based on our research of current house prices in France.

'We can't let the place go for so little,' I said to Al on the telephone that evening. 'We'd be selling ourselves short and losing our privacy into the bargain.'

'No, Lol,' she agreed. 'We'll have to think of another way. I've been making some enquiries about the possibility of obtaining a loan. I'll keep on looking, and perhaps that will be the solution.'

'OK,' I said. So we determined that we would not be obliged to sell part of our dream home under any circumstances. There must be another way to carry on with our programme of renovation.

Al stepped down from the glistening silver train as it drew to a halt alongside the platform at La Souterraine on the evening of her return. She was the only passenger to alight. We greeted each other with lingering hugs. It was so good to see her after our prolonged separation. Not really at home unless clad in faded denim, she wore her favourite jeans and from the breast pocket of the well-worn denim jacket poked a little stuffed animal, her mascot. We drove back to Le Mas Mauvis as the sun was setting and the sky glowed with a rich red, signalling that the next day would be fine and sunny.

When we arrived back at the *grange*, we discovered that Véronique had kindly left a 'welcome home' package for Al. Opening the bag, she pulled out a pale green vegetable shaped like a giant pear with a bulbous base like a gourd, and another the same colour, but small, squat and domed like a squash.

'What on earth are these?' she asked.

'I'll give you three guesses,' I replied.

Véronique, who normally retired to bed early, had stayed up to greet Al and, on hearing our car draw up, waddled over, clutching her lengthy walking stick at shoulder height. She and Al exchanged multiple kisses and hugs.

'Thank you so much for the vegetables, Véronique,' enthused Al. 'But what are these? I've never seen anything quite like them before.' Véronique shot me a knowing glance and smiled.

'Courgettes, perhaps?' I suggested.

'*Oui, c'est ça.*'

OK, I thought to myself. We'll get to the bottom of this! I excused myself and shot upstairs, returning moments later clutching one of the long, dark green courgettes I had bought at the supermarket.

'Ha, ha!' I said, wielding the vegetable as if it was a rapier. 'Ha, ha! Now what do you call this, then, eh?' I pulled a smug expression. Our neighbour stared blankly at me and blinked.

'It's a courgette, Monsieur Richard,' she replied with a suspicious tone to her voice. I picked up the courgette-squash and compared it to my own courgette-*authentique*. Surely the two could not be related?

After bidding goodnight to Véronique we retreated indoors and, like a thing possessed, I took up my trusty dictionary, determined to solve the courgette mystery.

'Damn! Don't you just hate it when you're proved wrong! Véronique's right! They're all courgettes,' I exclaimed, having located the word *courge* amongst the list of entries. '*Courge* is French for gourd, known in the US as winter squash. *Courgette* is the horticultural term for small marrow.'

It seemed that, whereas in England we had separate names for courgette, squash, marrow, gourd and pumpkin, the French simply lumped the whole lot together under one all-encompassing nomenclature. But how on earth could they differentiate between the weird and wonderful colour and shape variations? Just when I thought I was getting the hang of the French language, someone threw a spanner (or was it a courgette?) in the works.

Al was overjoyed by the transformation that the *grange* had undergone during her absence and touched by the romantic meal I had prepared to welcome her. We sat at the little rickety camping table and dined on a delicious warm chicken salad by flickering candlelight and recounted the events of our time apart. The strains of smooth jazz played gently on the hi-fi while we talked. We remarked on how our relatively civilised meal was a far cry from our first chicken salad in a plastic bag at the *grange* and, although we still slept in a tent pitched indoors on the timber floor, and still cooked by camping stove, we were able to switch on our electric lights whenever we wanted, could shower in piping hot water, and were now able to gaze out of three beautiful, white-painted windows, through panes I'd studiously polished in honour of my wife's return.

Life was good, our barn was becoming a home – but we still needed an injection of cash to fulfil our dreams of an idyllic life in France.

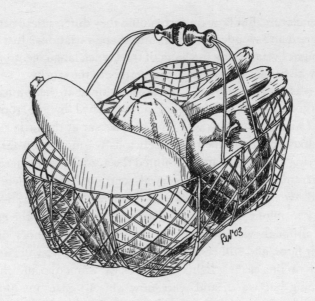

Chapter Thirteen

Verbal Gymnastics

Al and I spent a relaxing week swimming at various lakes, dining with our new friend David, and generally doing as little renovation work as possible. We were simply enjoying our time at Mauvis.

As a non-French speaker I had always admired and was somewhat jealous of my wife's fluency in the language. She spoke with such confidence in what appeared to me to be flawless French. Our French neighbours often complimented her on her accent and I would always boast to others about her bilingual capabilities.

A favourite tale she loved to recount involved a period during her early twenties when she worked as a chambermaid-cum-waitress in a small *auberge* in the mountains near Nice, brushing up on her schoolgirl French. At that time she was known by the nickname Ali (despised as much as her true given name, which I am forbidden from relating on these pages, known to us both as 'the dreaded A-word'). At the end of a tiring shift her employer would take great delight in saying to her each evening: '*Alors, Ali! Allez au lit!*' – 'Come on, Ali! Go to bed!'

As I became more conversant with the French language, I realised that Al's creative use of words was not just limited to her mother tongue. The *Alisme*, it seemed, was alive and well and issuing forth with gay abandon here in the heart of France.

Véronique had spent a short spell in hospital and on her return was eager for *un petit quatre* with her English neighbours. The poor lady was a martyr to her *jambes*, her legs, and was on the waiting list for an operation to implant new artificial knees. During our afternoon chat I distinctly heard Al rambling on about Véronique's *jambons*, or hams, in an enthusiastic display, which included dramatic gestures and facial expressions. Our neighbour's half-hidden smirk told me that she understood Al nevertheless, yet was too polite to correct her. I, however, had no such inhibitions and promptly pointed out the error.

Undeterred by her mistake, Al next embarked upon mellifluous praise for Véronique's brave and unstintingly positive attitude towards her constant and debilitating ailments, in which the dear lady was to be admired for '*souriant dans la forêt de vos maladies*', or, as I was able to translate it, the somewhat florid 'smiling through the forest of your maladies.' Now that I was wise to my wife's creative phraseology, I made a point of listening out for her meanderings and subsequently identified her frequent use of the all-encompassing word *truc*, or 'thingumajig' for items that had somehow evaded her considerable vocabulary. I decided to adopt the word myself, as a handy means of getting out of a conversational hole. Most of the time, however, it was no longer necessary for Al to translate for me, as she had been obliged to do in our early days in France, and we tended to work as a team, with me providing some of the obscure French words for building terms and myriad do-it-yourself items.

Al's verbal gymnastics were a sheer joy to behold and the flagging spirits of our poorly neighbour seemed considerably lightened after our visit.

One day, whilst I was involved in the tricky procedure of reconnecting an electrical socket, we received some unexpected visitors. An English couple and their toddler daughter had arrived to view our property.

'But we're not selling anything,' Al claimed.

'Yes you are, according to this,' said the man, handing Al a photocopied page of an estate agent's details bearing a photograph of our *maison du pain*. We had never seen the details before, had not agreed the description it contained, or the price that was being asked for our property. More importantly, we had not signed – nor even had sight of – a contract from the estate agent. We explained this to our visitors, who were very understanding and, after having looked around the *maison du pain*, commented that the price the agent was quoting seemed to them extremely low. They left with our promise that, if we did decide to sell, we would contact them in England and give them the opportunity to put in an offer.

When Al telephoned the estate agent for an explanation, the young lady who had visited to make a valuation was extremely defensive, although her publication of our house sale, and the issuing of details to potential purchasers without any kind of agreement was indefensible. Even our visitors' arrival without an appointment was well out of order. Al ended the unpleasant telephone conversation with a demand that the property be taken from their books – we would not be selling anything, and particularly not with her company as agent.

We had become so used to our rather primitive conditions at Le Mas Mauvis that we were blinkered to the possibilities our new facilities offered. It was while preparing a spot of tea for David one afternoon that, after ten minutes of waiting for the tiny camping kettle to boil on the little butane stove, which would produce only enough water for one and a half modest cups, that our guest came up with a revolutionary idea.

'Look, tell me to mind my own business, you two,' he said. 'But why don't you get yourselves an electric kettle? It's going to be dinner time when we get our cup o' tea.'

Al and I stared at each other blankly. We had to admit that David's suggestion made some sense. We had never considered it before. An electric kettle! Now there was an innovation! After that breakthrough and the realisation that we had been complete twits, we got to thinking how our life could be made a lot easier in the *grange* if we were to employ other new-fangled labour-saving devices. What was to stop us from buying an electric fridge to replace our existing means of keeping dairy produce cool, fresh and free from the attentions of vermin? The pair of lidded buckets that served as cool boxes had been only marginally successful anyway, and I always dreaded opening the one that contained a vile smelling (but delicious) two-week-old Camembert. The next day we dropped in at Monsieur Laborde's retail outlet in St Sulpice Les Feuilles and bought a cheap but functional refrigerator and a gaudy yellow electric kettle. With these purchases we felt that our *grange* at Le Mas Mauvis had finally joined the twenty-first century.

We had also come to realise that, using only a rather primitive sickle and a scythe, we were losing the battle to contain the spreading sea of nettles and thistles that threatened to engulf our property. So I borrowed my brother's petrol-driven strimmer and prepared to do battle with the rampant growth in a more efficient and, I thought, less physically taxing way.

'The old machine's a bit temperamental,' advised the Count over the telephone from England. 'But once you've got the hang of starting it, you should be OK. It's noisy and it gets really hot. I'd advise you to dress for the part: long trousers, boots, gloves, fisherman's socks, long-sleeved shirt – and wear the helmet and visor, too!'

Ridiculously over the top, I thought. Wearing long trousers held no appeal for me in the baking heat that France was enduring at that time, and I wasn't about to truss myself up with irritating long shirtsleeves, socks or clumpy boots. The visor, however, seemed a sensible precaution against flying particles of decimated thistle.

Véronique stood on her front porch and watched with interest (or was it incredulity?) while I, coolly attired in nothing more than cut-off denim shorts and trainers, rammed the helmet on my head, flipped the visor down and tugged at the strimmer's starter cord. The machine coughed politely but nothing else happened. I tugged again. Nothing. My visor steamed up and I could not see a thing. I flipped it up and studied the strimmer as if a solution would present itself to me. Now, I have never achieved any kind of affinity with motorised equipment and this little sod was no exception. I adjusted my stance, pressed the little priming button again, fiddled with the choke as if I knew what I was doing and tugged at the starter cord. The machine spluttered and its engine roared into life. Then it died. Véronique began to shake her head mournfully. After several failed attempts I succeeded in coaxing the infernal machine into life and, pulling the visor down once more, tramped off into the depths of the nearest nettle bed, swishing the tool from side to side, while its revolving nylon line efficiently sliced its way through the stems.

After about a minute the line snapped and I had to stop the machine and replace it. Starting the motor again was just as problematic as the first attempt, but I eventually got into a rhythm and was soon cutting swathes through the nettles. After about half an hour the cut stems lay around me like a carpet, the entire bed flattened by the ravaging strimmer. Véronique gave a satisfied nod and retreated indoors.

Unfortunately, I hadn't bargained for the fact that the juicy stems of the nettles would splatter my exposed and heavily perspiring skin with their disgusting sap and that their massacred leaves would coat me with a green mush. I soon discovered that this nettle paste, which had turned my bare legs green and had infiltrated the tops of my sock-less trainers, still retained the original plant's capacity to sting. My skin began to tingle uncomfortably. I was reminded of a time in my childhood when my brother had mischievously pushed me from a rock into a nettle bed when I was clad only in skimpy swimming trunks: my current predicament brought back fleeting images of my white-spotted body being rubbed with liberal handfuls of dock leaves by my mother and aunt in a futile attempt to neutralise the stings.

My brother had warned me to dress for the part and I had ignored him: perhaps he had been trying to make amends for his childish prank, or maybe he assumed I'd ignore his sensible advice (which, of course, I had) and that the last laugh would be on him.

I went to shower, then returned to the fray trussed up to the nines with overalls, wellington boots and gloves.

It was an unfortunate fact that our *région* of France, although blessed with a warm climate for much of the year, was also apt to receive a substantial amount of rainfall. Our farm buildings, situated at the lowest elevation in the hamlet, tended to be deluged by a goodly proportion of water running off the land. The gradual slope of the common land channelled surplus rainwater directly towards the ancillary barns attached to the main *grange* and caused a veritable river to flow down the space between the barns and the *maison du pain*, heading directly for the little pig pen house. Our foundations, such as they existed, were threatened by eventual subsidence unless the problem could be cured. Also, the communal track that ran past the grange became like a quagmire after heavy rain, worsened by the passage of our car and Monsieur Jérôme's marauding tractor.

So one day Al placed a courtesy call through to the Mairie with a general enquiry: would the local authority be willing to divert the flow of water away from our buildings? To her surprise, she was put through directly to Monsieur Rouaux, *le maire* himself. After Al had been grovellingly smarmy to this high-ranking and universally respected public official, the mayor said that he would be happy to come along and investigate our problem himself. He suggested a morning appointment in a few days' time. Honoured that the mayor had deigned to pay us humble peasants a visit, we determined to rise bright and early on the morning of his expected arrival and to dress appropriately in a sober but smart manner, rather than the scruffy rags we usually donned each day when working on the property.

Lying in our tent the evening before our rendezvous, I asked Al about the etiquette one should observe when meeting a mayor.

'How exactly should one address *le maire*? Does one say *Bonjour Monsieur Le Maire*? Or how about *Bonjour cher Monseigneur*? Does one bow, kiss his hand or, in your case, curtsey?'

'I'm sure I don't know, Lol,' admitted Al, obviously as unfamiliar as I was with the correct form for greeting powerful dignitaries of state. (Frankly, I had expected a more positive response from her: when she had been working for the British Consulate in Zimbabwe during her world tour, she had made something of a name for herself. During a party to celebrate the Queen's official birthday, attentive of the ambassador's request for staff to tend to the needs of visiting dignitaries of State, she had made a beeline for a poor, kindly looking elderly gentleman who was tottering about on a walking stick and dabbing his forehead with a large white handkerchief. Feeling sorry that the old chap seemed chastised by his peers, Al had spent half an hour chatting with him about the local agriculture and flora, for which he appeared grateful, and sought her out to shake her hand when he left the shindig. Later, revealing to admiring colleagues that she hadn't been able to catch the sweet old gent's name, she was told that she had been holding court with the vice-president, Joshua Nkomo, a man widely thought to have sold out to the notorious President Mugabe. OK. So maybe Al wasn't the person to ask about the do's and don'ts of meeting important people.)

'I expect *le maire* will be fairly smart and formal,' Al said drowsily from the adjoining pillow. 'He'll probably draw up in a shiny, chauffeur-driven limousine.'

'You think so, eh? That'll be exciting. The neighbours are going to be seriously jealous when they see us hobnobbing with the Chief Honcho. Do you reckon French mayors wear chains of office while out visiting the public, like they do in England?'

'Probably. Now hush up and go to sleep, darling. We don't want to oversleep.'

The following morning we arose early as planned, showered and dressed in our smartest clothes, and sipped coffee while we nervously awaited the arrival of *le maire*'s Rolls-Royce or perhaps his horse-drawn carriage. Just before the allotted time, I heard a vehicle skid to a halt in front of the *grange*. I peered out of the upstairs window and was disappointed to see a tatty white transit van with a pair of ladders and lengths of copper piping strapped to a roof rack.

'Oh bugger!' I hissed. A tall, grey-haired man dressed in blue jeans and a faded blue vest stepped from the cab of the van, slammed the door behind him and, cupping a hand over his eyes, gazed up at me squinting from the window.

'What's the matter, doll?' asked Al, putting the final touches to her coiffeur, a long plait down the back.

'Some scruffy old builder's just turned up and the flipping mayor's due any moment. Nip down and tell him to shove off, will you?'

'We're not expecting any workmen, are we?' asked Al as she headed for the ladder that led downstairs. I watched from the window. The man approached, smiling, and extended a hand. I could have sworn I saw the faintest hint of a curtsey from Al, as she shook hands with the tall man, then called up to me: 'Darling, Monsieur Rouaux, *le maire* has arrived!'

Monsieur Le Maire was a down-to-earth sort of guy, who, like most French mayors, held down another, full-time profession and devoted a proportion of his time to the service of the commune.

Monsieur Rouaux was indeed a builder, well qualified to identify our water drainage problem. He lost no time in rummaging around in various manholes to determine the flow of water across the common land and examined our perennial soggy patches. The solution was, as we had supposed, to divert the general flow so that it followed the line of the communal lane that ran in front of our property rather than crossing or seeping underneath it. Here it could drain into existing open storm trenches that were commonly dug along the sides of roads and paths, and so filter harmlessly away to earth or join the little stream that intersected our land.

'I will see to it that the work is done,' said Monsieur Rouaux. 'I cannot say when, but I will put it in hand. *Alors*,' he said, rubbing his big builder's hands together, 'can I be of any further assistance?'

We thanked the mayor graciously for his attention to our plight and, while we had his undivided attention, decided to broach another subject that had been troubling us of late: a semipermanent campsite which had been constructed by unknown persons in woodland at the back of our property. I had discovered not only the remnants of an open fire that had scorched several young overhanging trees, but also some thirty or forty empty beer and *pastis* bottles scattered about the ground and tossed into the undergrowth, where they had shattered. Our fence that flanked the *route de la Pentecôte* had been pulled down for access to the site and the perpetrators had also constructed a shelter in a little canyon, made from branches and saplings they had cut and woven into a substantial roof and walls that were lined with bracken.

'*Le camping* you say?' The mayor frowned. 'We can't have that! *Montrez-moi*, if you will!' Off he went at a determined pace, his long legs striding down the track. Al and I trotted along after him. We struck off onto our little pathway towards the back field and into the area of woodland.

Whether the mayor imagined that we would fall upon a gang of dangerous escaped convicts living off the land or a party of Gypsies, I do not know. But he seemed rather disappointed when he entered the clearing in which the campsite was situated.

'Oh, it's just the local *enfants, je crois*. The children, they have little to do around here, so they come to build a play area.'

'But they have lit a fire, as you see, which has burnt our trees, and which could cause a major blaze in the summer,' explained Al. We were well aware of the danger of lighting fires to burn grass and other cuttings in the hot summer months: it was, in fact, obligatory to inform the fire brigade if a summer bonfire was planned as the risk of a blaze spreading and becoming an all-consuming conflagration was ever-present.

'They have also made a considerable mess on our land – broken bottles everywhere. And they have damaged our fences,' I put in.

'*Oui! Ce n'est pas bon!* You have, of course, the right to stop these *enfants* from making this mess on your land.'

'While we don't have a problem with people walking across the land, it's a question of respect for our property,' explained Al. We were aware that in France people have a natural right to cross others' land, and did not dispute this. 'But would we be allowed to put up signs saying "Private" to discourage people from damaging our property?'

'*Mais, naturellement!*' agreed the mayor. 'You could do this. *C'est votre terrain*. And people would generally respect this. *Par example*, if you were to keep animals on the land you would obviously want to ensure the fences were not pulled down. *C'est normal*.'

We strolled down the Pentecostal way towards the hamlet, joined the road and walked around the communal land. As we passed, I noticed the shadowy figure of boiler-suited Monsieur Cédric, the lanky, moustachioed member of the extensive and close-knit farming family who lived in the little row of cottages at the centre of the hamlet. He was skulking at the side of his prodigious row of logs, which was covered with black polythene, watching our passage. He clearly recognised *le maire* and was curious as to his visit. Often seen loitering by the wood pile at odd times of the day, Monsieur Cédric would stride back and forth along the row as if calculating the number of cords it contained and determining whether it was sufficient to last the winter's heating needs. Of swarthy complexion and bearing a slightly bemused expression, Monsieur Cédric – never without his green boiler suit, wellingtons and a cloth cap – rarely spoke, and when he did his speech was delivered with extreme politeness and a debilitating stammer. As we neared, the farmer scuttled around the back of the logs.

'Whose equipment is this?' asked the mayor, pointing out the jumble of broken-down farm machinery, rusting and overgrown with long grass and nettles, that was scattered across the common land. Al and I smiled wanly at each other. The presence of the machinery – and the enormous pallets of fertiliser that lay about, broken and leaking – had been another slight bone of contention with us, marring the appearance of the grassy area, visible as it was from our property. Although not assuming that we Brits had the God-given right to take up residence in a rural French farming community such as this and then expect the inhabitants to clean up their act and sanitise the area by creating a beautifully manicured village green, most of the rusting equipment had not budged since we had bought the farm.

'I believe it belongs to Monsieur L'Heureux, the farmer who sold us our property,' revealed Al, with a tinge of guilt for potentially 'shopping' Monsieur Jérôme, whose equipment it surely was.

'And does he still have a farm here?' queried the mayor.

'No, Monsieur Rouaux,' admitted Al. 'His aunt owns the house opposite to us, and he still retains some fields around Le Mas Mauvis, but his farm is several kilometres away.'

'Hmm, I see,' said the mayor, stroking his chin thoughtfully as he surveyed the scene of disorder before him. Wearing his official hat, perhaps he could see how the small matter of the mess in our woodland drew parallels with the potentially larger problem of the mess on this area of common land. He sighed with resignation. '*Alors*. Unlike your woodland, this area is communal; it belongs to all the inhabitants of this hamlet. But it is not a depot and should not be used as permanent storage for one farmer's accoutrements.'

With that, Monsieur Le Maire bid us a warm *adieu*, clambered back into his builder's van and, promising to sort out our drainage problem in due course, headed off to put in a good day's work in his office.

Although happy with the outcome of our meeting, we had no wish to drop Monsieur Jérôme in the *fumier* for his somewhat haphazard farming practices. However, we had to admit that it would be marvellous if the common became more like a verdant oasis than a breaker's yard.

Our week's sojourn soon passed and Al and I headed back to England together by train. Deposited at La Souterraine station by David, leaving our car behind at Le Mas Mauvis, Al was to return to work in London while I was taking the opportunity to spend an all-too-brief day with my son before returning to France. It felt strange to be back in England after an extended period abroad, and our lodge house felt tiny and cramped compared with the vast space of the *grange* and the rolling fields in which it was set. Although I would miss Al terribly in the coming weeks, it was with a comfortable feeling of 'going home' that I boarded the Eurostar at London's Waterloo station and set off for France once again, after only four days back in the UK.

I was met at the station by David, who introduced me to his girlfriend, Dennie. Tall, slim and elegant, with auburn hair styled in a neat bob, Dennie had intense, smiling eyes that complimented her animated and kindly face. The couple had met while Dennie – originally from England but who had lived in France for almost ten years – was working for the English-run estate agency through which David was looking to purchase a property (and with whom we had recently had our disagreement).

Dennie was an impressively fluent French speaker who rolled her r's flamboyantly with the accent of southern France, where she used to live. However, she mocked her own proficiency in the language, claiming to be sadly lacking in the correct use of grammar. 'I'm really dreadful,' she confessed. 'I just don't think about what I'm saying any more. I just blurt it out and it's probably terribly wrong. I don't know how people understand me! Perhaps they don't!' She had been responsible for showing English clients around various houses and, although David had found nothing suitable, the pair had maintained their blossoming relationship despite the fact that Dennie subsequently moved to far-off Bordeaux, where she had secured a full-time job as a chemistry teacher. Dennie would make the lengthy journey from Bordeaux to see David most weekends. Together they would drive around the country lanes looking for houses off the beaten track, whether for sale or not, in the hope of finding a suitable property. It was quite common to find scrawled notes reading '*A vendre*', with a contact telephone number, stuck in the window of a deserted house, hoping to catch the attention of passers-by.

On the drive back to Le Mas Mauvis, David told me that they had been to view a house in the adjacent commune of Mailhac-sur-Benaize, after a tip-off from an acquaintance who suggested that the owners of the property might be willing to sell. After making a tentative approach, one of the owners had met the couple at the dilapidated and unoccupied property and shown them around. David and Dennie could see huge potential in the house and its overgrown garden and had lodged an offer for its purchase. However, it transpired that the property was actually owned by three brothers and a sister who did not see eye-to-eye. An ongoing family feud had meant that the house had been up for sale for some fifteen years: several potential purchasers had, during this time, gone through the motions of buying the place only to see the deal collapse at the last hurdle when the squabbling younger siblings disagreed with their elder brother about the small print. Now, with their hearts set on the house, David and Dennie were hopeful that the bickering family would manage to set aside their differences and allow the sale to proceed to its conclusion.

Worrying for David was the fact that he expected to complete the sale on his house in England within the next few weeks and was stuck for somewhere to store all his furniture. While he had been offered space in another English acquaintance's barn he was reluctant to store his possessions in what he knew to be a damp building with an earth floor.

'Why not store your stuff in our barn, then? At least it's nice and dry,' I suggested. 'We're not using the downstairs guest bedrooms or the hallway at the moment, so it wouldn't bother us.' Our friend graciously accepted my offer, and I could see that it was a weight off his mind.

Now that his work at Vic and Anne's house was nearly over, David had joined the French system and had taken on a full-time job working for an established English builder. His role was to tackle internal finishing – stud walling, plasterboarding, plastering, tiling and other decorative treatments – mainly in houses owned by English clients. As a man who prided himself on his meticulous attention to detail, this suited him admirably. Although concerned about how his brother and sister-in-law were going to manage the maintenance of their house once he was working elsewhere and had found his own property, he was keen to embark on this new stage of his own life in France. But there were still some aspects of living abroad that instilled in him a mild homesickness.

David was, as Dennie described him, the typical Englishman abroad. Although he loved France and had largely adopted the laid-back attitude of a Frenchman (although drawing a line at peeing on the roadside), there were just some home comforts he felt were missing from his adopted country of residence.

'Has David shown you his siege cupboard?' asked Dennie, placing a plate of chicken curry and rice in front of me as we sat down for a very welcome late supper. David looked up from his curry as if a vital trade secret had been revealed.

'No,' I said, curious.

Dennie opened the pine doors of a large cupboard to reveal shelves crammed with dozens of tins of Heinz baked beans, jars of pickles, boiled potatoes and other vegetables, steak and kidney, and other canned produce. There were bottles of Yorkshire Relish, jars of Marmite, English preserves and curry sauces. Several boxes of Yorkshire Tea were stacked up alongside cartons of English breakfast cereals. It was true that the shelves of French supermarkets rarely – if ever – featured these items, or other 'English' staples such as Chinese sweet-and-sour sauces and Indian curry mixes.

'I've always had a siege cupboard,' admitted David. 'Even in the UK. In that cupboard there's everything you'd need to make a meal.'

'And, of course, David always comes back from trips to England with dozens of loaves of white sliced bread,' said Dennie, revealing more of her partner's charming idiosyncrasies.

'Aye, but you just can't get ordinary white sliced bread here,' responded David in his defence. 'Baguettes are fine, and I love their walnut bread. But you can't make decent sandwiches with them. I stick loaves in the freezer so I've always got the means to make sandwiches.'

'You mean *I* make your sandwiches,' corrected Dennie. 'Since David's been working five days out of seven, I make up sandwiches for the entire week and put them in the freezer –'

'It's only sensible, love!' cut in David. 'I take one out each day and by the time it gets to dinner break it's defrosted and ready to eat.'

'And then there's your English cheeses, David.'

'Aye, there's my cheeses.'

'You bring English cheeses to France?' I asked, incredulous. David was looking distinctly persecuted.

'Aye, kid. A nice firm Cheddar, a nice crumbly Cheshire. Or a Wensleydale. You're a Northerner. Surely you can appreciate a nice bit of Lancashire? The French just don't make nice hard cheeses, nor lovely crumbly ones ... ones with a bit o' bite.'

'What about Cantal or Comté?' I suggested. Both of these French cheeses were of the hard or semi-hard type, respectively.

'Aye, but ...'

'It's just not English cheese, is it, David? That's what you miss, isn't it?' Dennie stroked the Yorkshireman's arm affectionately, smiling sweetly.

'Aye, lass. And I sometimes miss popping down the pub for a pint.' There was a touch of sadness in his puppy-dog eyes.

'We could always go for a beer at the *bar-tabac* in Magnac,' I offered.

'Aye, but it's not the same as a traditional English pub.'

On the way back to the *grange* after that pleasant evening, replete with curry, I reflected on what I would miss from the UK. Certainly I liked to quaff a pint or two of bitter down at the local pub, but in reality only ever did so infrequently. I would be happy if I never saw another loaf of processed white sliced bread. The choice of bread in France is far broader than the archetypal baguette, which stays fresh for barely a day. The selection of bread at most *boulangeries* includes brown wholemeal *pain complet* and *pain au son*; close-textured *pain noir*, made from buckwheat and rye; *pain au six céréales*, crammed with sesame and sunflower seeds, barley and oat flakes; and vitamin-rich organic *pain biologique*. Rustic country loaves include crusty white *pain de campagne*, a large, flat sourdough loaf with a tangy flavour, which remains edible for up to a week; while a Dordogne speciality, *pain périgourdin* has a defiantly hard crust that demands careful crunching to reach the spongy middle. Sheer delight to mop up olive oil or dip into hearty soup. The humble baguette is often seen in other guises: skinny *ficelle*; plaited *pain perle*; *bout pointu* with sharp, pointed ends that are irresistible to nibble off on the way home from the *boulangerie*.

Tea sold in France – mainly individually wrapped bags on strings – just did not seem to have the strength of flavour to compete with a nice strong pot of PG Tips or Yorkshire Tea. But, in my mind, even English tea brewed abroad could never compare with the home-brewed version because not only did the fresh milk available in France taste completely different to the English variety, but so did the water itself, although pure and eminently drinkable. Fresh milk was available in the supermarkets, usually sold in plastic bottles, but it was not stocked in the large quantities we were used to in England. One had to be quick in the mornings to grab a few bottles. Most locals seemed happy to drink the cartons of long-life UHT milk, which did not need refrigerating, but the taste of it repulsed me: if offered this I would invariably politely decline and drink my tea or coffee black. When fresh milk was not available we would opt for powdered milk, which gave a rich, sweet flavour to coffee.

What else would I miss? Isolated in our little hamlet, I would perhaps miss the convenience of buying fresh herbs, chillies and the more unusual varieties of mushrooms and fruits commonly sold in even the smallest English supermarkets, but in our part of France only available from the hypermarkets located in big cities such as Limoges or Poitiers: both more than an hour's drive away. We had learned to live with alternatives to some of these ingredients: Tunisian harissa, for example, the piquant paste made from red hot pimentos, coriander, caraway seeds and garlic, was widely sold in little cans and tubes and made a fine substitute in a dish that normally required fresh chillies, and was fiery and delicious when stir-fried with the huge tiger prawns that were sold deep frozen at a third of the price they were in England. I consoled myself with the fact that there was no reason why we could not grow some of the more elusive ingredients ourselves. As for mushrooms, I knew that our own woodland yielded masses of wild *champignons*: various villagers would saunter down the track on a Sunday morning and come back laden with bags full of the luscious fungi. If only I knew how to identify the edible varieties!

After I had climbed the ladder up to the *grenier* and crept into the tent I concluded that certainly there were things I would miss, even long for, about the land of my birth. But at Le Mas Mauvis Al and I were forging a new and exciting life for ourselves. While there were undoubtedly familiar things to let go of, there were many more new and thrilling aspects of life in France to embrace.

Chapter Fourteen

Herd Instincts

Bernard Morestin's llama farm was located down a cul-de-sac, a single-track lane leading off a quiet country road that passed several humble farmhouses that seemed to have been frozen in some bygone age. I had headed south on the A20 autoroute, which carried me through the industrial zones of Limoges, with the bustling city to the right, towards the distant mountains of the Dordogne in the direction of Brive and Toulouse. The motorway sped over a viaduct with the rooftops of the historic village of Pierre-Buffière nestling at its base and shortly afterwards I turned off near the town of Magnac-Bourg and headed along undulating country lanes towards the affluent medieval town of St Germain-les-Belles. Since leaving the autoroute I had witnessed the contours of the hills deepen into generous folds, with the rivers of La Grande Briance and La Petite Briance wending their way through the valleys between. A notable difference in this area, compared to our part of the Haute-Vienne, was the fact that the roads were less ramrod straight, with the need to circumnavigate the more hilly terrain.

Driving down the lane towards Bernard's farm, I kept my eyes peeled for the sight of llamas over the lush hedge lines, hoping that I wouldn't see instead gangs of orange-robed monks toiling in the fields. I saw neither, until the lane eventually petered out in front of a vast *grange*. Climbing out of the car, I was greeted by a friendly dog covered in black dreadlocks. It was apparent that the animal functioned mainly by sense of smell, for his eyes were entirely concealed behind a curtain of corkscrew curls: a wet, black nose protruded from the dreadlocks and a long pink tongue lolloped from his mouth as he panted enthusiastically around my legs.

'Jaffa! *Allez!* Leave the man alone will you, for God's sake? Sorry, 'ee ees a flippin' nuisance!' said the man who approached from a little lean-to attached to one end of the barn. Behind him, two fully grown llamas stood gazing forlornly over the gate of the lean-to. Jaffa scuttled off and flopped down on the grass, panting, as his master shook my hand. '*Bonjour*, I'm Bernard. And you must be Richard. Pleased to meet you.'

Aged in his fifties, Bernard had short, iron-grey hair receding at the temples, black eyebrows, and a warm, open, smiling face with ruddy cheeks. He wore a pair of khaki utility trousers and a baggy sweatshirt.

'*Bonjour* Bernard. It's good of you to see me,' I said.

'Orh, but eet ees no problem,' he responded with a Gallic shrug. 'Anyway, we talk in English, *non*? Eet ees bettaire for you, I think.'

'Was my telephone message that bad?' I said, embarrassed by the garbled message in appalling French I had left on Bernard's answering machine a few days previously.

'*Non, non, non!* Did you rehearse thees message?' he asked. I shook my head. 'Well then, I understand eet. *Non*, you were very fluent.'

'*Merci.*'

'*Pas de problème*. But we speak in English. Eet ees easiere. Come, we go in 'ere a minute.' He beckoned me towards the barn and we entered the top floor of the split-level building via a hole in the wall covered by a sheet of thick blue polythene nailed at the lintel. Bernard held back the polythene for me and I ducked inside. I was ushered into a makeshift yet fully functioning kitchen in a dimly lit niche formed by antique cupboards. Partitioned off from the rest of the barn with stacks of hay bales was a sitting room containing a pair of shabby sofas, a television set and a stereo grey with dust and littered with strands of straw, and a large, round dining table and chairs. The floor comprised wide oak boards with large gaps between, through which it was possible to see directly into the pens below where several llamas sat chewing the cud. The sitting room was open to the interior of the vast barn on one side, forming a gallery overlooking a cart entrance at lower ground level.

The atmosphere in my host's home was a cool and welcome retreat from the hot sunshine. His bed, half hidden in a niche beyond the sitting room, was draped with a mosquito net suspended from a beam. Although protected from the attentions of stinging insects, I wondered how Bernard coped with the undoubted presence of mice and probably rats while he slept. The barn was open to a vaulted oak-beamed ceiling rather like our own at Le Mas Mauvis; gaps at the verge, where the sloping roof met the walls, were stuffed with hay to keep out draughts.

'Just like home,' I remarked. 'I thought my wife and I were the only ones who lived in a barn.'

'Ah, eet ees not much, but eet ees 'ome,' laughed Bernard. 'Needs must. I lived in a rented 'ouse up the road until a few years ago, but one thing led to anothaire and I 'ad to move out and thought, well, I might as well camp in 'ere. But of course I only live 'ere in the summere. Eet's too flippin' cold in the wintere! I move into a caravan when eet gets cold. I'm renovating a little 'ouse at the back – you can see this latere – but I don't seem to 'ave much time. The llama, they keep me pretty busy. Eet ees not so bad livin' in 'ere, but the flippin' mice! Blimey, I can't believe eet! They are so cheeky! They come and they nick all my food, the little beggaires!'

'Yes, I know how you feel. We have the same problem.'

'You like the duck?' he asked suddenly, changing the subject. 'I'm cooking a leetle lunch for us.'

'Mmm, yes,' I said. 'That's very kind of you.'

'Oh, eet ees normal! The famous French lunch, you know …'

He pulled down the door of the little gas oven that stood in one corner and squinted in the half-light at the contents of an enamel pan sizzling with the juices of two plump duck breasts. A delicious aroma wafted out.

'Come, Richard, we'll go and meet the guys and gals and then come back 'ere for a bit of nosh. Then you can ask me all about keeping the llama, *oui*?'

'Sounds good to me!' I said, following him back through the polythene flap into the bright sunshine where we were rejoined by Jaffa, who padded alongside us. We made our way to a field in which four llamas were tethered at intervals to ten-metre-long ropes secured to the underside of their halters. Each animal was in the process of grazing down the lush grass within the radius permitted by their tethers, which were attached to trees at the perimeter of the field. They raised their heads on long, broad necks as we approached, then calmly returned to eating. Bernard opened the gate and we entered the field. Grabbing the tether of the nearest llama – a woolly-coated, chocolate-brown character – he reeled the animal in until it stood between us.

'Hello Chocolat. 'Ow are you?' said Bernard, patting the animal gently on its long back. 'Thees chap comes from England, so I speak to 'im in English. But I'm not so sure 'ee understands … 'ee usually ignores me.'

Although I had been fascinated by llamas for some years and had visited llama farms in the UK, this was the first time I had been in such close proximity to one of these elegant animals. Standing over a metre tall at the shoulder, Chocolat's thick, woolly neck raised his head almost another metre above me. He gazed down at me placidly with a pair of huge shiny black eyes with heavy upper lids fringed with long, curling lashes. Whereas the llama's body was thick with a mass of shaggy fibre or 'wool', his gentle face was covered with short, thick hairs, rather like the fur of a teddy bear. High on his head a pair of distinctive banana-shaped ears were angled forwards as he listened to his owner's musical voice.

'Oh, you silly chap!' Bernard sang as he busied himself releasing the tether line from where it had become entangled around the animal's legs. The llama stretched its muzzle forwards and curled his top lip to reveal a pair of enormous yellow incisors. ''Ee's always doin' thees thing. Yes, you can look at me like that, Chocolat, but you still keep getting in thees mess! I can't believe eet!' The llama leaned forward and nuzzled the man's cheek affectionately. 'Oi, watch eet, mate!' he retorted. 'Boys don't kiss boys! Well, some do, but not thees boy anyhow!' The animal's ears flopped backwards as if reprimanded for some misdemeanour.

Bernard came across as a charming, easy-going man, obviously only too pleased to show me around his property and proud to introduce me to his herd of some fifty llamas, each member of which I was certain he adored. He spoke with a light, sing-song voice that rose to a high lilt at the end of every sentence. His command of English was impressive, laced as it was with amusing colloquialisms and slang phrases.

'People in llama circles think of me as a bit of a rebel, you know, Richard,' he confided. 'Few others tether llamas like I do. Maybe they think eet cruel. I don't know. But in my view the llama ees a work animal. Eet ees domesticated. Eet 'as never been a wild animal. My llama they 'ave their freedom in the fields most of the time, but I also use them like thees to keep the land clear. I don't know 'ow you feel ...'

'I don't have a problem with it,' I confirmed. My research into llama keeping had taught me that these strong, intelligent and hardy animals were traditionally used for packing and were accustomed to being tethered during journeys or at homesteads. The Incas were responsible for first domesticating these wild animals, developing over thousands of years of selective breeding two species: the llama *(Lama glama)* and the alpaca *(Lama pacos)*. The llama – the largest of the South American camelids, weighing up to 180 kilograms and standing nearly 1.5 metres at the shoulder – was mainly used as a beast of burden, but was also kept for its meat, hide and sinew. Andean people still rely on the llama for taking produce to market. The smaller alpaca was bred for its fine fibre, used to make wonderfully soft and warm knitted garments. Although not as fine and luxurious as alpaca fibre, llama fleece is also used by hand spinners, often mixed with sheep's wool, to which it lends lustre and sheen.

The llama has a gentle temperament and an inquisitive nature and, easily adapting to the halter, can be led. Llama trekking is a growing recreational pastime, both for short walks or long-distance hikes lasting days or weeks. Although they are not riding animals, llamas can be taught to pull a small two-person cart. Many people simply keep llamas as companions. Al and I, as keen long-distance walkers, were interested in the trekking as well as the lawnmower aspect.

'Chocolat is not too good for the trekking,' said Bernard. ''Ee ees strong but 'is woolly coat is too thick; eet would get caught on brambles and things and would be too 'ot, especially with the packing saddle. 'Is back dips a bit as well: you want to look for the good, straight back.'

We left the llama to chew the cud and strolled over to one of the other tethered males. 'This is Radjah. *Bonjour Radjah, comment ça va?* 'Ee'd make a good trekker.' The llama's coat – predominantly off-white with a large grey patch down one side of his body – was less woolly than the first animal's. He stretched his long neck towards us as we approached and allowed us to stroke his soft, whiskered muzzle, which had dark brown blotches to match his brown ears. 'You see, 'ee 'as good conformation: strong, straight legs, strong pasterns.'

'Pasterns?' I queried.

'The ankle, see how straight 'is ankle ees? Some llamas suffer from dropped pasterns, which ees no good for the trekking, of course. This one 'as a good straight back, a medium-width frame. If 'ee 'ad too broad a chest, for example, 'ee would not 'ave, how you say eet? The endurance, the speed.'

Bernard went on to explain how his own interest was in breeding llamas and selling on the offspring to people like myself, who might be interested in trekking, showing, fibre production, or in starting off their own breeding herd. Selective breeding ensured that desirable characteristics such as good leg conformation, thickness of wool and temperament were passed on to the young llamas.

Bidding farewell to the tethered males we visited a large paddock where twenty or more females stood huddled with their assorted young under the shade of overhanging trees. Some of the crias were no larger than spring lambs, and peered nervously from between their mothers' legs as we approached. A pretty, spindly-legged cria, white overall with brown saddle patch, chest and head, crept from behind its mother and took a few tentative steps towards us before thinking better of this action and scampering off again.

'That's Sémiramis,' said Bernard. 'She's only nine days old. And that's her mother she's 'iding behind, Miss Batman. The baby ees cute, *non*?'

'Very,' I agreed. Several eager young llamas suddenly surrounded us, jostling to get close to Bernard.

'This ees what I love the best, Richard, to see them run up to me as I arrive and fight for my attention.' The nearest animals rested their chins on the man's shoulder or nuzzled his face while he petted them lovingly. A few of the girls at the back of the queue grew impatient and started to emit throaty gurgling noises before spitting at each other in a most unladylike fashion, ears flattened back against their heads, necks extended.

'I was going to ask if they spit,' I said, ducking out of the way of a gobbed projectile.

'Well, yes, they do,' laughed Bernard. 'But eet ees more like the puking really. And they usually don't spit at the people, just each other. Of course, you can get caught in the crossfire!'

After a few minutes of attention, the llamas wandered off to join the rest of the herd. 'Look, they 'ang around by that gate 'oping I'm going to let them into the next field,' said Bernard. 'Well, I guess they 'ave grazed thees one pretty good. Let's give them the treat!' We fought our way through the throng and Bernard opened the gate. The llamas barged past, then pranced like gazelles through the lush grass with unabashed excitement. After a few minutes' exploration they calmed down and began to emit gentle humming sounds; some of the adults lay down, while others grazed. Mischievous crias did their best to make nuisances of themselves. It was a magical experience to be amongst these contented creatures and as we watched, Bernard pointed each one out in turn, reeling off their names and their relationship to others in the herd.

'I often come 'ere and just sit and watch them graze,' said Bernard. 'Eet ees very relaxing. We 'ave a kind of silent conversation. And in the evening the youngsters perform thees – what can I call eet? – the lap-dance.'

'Lap-dance?' I repeated doubtfully. Perhaps there was more to llama raising than I had realised.

'Oh, no, sorry, thees ees something else, I think. Leap-dance, I mean. Eet ees wonderful to watch them leaping and tearing about the field.' He glanced at his wristwatch. 'Look, Richard, now the llamas are 'appy with thees new grass, perhaps you and I should go eat, eh?'

Over a delicious lunch of coarse pâté and rustic bread, followed by roast duck breasts, potatoes and green beans, Bernard told me a little about himself. During the seventies, this quiet man had worked for British Airways as cabin crew – 'I was the original trolley dolly,' he grinned – and basing himself in London, had soon learned the lingo. He met an English girl and eventually they married and started a family. Divorce sadly followed, however, and Bernard, who had by then traded his wings in for a job in cabin crew training, eventually found himself back in his homeland. Having bought a few llamas almost on a whim some ten years ago, he had soon realised that breeding these companionable animals was where his future lay, and he came to rest in this idyllic corner of Briance-Ligoure, where the undulating countryside was a mere stone's throw from the rugged hills of the Dordogne to the south-west and the Correze *département* to the south.

Bernard then patiently answered the barrage of questions I had about keeping llamas. He advised me about such matters as fencing requirements, shelter for the animals, other facilities and equipment I would need, feeding and nutritional requirements, health problems, breeding and herd management.

'What about land clearance, then?' I asked, intrigued as to how effective llamas could be in helping Al and I keep our farm in trim.

'Oh, they are by nature curious animals,' he explained. 'They love to gnaw at and taste all sorts of vegetation: they will nibble the young shoot of the nettle so the plant dies back; they do the same with the bramble. So they are good for lawn mowing and clearing undergrowth without damaging land or big trees. I mean, flippin' 'eck, Richard, you'd 'ave to keep them off the flowerbed, though! But, like us, they 'ave the preference. They love green grass the best, and a little hay.'

One of my major decisions, he indicated, would be the type of llamas I wanted to keep: classical or woolly. After our leisurely lunch, I walked with my host to meet Tarzan, the herd sire. This majestic beast stood well over a metre and a half at the shoulder and had chiselled facial features and a powerful, muscled physique that was covered with an extremely shaggy russet-brown coat. Presently seconded to Bernard's next-door neighbour as a lawnmower, the huge animal was contentedly chomping his way through the long grass within the broad arc permitted by his tether line. He gazed at us nonchalantly, his lower jaw moving from side to side as he chewed.

'You see, thees chap ees the classical llama – well defined muscular shape and thees haughty kind of a look. 'Ee think 'ee's the knees of the bee! The woolly llama are softer, more subtly defined.'

We carried on to another paddock where a gang of juvenile males paced back and forth awaiting the treat of tasty pellets Bernard had brought with him. While the energetic youths pushed and shoved each other to get at the bucket of nutritional supplements, Bernard pointed out the physical differences between them: some, like Tarzan, had only light or medium wool coverage with no wool on the legs, while others possessed heavy coats of wool over most of their extremities, including long, silken locks sprouting from their faces, ears, eyebrows and legs.

'Most of my stock ees a mixture of European, mainly British llama, some Chilean and some from Argentina. But all the types can be woolly or 'ave not much wool coverage.'

'So what about if I decided to breed my own llamas?' I asked. 'What would I have to look out for in a good breeding male?'

Bernard's eyes lit up. Obviously I had touched on a subject close to his heart. 'The thing you got to look for in the good breeder, Richard,' he said, indicating the exposed rear end of a likely looking subject, 'ees a good, rounded pair of …' he looked thoughtful, motioning as if squeezing a ripe avocado. 'Bloody 'ell, Richard, now what ees that word?'

'Testicles?' I ventured. The llama looked around suspiciously, allowing his companions to dive into the bucket of pellets. Perhaps this character originated in the UK and knew this word. His banana ears flattened against his head.

'No, no, no. That's not the word,' said Bernard, squeezing his invisible avocado more vigorously. 'Balls!'

'Ah, balls!'

'Blimey yes! 'Ee's gotta 'ave the good plump pair of balls!' The llama's short tail flicked down to cover his exposed genitals and he sidled off, keeping a low profile. 'Mind you,' continued Bernard, thinking of some extra information on the subject of the llama's reproductive organs, 'a llama 'as the ability to draw 'is balls up inside him.'

'It's a good trick if you can do it, I guess,' I remarked, quite impressed with the llama's versatility.

'Yes. Any 'ow, often you 'ave to give them a bit of a ...' he looked thoughtful again, searching for the English word.

'Squeeze?' I suggested.

'Palpation,' said Bernard. 'Flippin' 'eck, the poor guy mightn't 'ave got any bloody balls! Might be a genetic defect. So you got to find them if you want to buy a good breeder. You don't want to get 'im back 'ome and find out 'ee 'asn't got the means to, you know ...'

'Oh, definitely!' I agreed.

There was no stopping the llama breeder now. 'So what you got to do is you reach from behind, over the scrotum and you slide your finger back, putting on a bit of pressure.' I winced at the very thought, and I noticed how most of the llamas, who had been hovering around us, had strangely sauntered off. 'If the guy's got any balls they pop back into the scrotum. *Voila!* Then you grab them and give them a bit of a feel to make sure they are the uniform size and shape.'

'Oh,' I said, coming over a mite queasy in empathy with the llamas. 'You grab them ...'

'Yes, of course! Blimey, eet ees the only way! Mind you, eet ees best to let the veterinarian do that if eet ees your first time. You don't want to squeeze too hard, do you? Monsieur llama, 'ee would not appreciate thees, *non?*'

'No. Thanks for that, Bernard,' I said, wiping a tear from the corner of my eye and adjusting the hang of my jeans.

After bidding a fond farewell to the herd of llamas and promising Bernard that I would return, I set off for Le Mas Mauvis determined that as soon as our domestic situation allowed, our farm would have its very own small herd.

Al returned to Le Mas Mauvis by train after three weeks to find me physically exhausted from two months of virtually non-stop hard labour. It was a whistle-stop tour for her because we were due to leave the very next morning on the long drive back to Calais and the ferry to Dover. It was high time that I contributed once again to our finances, and I had a freelance contract to fulfil that would enable me to work from home most of the time and – should the magazine development become a national success – offered me the possibility of being able to work from France. Only time would tell. We had abandoned the idea of selling part of our property in order to finance further renovations: rather than converting the *maison du pain* into a habitable building we would never actually use as such, we had decided that it should be adapted instead as stabling for our future herd of llamas and for the horse that Al would one day own, thus fulfilling her own personal dream of riding along the quiet roads and bridleways of the Haute-Vienne.

Recognising that because of my family situation I found it difficult to be in the UK and that I was happiest at Le Mas Mauvis, Al suggested that I should try to spend as much time in France as possible. With an Internet connection on our telephone line, there was no reason why I could not carry on with my magazine and book work from the *grange*. Al had promised her parents that she would not move to France for a number of years after her sister's death, but was open to the idea of spending longer periods of time at Mauvis and would even contemplate commuting, returning to France each weekend: surely it couldn't be any worse than the horrendous daily London commute?

In *Jean de Florette*, Marcel Pagnol's magical book on the hardships of life in nineteenth-century Provence, the eponymous hero had to contend with the dastardly actions of his neighbours, who selfishly blocked off the natural source of spring water to his land in order to avail themselves of it, causing the poor hunchback to trudge miles in search of an alternative source, resulting in his tragic demise. At Le Mas Mauvis, however, just the opposite was true. We had far, far too much water.

On returning to our farm the following spring, we were amazed and thrilled to find that Monsieur Le Maire had, true to his word, sorted out our initial water problem in one fell swoop, only to highlight another similar problem. According to Véronique, a large digger had arrived unannounced one day to carve a broad, deep trench across the front of her house in order to insert a system of pipes that would divert the excess water flow from the communal land into the existing drainage trench. This was no small inconvenience to Véronique, who had had to traverse the trench for several days while the work was carried out. Although this cured our immediate problem, it showed up the fact that our property suffered from another drainage inadequacy.

A single length of plastic gutter ran along the front of the *grange* where it joined another that ran along the roof line of the hangar. Thence the rainwater poured into a single puny downpipe, only to discharge many hundreds of litres of water directly onto the ground, which was still sodden after the winter rainfall. The soil of the Limousin is not known for its good quality and consists of thick clay beneath the rather sandy topsoil. The rainwater, then, tended to lie on the surface of the field at the back of the barn, where it was joined by a similar deluge from the rear roof slope. The asbestos gutter at the back was intended to drain into two downpipes fixed at each end: one had snapped off halfway up, the other was non-existent. Water not only gushed onto the soggy earth but also poured down the walls of the building. The ground at the back of the *grange* had become a mire, worsened by the fact that the impertinent Monsieur André appeared to have continued to allow his cattle to graze the field in our absence and deep hoof prints peppered the surface.

We decided that the only way to solve both of our current problems was firstly to install new guttering in conjunction with a system of underground land drainage pipes to channel the liquid into the stream, and secondly to erect substantial fencing around the perimeter of our property to keep the cattle out once and for all. We decided to tackle the drainage predicament first.

Deciding that we could manage the job without recourse to hire a costly mechanical digger (for which we had not budgeted anyway), Al and I set to with shovels and spades to dig a trench from the location of the missing downpipe heading in the direction of the little stream, towards which the land naturally sloped. Only able to work in the early morning, when the heat of the sun was not too intense, we progressed depressingly slowly with our task. I determined that we would need to dig a trench about ten metres long and half a metre deep, terminating in a soakaway – a hardcorefilled pit a metre deep and measuring about a metre square – which would filter the water away harmlessly. By the end of the first day we had completed a knee-deep length of trench, a spade's width across and about three metres long. The work was backbreakingly arduous. Beneath one spade's depth the topsoil became thick, gooey clay. The trench filled with muddy water that leached from the sides of the excavation. Soil from the sides had the irritating habit of falling directly into the tops of my wellington boots, and my heavily perspiring feet turned it to a sticky sludge around my toes.

'You want to get a mechanical digger in there, kid. Be a piece o' cake. You're going to be right knackered doing it by hand,' offered David helpfully, having come along the following day to inspect the earthworks, and looking singularly unimpressed with our progress. He plucked a cigarette from behind his left ear, stuck it in his mouth and lit it, drawing heavily.

'We can't afford it. We're being economical. It won't take long, anyway. It's quite easy, really,' I lied blatantly.

'Anyway, how far are you planning on going then? All the way down t'little stream?' He chuckled. The little stream was some 65 metres away. I sneered at him from the depths of my trench.

'No, David, I don't think so, do you? That would be a bit unnecessary,' I said, mildly irritated that our friend was poking fun at our project.

After three days our trench extended about twelve metres into the field and constantly filled up with water leaching out of the surrounding soil. It steadfastly refused to drain away into the earth. The walls of the trench constantly collapsed with the efforts of tunnelling moles. The waist-deep soakaway I had dug and half-filled with a filtering layer of broken concrete and stones at the six-metre point had promptly filled to the brim with muddy brown water. I filled it in again and continued the trench beyond it, releasing the contents of the soakaway into this new branch, which became like a fast-running river. We lined the base of the trench with gravel, then laid in plastic drainage pipes with slits cut in one side, through which water could filter. At one end the pipe line would be connected to a gully into which the end of a new downpipe would slot. Water would then be carried directly from the roof via the gutter and downpipe, into the buried drainage pipe, which would channel it along the trench. At least that would take the water well away from the foundations of the building and allow the ground to dry out.

Monsieur Jérôme swaggered down the side of the hangar one day with his nephew François following dutifully behind. The big man stood with hands on hips and studied our trench-digging.

François, or Frank, was a tall 23-year-old with the physique of a male model: he had a swarthy complexion, deep, piercing hazel eyes and shoulder-length, shining black hair. He seemed to me to have grown from a spotty youth into a man in a matter of a few months. When not amusing himself with his trendy mates and an entourage of drooling young girls at the Lac du Mondon, the lad had taken up the profession of farmer, like his macho uncle, who Frank seemed to hold in considerable esteem. Al and I greeted the pair with back-of-the-wrist handshakes.

'Why is this land so wet?' asked Monsieur Jérôme, stamping in the sodden earth to demonstrate its obvious dampness. 'This is *pas normale*. You must have a *fuite* somewhere.'

'*Qu'est-ce que c'est "fuite"*?' asked Al, unfamiliar with the word.

'*Fuite*,' repeated Monsieur Jérôme and, when we both returned gormless expressions he sighed and said: 'You 'ave ze leak.' It was always something of a triumph for us when he was obliged to break into English, not because we wanted him to converse in our language, but because he generally refused to help us out when he could see that we were struggling with a particularly difficult French word, despite the fact that we knew full well by now that his command of English was excellent.

'No, this part's always been damp,' I said. 'I don't think we have a plumbing leak. But there's no gutter, as you can see. All the rainwater from the roof discharges here.'

'*Non, non, non, non*,' said Uncle Jérôme, wagging a chunky, oily finger at me. He appeared to be playing to the crowd: namely the admiring Frank, who was trying to mimic his mentor's stance. 'It was never this wet when I owned the farm.'

'It was,' I insisted, clambering out of my trench and looking for a stone or some high ground to stand on so I wouldn't feel so dwarfed by my adversary. I felt a bit ridiculous, as it happened, due to the fact that I was wearing only knee-length blue shorts, wellingtons and a pair of tattered gardening gloves. I had also been digging with a garden-gnome-sized border spade, which I wrongly assumed would be less prone to collapsing the trench sides than a conventional spade. In reality it was akin to using a teaspoon.

'It was not,' Uncle Jérôme said firmly.

'Was,' I said under my breath.

'It's only been like this since you got *le maire* to dig that trench in front of my aunt's house and make a mess of the drainage.'

Aha! I thought, gloating. I knew that he had been rattled by the diversion of the water because it highlighted the fact that he –

the one responsible for maintaining Véronique's house – had not adequately arranged the waste water drainage from the property. Our suspicions had been aroused by the river of soap suds that bubbled in the lane at the front of our *grange* whenever the dear lady used her washing machine or shower. We also suspected that the contents of her toilet followed this same untreated course rather than being fed to a septic tank, as was standard practice.

'Oh dear, Jérôme,' said Al with mock concern. 'Do you think we should ask *le maire* to come back and have another look then?' We knew that Monsieur Jérôme had an allergic reaction to officials: we had had cause to bandy about the dreaded name of Madame Marsolet, the *notaire*, on various occasions in the past when our vendor had been lazy in fulfilling the conditions of our sale contract, and he had displayed symptoms of real anguish. Dealing the trump card of *le maire* was an excellent gambit for Al to bring into play: I bristled with pride.

'*Non, non, non, non, non! Ce n'est pas necessaire!*' Monsieur Jérôme looked aghast and shook his head furiously, backing off. Frank adopted a similar expression, although his was more theatrical. '*De toute façon*, it's your land. But I'm only saying it looks like *une fuite*. It was never this wet when I owned the farm.'

'Was,' I muttered, just out of earshot. With that, the farmer and his sidekick turned and tramped back up the lane to perform their farmerly duties, which seemed to involve spilling lots of white fertiliser all over the communal land.

Ignoring Monsieur Jérôme's unfounded opinion that our plumbing had sprung a leak somewhere, I calculated that we needed to dig another trench starting at the foot of the broken-off downpipe, which would divide the water from the roof of the *grange* between two separate drainage points, once new guttering was installed. We extended this secondary trench – which relied upon me hacking away at the solid bedrock under a light dusting of topsoil with a pickaxe – towards another soakaway. This pit was marginally more successful than the first in its ability to soak water away.

A third trench was dug along the end of the hangar to collect the water from the front roof slope and channel it into a large plastic water butt, the contents of which could be siphoned off for our future garden-watering needs. Once the butt was almost full, an overflow pipe I rigged up would allow the excess water to enter an underground drainage pipe.

Heavy rainfall, however, told us that this complex network of pipes and trenches had failed unreservedly in its allotted task: although the pipes successfully carried the water away, it collected at the end of the first trench in a sodden mess.

'It's no good, Al,' I announced on inspecting the muddy lake that was forming around the mouth of the ultimate drainage pipe. 'We'll have to extend the trench further. If we leave it open, it'll act as a kind of storm drain like they have at the sides of the roads, and the water will have a chance to filter away.' And so we kept on digging, making our trench a shallower one-foot depth, and heading inexorably towards the little stream, which loomed ever closer with each day that passed.

After ten days Al returned to England, leaving me behind digging, digging, digging. One evening, drained of energy, I collapsed into a chair and telephoned her with the happy news: 'Hello, darling. I've reached the stream at last. Now the water will definitely drain away.' Or so I thought.

Chapter Fifteen

Flight of Fancy

Shinning up and down the aluminium ladder to access the *grenier* had become second nature to Al and I and we tended to overlook the fact that many visitors found the climb a mite daunting. Some would approach scaling the ladder with the same trepidation one might expect if asked to ascend the outside of the Eiffel Tower; others would take an age to clamber up one tentative step at a time and, once at the top, would fret about an appropriate method of descent. Sticklers for safety would demand the wholly unnecessary repositioning of the ladder to a wider angle; timid souls just froze halfway up and had to be assisted the rest of the way.

'Why don't we just go out and buy a staircase?' I suggested after David and Dennie, dining with us one evening, had consumed rather more *vin rouge* than was good sense with only a ladder to enable their descent to terra firma. It had taken them long enough to get up there in the first place, and reaching ground level again had been a major undertaking. We would also have loved to entertain our neighbour Véronique but we doubted that someone of her advanced age and frailty could manage the ladder. (Although Al's plucky 82-year-old father, the good Doctor Winter, succeeded in ascending to base camp during an early visit to us.)

There had been much previous discussion about the precise position of a staircase in the *grange*. Al and I were adamant that we wanted the flight to consume as little of the massive *grenier* floor as possible, and had planned for it to rise to the right-hand side of the hallway on entering the building, hugging the inner face of the front wall. In preparation for this I had removed a number of the vertical oak beams that originally divided the outer and central bays (through which the cattle used to poke their heads to access the mangers), and had demolished a section of the low stone wall on which they and the mangers had been built. But Monsieur Laborde had, for reasons best known to himself, placed the fuse box high on the wall, slap-bang in the intended position for the top of the flight, despite the detailed floor plan of the conversion we had furnished him with. It was going to be touch and go whether or not a staircase could fit over the box. Moving the fuse box itself was clearly not an option, for every single cable of our electrical system sprouted from this junction: the excitable Cyrille would likely self-combust in a fountain of sparks if we were foolhardy enough to suggest that he might have blundered.

I decided to seek the counsel of someone experienced in the art of staircase installation.

The Count, a skilful self-taught carpenter, had constructed a staircase for his French abode, cleverly making all the parts from scratch back in England. He had studied several meaty and technical tomes on staircase construction, had a workshop equipped with all the tools, and had obviously got it just right. Transporting the parts to France on the roof of his car, he was able to assemble the flight entirely on his own. Rising from the living room, the open-balustrade flight was certainly impressive, despite a few characterful creaks which the Count turned a deaf ear to, and was a credit to his dexterity. But no amount of cajoling would convince my brother to repeat his triumph and build a staircase for our *grange*.

'You must be bloody joking, pal!' was his rather blunt response. Staircase construction was not, apparently, something the Count would ever like to repeat again.

Unable to afford to have a staircase built by a local carpenter, Al and I decided that we would have to go it alone. Although I am not a carpenter of the same calibre as the Count, I considered myself quite capable of installing a staircase: after all, I'd written about it in do-it-yourself books numerous times in the past.

Stringing a line of trusty blue binder twine between ground floor level and the underside of the floor joists at the perceived angle of the flight, I scribed on the wall the positions of each tread and riser. Everything seemed to fit nicely. The only problem I could foresee was with the length of the opening I would have to cut in the upper floor. With the top of the flight narrowly missing the infernal fuse box, the presence of a chunky oak beam would unfortunately coincide with the head height of anyone using the staircase, unless they were extremely vertically challenged. It would not be merely a case of 'duck or grouse': the beam would simply have to go.

Armed with the essential dimensions our staircase would need to comply with in order to avoid the fuse box, Al and I began to research what was available in the ready-made staircase market. Leafing through various brochures from specialist joinery chains we discounted the hideously expensive flights in *bois exotique* that predominated. We flirted briefly with the romance of a spiral staircase, then thought of the practicality of hauling furniture up and decided against such an extravagance. Rather impetuously, when viewing showroom models in Limoges, we plumped for a simple straight staircase in fir, found flat-packed amongst the racks in the cavernous Mr Bricolages store. The kit seemed to conform to our specifications, allowing for lopping off the thirteenth step. Strapping the packs to the roof rack of our car, we set off for home with fingers firmly crossed that it would actually fit.

Al conveniently departed for England, leaving me to interpret the rather brief assembly instructions that came with the staircase. The task seemed straightforward enough: the flight consisted of two wide boards set on edge, which formed the sides of the staircase. These *limons* (called 'strings' in the UK) had rectangular slots cut on their inner faces, into which the projecting tenon joints at each end of the treads would slot. The treads also had a groove cut under their rounded front edge 'nosing', into which a tongue cut along the top edge of the vertical part of the step would slot. The whole shebang would be glued and screwed together (despite the fact that the instructions neglected to mention the need for glue).

My first task was to mark out the length and width of the hole I would need to cut in the *grenier* floor, and to cut away the floorboards. Once this was done, I propped up the central joist that was to be cut back to the length of the opening and sawed through it. I then used a portion of the joist as a 'trimmer joist' to fit between the outer joists, which closed off the opening and supported the cut end of the central joist. With the opening so formed, I could then assemble the staircase itself. I discovered that this was not easily a one-man job. With one *limon* lying on the floor, I daubed woodworking adhesive into its joint slots, then applied more to the projecting ends of the treads. I slotted the treads into position. Fine so far. Then, after gluing the other *limon* and the exposed ends of the treads, I lifted it up and attempted to slot it onto the treads – just as it showed in the little illustration on the instruction sheet. When I had managed to mate two or three joints, I found it impossible to get the other treads to slot into place. As I worked along the length of the flight, the previous joints sprang apart. The whole assembly was wobbling so much that it eventually collapsed, smearing wet glue everywhere it wasn't supposed to be.

I persisted with the prescribed method of assembly until, after several failed attempts, I gave up and tried my own technique, which involved standing the *limons* on edge and slotting the treads between them. This was only marginally more successful than the correct method, but enabled me to drive a few screws through the *limons* into the ends of the treads at strategic points, giving the assembly sufficient stability to allow me to insert all twelve treads. The risers were supposed to slot between the *limons* and into the underside of the treads. However, all twelve were, inexplicably, about one centimetre too large. But such inconsistencies are the curse of self-assembly kits the world over. Cursing, I was forced to mark each riser carefully and cut it to size. My sawing technique had improved since my friend Jean Le Grand's lesson some years before when building the stud partition walls, and I eventually succeeded in completing the flight after several frustrating hours.

The following day, David happened along just as I was wondering how I was going to single-handedly hoist the staircase into position.

'C'mon then, kid. Let's get 'er lifted up!' said David.

Together, we grasped the sides of the flight and eased the bottom end through the opening in the dividing wall. Then, hoisting it above our heads, we shuffled underneath and pushed upwards. The flight was heavy, and it took all our strength to get it hooked on the inch-wide batten I had secured to the trimmer joists at the top. It seemed like such a flimsy fixing for such a heavy staircase. We stood back and admired the structure. Oh joy! I was relieved that the top step fitted over the fusebox with several centimetres to spare. We went around into the hall and looked at it from that angle. I fetched my spirit level and placed it on the treads: perfectly level. I was proud. I couldn't wait to tell Al on the phone.

'Can I be t'first to go up?' said David, pulling off his boots in anticipation.

'Shouldn't we fix it in place first? It's just hanging off that little bracket at the moment.'

'No, lad! She's solid as rock. She's going nowhere.' And with that, he was off up the stairs, bold as brass. I gritted my teeth, imagining that the whole lot would come tumbling down at any minute. Once David had successfully negotiated the flight to the top, he gingerly crept back down again and we set about securing the structure to the joists at each side with large coach bolts, and at the bottom to the vertical oak posts that formed the opening to our new stairway.

That night, for the first time in almost four years of owning the farm, I was able to ascend to the *grenier* by my own staircase. Over the next few days, however, habit prevailed and I would constantly head for the ladder, which was still propped in the open hatchway. Because of my forgetfulness, I had decided to leave the ladder there until I could construct a trapdoor: it would be unfortunate if, rising sleepily at night to descend to the toilet, I clean forgot about the staircase and took the painful shortcut down the gaping hole usually occupied by the ladder.

I panelled in the stairwell with plasterboard, also utilising lengths of the oak posts I had removed from the dividing partition of the hallway to suggest a touch of rustic authenticity that visually linked the stairwell to the hallway. At the top of the stairwell I fixed a balustrade of turned spindles and a smooth handrail between two stout newel posts. Then all I needed to do was to locate a suitable tone of wood stain that would blend the light softwood with the honey-coloured exposed beams in the *grenier*.

The troublesome beam that limited the head height of the staircase was not as easy to remove as I had imagined: it measured about thirty centimetres square and was made from extraordinarily tough and aged oak. I was reduced to sawing by hand, then chopping out great chunks with a chisel and mallet, slowly reducing its girth. Once I had sliced through the beam, however, I discovered that the other end was housed about sixty centimetres into the external stone wall. Eventually, by wiggling the beam and tugging down on it, I managed to free it, just nipping out of the way in time before it crashed to the concrete floor of the hallway. This small piece of wood – only about a metre long – weighed a considerable amount and I had trouble even lifting it out of the way.

News of the staircase spread – disseminated by Véronique, who had come to view the fine edifice, although because of her dodgy knees she felt unable to negotiate the steps. During the next few days a troupe of neighbours appeared at the door to inspect the flight, nodding approvingly, although none were brave enough to scale its heights. Change happened slowly in Le Mas Mauvis and it would no doubt take time for the presence of the staircase to sink into the local psyche. Few of our neighbours could, in any case, work out why on earth Al and I wanted to live in a cold, draughty barn in the first place.

'Would you like to go up?' I said, trying to tempt Bruno and Jolanda Bussiere into my lair upstairs, after they had paid me a visit one morning with the gift of half a kilo of tomatoes and a huge lettuce, crawling with little slugs.

'*Non*, I would not,' said Jolanda adamantly. Admittedly she was quite a frail soul and, living in a bungalow, probably rarely had recourse to climb stairs. The notion was obviously abhorrent to her, and she was not at all curious to see what went on up in the *grenier*. Her husband, on the other hand, looked a little hesitant and she placed a restraining hand on his arm, just in case he should falter.

'Let go, woman!' he growled, wresting himself from her grasp. He was tempted, I could tell. Good sense got the better of him, however, and he politely declined the offer. 'No zank ewe very much, Richard,' he said with a sterling stab at English. '*Un autre jour, peut être ...*'

Even Monsieur Jérôme looked impressed when he came to see my handiwork, offering a compliment: '*C'est très bien*, Richard. You have *une maison* now. It is no longer *une grange*. *Bon courage!*' Praise indeed from the big man, and gratifying to hear. Perhaps these particular *Anglais* were not 'ducks ready for plucking' after all.

If the grandeur of our staircase had been a subject whispered along the grapevine of Le Mas Mauvis, then another topic surely just pipped it to the post in terms of intrigue: the mysterious disappearance of Gordon and Maureen. Although the reluctant bullfighter had divulged to Al and me that he and Maureen were thinking of selling up and moving to the far south of France in search of a warmer climate more beneficial to his wife's illness, we were shocked to find that they had apparently upped sticks and left without saying a word to a soul.

Their house, in which they had invested a good deal of time and a lot of money over the previous four years, stood empty, its metal shutters closed across its windows. The garden, overgrown and neglected when it was once lovingly cared for, was closed off from the lane by a line of rope. The only sign that they had been there at all was the presence of their caravan, which remained parked on the drive, green with mildew.

'*C'est bizarre!*' opined Véronique, to whom Gordon and Maureen had been kind and considerate in the past. 'They left without a word, and did not leave a forwarding address.'

'No one knows where they have gone,' confirmed Bruno Bussiere sadly. He had regularly visited the couple with baskets of vegetables, and considered them his friends. He could not understand the situation. '*C'est étrange! C'est triste.*'

'It's said that the house is still full of their furniture,' cackled Madame Météo, somewhat over-theatrically, a sinister tone to her voice. Her eyes widened. 'They simply *disparu!*'

'I have no idea where they've gone,' said Monsieur Jérôme, feigning disinterest. '*C'est très, très bizarre*. They were *bizarre!* And the *dame*, she had it in for me! *Pourquoi?* I'm sure I don't know! But I've heard that the place is up for sale – *Et le prix!* Do you know how much is being asked for it? *C'est dérisoire!*'

'It's certainly odd, kid,' admitted David, who knew the couple only vaguely, drawing pensively on a cigarette. 'But maybe you should ask Monsieur Thierry where they've gone. Since Gordon saved him from t'bull, pair have forged some kind of bond. Thierry was always round mowing the grass or summat. He seems to be keeping an eye on the place now.'

Needless to say, Al and I declined to approach our grass-rustling foe about the strange disappearance of our English neighbours. Gordon and Maureen obviously had their reasons for departing so suddenly, and we just hoped that it had not been because of a rapid decline in Maureen's health.

Once we had put into motion our land drainage project, the problem of ousting Monsieur André's cattle from our property loomed. It seemed that the only way we could stop the infuriating man from allowing his beasts to sneak into our fields when our backs were turned was to erect a barbed-wire fence around the perimeter. This was fortuitous, as I was also keen to commence the fencing in preparation for the arrival of the llamas we hoped to purchase from Bernard. However, the books I had read on llama keeping had unanimously advised that barbed wire was to be avoided at all costs, due to the fact that the animals' long fibre might become entangled in the barbs. When I called the rebellious Bernard he pooh-poohed the namby-pamby notion of barbed wire's unsuitability, while broadly agreeing with my reference works that a fence suitable for containing a frisky llama (which could easily jump a five-bar gate) would need to be at least 1.5 metres high.

The part of our land where the cows could cross unhindered was the boundary that bordered Monsieur André's huge byre and pig barn (adjacent to Gordon and Maureen's house). A three-metre-wide parcel of land owned by Monsieur Jérôme was sandwiched between our land and the rough track that led to the farm buildings, which we understood was owned by the wily pig man. Monsieur Jérôme had retained this corridor – an unruly patch of grass and weeds at the best of times – as a safeguard against potential problems accessing the track in the future; the farmer needed to retain access to his fields which lay beyond. Al and I consulted the cadastral plan and discovered that our boundary was a higgledy-piggledy line that roughly followed the route of the trees and hedging. Parcels of land in France are frequently oddly shaped, for no obvious rhyme nor reason. Originally plotted using buildings, mature trees and established hedges as datum, the landscape and its features naturally changed over the passing generations. Subsequent storms or a policy of tree-felling for firewood, and the fact that elderly, neglected buildings tended to collapse in a heap, meant that these datum disappeared. Nevertheless, few astute landowners forgot precisely where these blurred boundaries lay, and such information was no doubt passed on through families.

It was whilst Al and I were marking out our boundary alongside Monsieur Jérôme's access corridor (in preparation for erecting the fence), that the farmer appeared. Hands on hips, he examined the circuitous route by which we were stringing a line of twine, and grubbing out the overgrown hedgerow in the centre of which we had discovered an ancient mesh fence. At one clearly defined kink in the boundary line, as defined on the copy of the cadastral plan, there had once been a substantial and centuries-old oak tree. All that remained of it now was a rotting stump. I imagined a scene hundreds of years ago when the original landowner mapped out the extent of his property, taking as his datum an oak sapling, which had grown to become a cornerstone of his and future empires. Even though the tree had long since fallen, its ghost lived on in this kink on our cadastral plan.

'Why do you mark this boundary?' asked Monsieur Jérôme.

'We're going to erect a fence to keep the cows off our land,' explained Al. The farmer squinted down the wiggly line of twine and shook his head. Was he about to dispute our interpretation of the boundary? I showed him the plan, which he dismissed with a wave of the hand.

'*Oui, oui, oui, oui! Je comprends! Ce n'est pas nécessaire!*' He raised his voice, sounding quite angry. What transgression had we committed now? Suddenly the ogre whipped a knife from his jeans pocket and flicked out the sharp blade. My God! I thought. He's going to stick us both and feed our corpses to Monsieur André's squealers! Instead, Monsieur Jérôme grasped the line of twine and sliced through it with his blade. Then he dragged the loose end across his strip of no man's land and stretched it out along the grass, about a metre in from the hard track.

'*Posez la clôture ici!*' he said, calmer now, and indicated a straight line parallel with the track. He closed the knife and pocketed it. I sighed with relief. Perhaps we weren't going to become pig fodder after all.

'But that's your boundary, Jérôme,' Al pointed out.

'*Oui. Je crois,*' he said. '*Mais,* if you fix your fence here, it will be easier for you – a straighter line – and we will both benefit. You will keep *les vaches* off your land, I will keep them off mine. *Et aussi,* you can use this land for your llamas, *non?*'

'Well, Jérôme, I don't know ...' Al said hesitantly, looking to me for support. I wasn't sure. Would we be making a rod for our own backs?

'I'm not selling you this land, though!' added the farmer.

'That's OK, because we don't want to buy it,' replied Al.

'I'm not giving it to you either. It will still be mine,' he stressed, lest we should misconstrue his motives.

'Fine!' Al said. It seemed like a reasonable, friendly offer. What could go wrong? If there should be a dispute in the future, we could always move the fence over to our higgledy-piggledy boundary. So a deal was struck. We would erect a straight fence line that, while barring the access of the cows, would provide us with a bonus in extra grazing for our llamas. Monsieur Jérôme would retain access to his strip of land, which was an ideal and inconspicuous site for storage of the sacks of fertiliser and other farming equipment that would otherwise litter the communal green. Not only that, but the farmer also volunteered to help me with the erection of the fence, and advised on the best quality barbed wire to purchase, and the size of fence posts we would need.

'*Samedi matin*,' he announced. 'I will arrive at *le weekend*, *samedi matin*, you understand? And we shall erect this fence, Richard. Do you have a *tendeur*?'

'*Non*,' I replied '*Je n'en ai pas*.' I checked my trouser pockets for some obscure reason.

'*N'importe*. I have one. I will bring it. We will need it, *bien sûr*.'

'Orh! *Naturellement!*' I agreed with my best Gallic shrug, trying to sound macho and knowledgeable, although I hadn't the foggiest idea what he was talking about.

'What's a *tendeur*, Rich?' asked Al after we had shaken the back of the farmer's wrist in farewell.

'Haven't a clue,' I said. 'But I don't think I've got one.'

Al and I bought thirty posts of the length recommended by Monsieur Jérôme, a box of staples, plus a 50-metre roll of viciously pronged barbed wire and began to set the posts in place, in preparation for the farmer's arrival at the weekend. This was easier said than done. After marking the line of the fence with twine, we decided on the position for the first post and I used my trusty iron levering bar to pierce the hard earth, ramming it in and then revolving it to widen and deepen the hole. When I thought that the hole was deep enough, I positioned the first post and attempted to drive it into the ground with my sledgehammer. Unfortunately, I am not especially tall and could only just heft the weighty tool high enough to strike the top of the post. The few glancing blows that I was able to make – with Al crouching low to support the post, nervous of the real danger of being clobbered herself – merely split the wood.

'I need a bit more height,' I said, wheezing at the effort.

'You're just the right height for me, darling,' said Al, squatting by the base of the post, head protected from expected hammer blows by her arms.

'No, you nit. I mean I need to be able to get a good swing at the top of the post. I'm not tall enough.'

Just then, Monsieur Jérôme pulled up outside his aunt's house, delivering the children. Spying our activities with an expression of amusement, he wandered over, grinning broadly. Oh, here we go! I thought. More ritual humiliation in store for me!

'Don't laugh, because I'm not tall enough, Jérôme. And the hammer is very heavy, I'll have you know,' I whinged unconvincingly. Smirking, he grabbed the sledgehammer from me in one big mitt and gripped the girth of the post in the other. Hefting the tool above his head like it weighed a mere whisper, he gave the top of the post such a well-aimed wallop that it sank into the ground a good two feet. Another smack and it was well and truly home. He handed back the sledgehammer, which I almost dropped on my foot, then tested the stability of the post.

'*C'est tout!*' he said. In my defence, I indicated the considerable height difference between the two of us – I only came up to his shoulders, after all – and the fact that his biceps were the size of watermelons. He laughed. 'You need *une brouette*,' he suggested.

'A brunette?' I looked at Al, sure that she wouldn't approve. Besides, we had work to do.

'*Non, non, non,* Richard. *Écoutez! Une brouette,*' then in English, 'veelbarrow.'

'Ah, *oui*! A wheelbarrow to stand in. *Oui*, of course! I was just going to get the *brouette*, actually.'

'Liar,' muttered Al. I fired her a wilting look. Shaking his head with a sigh of despair, the farmer left us two amateurs with a wave, saying that he'd return at the weekend to help with the barbed wire. Damn! That big lump was always showing me up.

Right, I thought, I'll show him I can do something without his help!

'Al,' I commanded, hoisting the sledgehammer onto my shoulder. 'Be so good as to fetch the *brouette*!' I marched off to the next post position three metres away, tripping over my own wellington boots en route and stumbling into the pile of posts.

Standing in the wheelbarrow certainly gained me sufficient height to reach the tops of the fence posts, although it being a cheap aluminium one rather than a sturdy builder's type, it wobbled disconcertingly. Balance has never been a strong point of mine and each swing of the sledgehammer created a rapid swaying motion in the wheelbarrow akin to a rowing boat on choppy water. However, despite the effects of mild seasickness, I was soon progressing well in sinking the posts along the stringline, ably assisted by a crouching Al. It was with a sense of accomplishment that, after a few hours, I stood by the final post, proud wife on arm, and gazed along the perfectly straight run. Mission accomplished. Nevertheless, I had to admit to feeling considerably drained of energy and was forced to retire for a well-earned lunch.

The following day my muscles ached so much that I could barely lift my morning bowl of coffee, much to Al's sadistic entertainment.

'Never mind,' I consoled myself. 'At least that's the difficult bit over. Nailing on the barbed wire's going to be a doddle!'

How wrong I was.

Saturday arrived and Al had conveniently departed for England, leaving me at the mercy of Monsieur Jérôme's veiled jibes about my abilities. He turned up, as promised, clutching a strange, extremely rusty device that consisted of a metal handle with two chains dangling from one side and another chain fixed to the opposite side; all three chains sported a hook at the end. Another separate length of chain he carried had two metal elliptical loops at one end, each with a curved metal piece attached.

'Do you want to put up the fence, Richard?' asked the man-mountain, swinging his chains.

'Now?' I queried. I was sure that he was trying to catch me out. Usually if the farmer suggested tackling some work together, he meant 'in a few months' time' rather than 'right now'.

'*Oui, oui! Si vous voulez,*' he said offhandedly, putting the onus back on me.

'OK. I'll come right now.' I collected the wheelbarrow, which contained hammers, staples, the prising bar, the roll of barbed wire and two pairs of thick gardening gloves, and followed Monsieur Jérôme around to the fence line.

'*Bon travail!*' he said, testing the stability of the posts. '*D'accord.* I'll show you how we do this.' I felt honoured, as if I was being inducted into a secret society. He hauled the barbed wire out of the barrow, released the end and wrapped it around the first post. He spurned the need for sissy gloves, despite the fact that the vicious barbs dug into his flesh and drew blood. As though this was a mild inconvenience, he merely wiped the blood off onto his grubby jeans. I noticed with concealed amusement that one of the back pockets had been removed and skilfully reapplied centrally on the backside, presumably to patch a hole, which gave his figure a lopsided look. He whipped a pair of pliers from the pocket, grasped the end of the wire and twisted it together. Next, he inserted my prising bar into the centre of the roll and together we unreeled it down to the far end of the fence run some twenty-five metres away. Here's where the chain device came in, for this was *le tendeur*, the tensioner, he explained.

'You know how this works?' he asked.

'*Oui, certainement!*' I lied, shrugging Gallicly. He studied me briefly with a look of doubt on his face, then began to wrap the device around the last post and secure the hooks in some technical manner I did not quite catch (partly because – purposefully, I thought – he hid the technique with his body). I could just see that the end of the barbed wire was inserted in the little curved cups at the end of the separate chain, which retained it like a clamp. Heaving on the end of the wire, which was attached at the opposite end of the fence run, the farmer connected the chain to the two hooks on the *tendeur* and began to apply leverage to the handle. As the wire fence became taut, he was able to release each one of the hooks in turn and reconnect it further along the length of chain. Once the wire was sufficiently taut (he twanged it like a giant guitar string and it reverberated metallically) he hammered metal staples in to secure it. He disconnected the *tendeur* and grabbed a handful of staples.

'*D'accord*, Richard. Now we nail the wire to each post.' He indicated that it was important for the wire to be fixed at a consistent height from the ground along the length of the fence. With one wire attached, we laid out the second wire. 'This must be positioned thirty centimetres above the first,' he divulged. Suddenly a car pulled up at the end of the track and Jérôme's wife waved and hollered something from the open window.

'*Merde!*' said Monsieur Jérôme. 'I have to go. It is my children's school sports day.' Great, I thought. Now he tells me. We've only just started the job and already he's bunking off.

The big man handed me the *tendeur* as if he was investing me with a special privilege: 'Take this *tendeur* and use it wisely, my apprentice!' I imagined him intoning. Instead, he just said: 'You won't be able to do this on your own. I'll be back in a few hours. *A plus tard!*' And with that, he was gone.

After the farmer had departed I stood and looked forlornly at the incomplete fence. Right! I said to myself. I'll show him! I can do this on my own! I attached the second wire to the outer post, copying the method my tutor had employed, and stretched out the wire. Attaching the end of the wire in the little clamp device was quite straightforward: it gripped a barb firmly in its jaws. Next, I wrapped the single chain attached to the *tendeur*'s handle around the post and secured it onto one of the other two chains. Wrong move. I realised too late that the chain should have been hooked onto itself. The whole tool was immobilised. I disassembled the device and tried again. After about half an hour, however, I had managed to crack it and was progressing well. Eventually, I was able to secure the wire to the posts with staples, remove the tool and start on the third wire.

Then disaster struck. I bent down to pick up my hammer and, on straightening up, did not realise that my head was directly underneath the topmost wire. A razor-sharp barb dug into the unprotected bald patch at the crown of my head and ripped agonisingly through the flesh. I screamed in pain and grasped the top of my head, falling backwards into the long grass. I could feel blood pouring from a laceration that felt deep and broad, enough to scratch my skull. Staggering to my feet, I headed for the *grange*, feeling my head throbbing and the sticky wetness trickling down my face.

Grabbing the first-aid kit we kept in the bathroom my first thought was to clean the wound. I bent over the basin and turned on the tap, aiming the cold stream of water at the gash. The water ran red with blood. I felt nauseous. I fumbled in the first-aid kit and located a sterile dressing, which I ripped from its packet and applied to my head, applying pressure. After a few minutes, I peeled the dressing off and inspected the laceration in the tiny shaving mirror that hung from the wall above the basin. Still seeping blood, the cut was about six centimetres long and appeared quite deep. Did it need stitches? Who could I ask?

Just then I heard a loud rap on the door. I staggered out to the hallway to find Monsieur Jérôme grinning in the open doorway. His ten-year-old son Didier stood at his side, smiling from ear to ear.

'Do you want to put up this fence today or not?' said Monsieur Jérôme, consulting his wristwatch.

'I've cut my head on the barbed wire, actually. And I don't know how serious it is. I might have to go to the hospital, as it happens.'

'*Où?* Let me see.' I removed the dressing and bent forward. Father and son studied my bald patch. 'Pah! *L'hôpital?* But it's just a little scratch! Come on, Richard. Let's get this fence finished. I have other work to do.' I mouthed a horrendously foul obscenity at the departing farmer.

Round at the scene of my accident, after I had applied antiseptic cream to my 'little scratch', I found the farmer admiring the extent of my labours, although vaguely amused at the method of applying the tensioning device.

'It's nearly complete!' he said, with a surprised tone in his voice, as I approached. Clearly, as an apprentice, I had learned well. '*Très bon*, Richard! *Alors*, you don't need me. You can do this yourself, and I can get back to my cows!' After giving me a supplementary lesson on the prescribed technique for attaching the *tendeur*, he left the device in my capable hands and asked me to leave it with Véronique when I had completed my task.

'*Faites attention!* Be very careful with the barbs, Richard. They are very sharp!' He winked, then began his John Wayne-swagger back up the track, the patch on the backside of his jeans seeming to exaggerate the swaying motion. Half turning, as if he'd forgotten to relay some important technical information, he said: 'Oh, and by the way, Richard … *Bon courage!*'

'Well, that should keep the sod out!' I said to David, slouching in my chair, having just described my day's experiences as a trainee fencer. I had popped up to see my friend for an aperitif that had transmogrified into a full-blown Yorkshire-style meat-and-two-veg dinner with copious amounts of wine. We sat in the garden under the shade of the linden tree, watching a fine sunset over the rooftops of our barns. I threw a handful of peanuts into my mouth and crunched.

'Who're you talking about, Rich? Monsieur Thierry André?' asked David, pouring a glass of white wine.

'Monsieur André Thierry,' I corrected, taking the glass that was handed to me and slurping from it.

'Farmer's name's Thierry André.'

'No. André Thierry.'

'No, kid. His first name's Thierry. Second name's André.' David peered at me over his spectacles like a wise old owl instructing an idiot pupil. A terrible realisation suddenly slapped me about the face.

'Are you sure, David?' I asked. 'For the last four years Al and I have thought his name was Monsieur André. André first name, Thierry second name.'

'No, lad. First name's definitely Thierry. Second name's definitely André. But don't just take it from me.' David grabbed the telephone directory and leafed through the pages. 'Look, here it is. Monsieur Thierry André. See? Get it, kid?'

'Well, bugger me!' How could we have got that one so wrong? No wonder the wily farmer looked at me so oddly whenever I marched up to him and said: 'Bonjour André!' How rude! It would be akin to him greeting me with: 'Hi, Wiles!' Then I got to thinking. It was true that Véronique called me Monsieur Richard, and my Yorkshire buddy Monsieur David, but David reckoned that this was merely because the French have trouble with the letter 'W' and could not correctly pronounce our surnames Wiles and Wrightam. I recalled Bruno's facial contortions when he had been trying to get his tongue around the pronunciation of the Yorkshireman's surname. David cited the case that Véronique called Bruno by his surname, Monsieur Bussiere, rather than Monsieur Bruno. But I was not so sure. I put that down to an old-fashioned sign of respect. Also, when the French write down their names, they give the surname first and the first name second, the two separated by a comma. No, I put our mistake down to the fact that the sneaky farmer possessed not one but two *prenoms* and tried to pass one of them off as his surname.

Chapter Sixteen

At Whit's End

Easter 2002 heralded a series of religious ceremonies peculiar to the Limousin in the form of the *ostensions*. Held every seven years by the faithful inhabitants of towns and villages in the Haute-Vienne and Creuse *départements*, these festivals honour numerous local saints, many of whom founded monasteries in the region, in addition to the hermits who lived in the Limousin and Marche Forests. Commencing on Easter Monday and lasting for fifty days, they give rise to colourful processions and ceremonies at which relics of the saints are displayed and venerated in their shrines and reliquaries. The *ostensions* originated as far back as the tenth century, when the relics of Saint Martial were brought into play as a holy weapon to combat a deadly epidemic gripping the heart of Limoges. Subsequent visitations of plague became occasions for repeating the ceremonies, which eventually became tradition, and often focused on local folklore in addition to religious exposition.

Le Dorat, ancient capital of the Basse-Marche, honouring its own saints Israël and Théobald, was to be the setting for the closure of the *ostensions*, when more than fifty neighbouring parishes converged on the town. The little winding streets had been bedecked with bunting and elaborate floral displays. Entire streets and squares were closed to traffic as medieval gatehouses fashioned from plywood – complete with realistic portcullises – were erected across the entrances. Dressed in colourful costumes, processions of *ostensionnaires* snaked their way through the cobbled streets to the sound of fanfares and drums, waving banners representing their particular craft guilds or specific causes.

When driving through the town one day in the midst of the celebrations, Al and I were surprised to find our way temporarily blocked by a platoon of sappers and drummers dressed in the full regalia of Napoleon's First Empire. The soldiers and other mounted musketeers formed guards of honour that escorted the myriad processions along their route, marching from house to house making collections and bestowing blessings and good wishes on the occupants.

During the *ostensions* another religious festival was held in the Haute-Vienne, in which our own hamlet played a key role. The *Pentecôte* – the religious feast commemorating the descent of the Holy Ghost upon the Apostles, fifty days after the resurrection of Christ – was an important date in the calendar of Le Mas Mauvis, at least for those God-fearing souls who resided there. It provided an interesting spectacle even for confirmed agnostics such as myself. Over the Whit weekend the hamlet became part of the *Procession des Neuf Lieux*. Each year on the eve of Whit Sunday hundreds of religious devotees took part in an overnight march that started after midnight mass in the twelfth-century church in the nearby town of Magnac-Laval. Covering a distance of about 54 kilometres, the procession – reputed to be the longest in Europe – would return via a circuitous route to the church at eight o'clock the following evening. Held to worship the memory of the good Saint Maximin, one of the most illustrious bishops of the fourteenth century, who once resided in Magnac-Laval, the procession was believed to have been first established as early as 1591 by monks wishing to spread the Christian doctrine to the heathen masses.

Following a meandering network of historical pathways, and traversing fields, woods and existing tar roads, the long, winding procession visits sites at which the saintly bishop is believed to have performed his religious rites. Prayers are chanted, religious songs sung and meditations performed by the assembled masses, presided over by the priest of Magnac-Laval. Hamlets all along the route play host to the passing procession, which pauses only briefly in order to bless the total of some 48 crosses adorned with flowers and greenery, erected by the inhabitants.

Preparations for the *Pentecôte* started the week before, when Monsieur Jérôme rumbled onto the communal green in his tractor and cut the unruly grass to within an inch of its life. Unfortunately, the pollen released into the atmosphere was sufficient to bring about a severe attack of asthma in his aunt, and poor Veronique was whisked off to the hospital in Le Dorat where she remained for four days linked to an oxygen supply.

On Whitsuntide morning David, who had witnessed the *Pentecôte* at Le Mas Mauvis in previous years, had been recounting to me (a Pentecostal virgin) the usual programme of events. He, Dennie and I were sipping coffee on the garden bench David had positioned just outside his brother's house near where the hamlet's cross would be erected in time for the following day's procession.

'The previous owner of the house was an atheist,' explained David. 'And he used to sabotage the cross when others had put it up. Couldn't bear it stuck outside his house. So I think the locals are pleased I try to help out like, and put out seating for old 'uns and serve fruit juice when the procession passes by.'

Monsieur Jérôme screeched up in his people carrier, leaped out, and began to prune branches of elder blossom from the trees surrounding the communal green. He carried armfuls of these huge bouquets to the area of grass in front of the house and laid them by the stone slab that was set within the turf. The big farmer greeted us briefly before setting off again to cut swathes of green foliage from the nearby hedgerows, returning to set them alongside the blooms.

As David and I positioned some garden seating in the shade of the trees adjacent to the stone slab for the benefit of elderly visitors wishing to view the ceremony, cowman Monsieur Cédric, dressed in his regulation green boiler suit, wellingtons and cap, appeared from his workshop carrying a large, brown-painted wooden cross on one shoulder.

David nodded towards the approaching figure. 'Here comes Cédric with the cross. Takes his job serious, he does. He'll be there tomorrow with a banner, leading the procession to the cross, then down the Pentecostal way and over the fields to Sejotte, where they all have their dinners.'

Monsieur Cédric solemnly trudged across the green and slotted the base of the cross in the square hole that was formed in the stone. From his pocket he produced some wooden wedges and David and I helped him to stabilise it. He stammered a polite if lengthy '*merci beaucoup*', commented on the favourable weather forecast for the procession the next day, then set off across the green again. Just then another car drove up and out spilled a gaggle of young ladies and numerous children and toddlers. While the kids played on the grass, their young mothers earnestly selected the finest blooms from the pile and attached them to the cross with wire ties, assisted by the manful Monsieur Jérôme. Skilfully they wove the stems together until after about an hour the cross was resplendent with white, sweetly perfumed elder interspersed with the fragrant heads of red and cream roses taken from Véronique's garden and accented with strands of lush green foliage.

'Could you to keep *le croix* in your barn overnight?' asked Monsieur Jérôme, who had taken David up on his offer of a cold beer on completion of his floristry duties. We three sat in a row on the garden bench watching the cross decorators pack up their belongings.

'Of course,' said David. 'And I'll spray the flowers with water to keep them fresh.'

'Ah, *bon*!' said Monsieur Jérôme, raising his beer bottle in salute. When the florists and their offspring had departed, our drinking companion thanked us for the beer, bid us a fond farewell and leaped back in his people carrier. '*A demain!*' he called, haring off back up the lane. David and I lifted the cross out of its slot and carefully carried it into the barn adjoining the house, which served as a store for garden tools and equipment. We leaned the cross against the wall and David fetched a plant sprayer and doused the blooms with a fine mist of water.

'Pop round at nine sharp tomorrow,' suggested David, as I prepared to head off home. 'And we'll watch the day unfold.'

I must admit that, in my time at Le Mas Mauvis, I had managed to unlearn the habit of doing anything at all remotely 'sharp' when it came to timekeeping. But still, the next day I managed by supreme effort – assisted by the rarely used alarm clock – to be there as instructed, only to find David still in his dressing gown, smoking his first cigarette of the day, while Dennie still languished in the shower.

'Bloody 'ell, you're up bright and early, Rich!' said the Yorkshireman. 'Couldn't sleep for t'excitement of the day, eh?'

The florists and their entourage of children returned at ten o'clock when the sun was already baking hot. There was not a cloud in the turquoise sky. It promised to be a stifling day. Once David and I had replaced the flower-bedecked cross in its mount, the girls laid out a lacy tablecloth on the stone slab and artfully positioned a collection of ancient leather-bound bibles and prayer books, little religious icons and sprigs of flowers in silver vases. The children contributed a few garish plastic teething rings and tacky toys, which looked rather incongruous. But who was I to judge?

Various floral wreaths were placed around this makeshift altar, and some were even suspended from the cross itself. Bruno Bussiere shuffled up, looking rather embarrassed, holding a homemade and slightly elliptical wreath that seemed to have been formed from a wire coat-hanger; it was rather sparsely adorned with flowers and a few bits of greenery. The offering, which he was at pains to insist was from his wife and not him, was proudly dangled from one of the arms of the cross.

Monsieur Cédric appeared, still wearing his green boiler suit, wellingtons and cap, and I wondered if he ever took them off. The collar of his shirt was frayed and dirty and the cuffs similarly disreputable, where they hung in threads from the arms of the boiler suit. He supervised the wedging of the cross to ensure that it was stable, then departed to carry on with his farming duties.

'He'll change for the procession,' David assured me. Somehow, I doubted this. Numerous people began to assemble around the cross, arriving on foot or by car, all dressed in their best clothes. An excited chatter sprang up as little groups of people greeted each other with kisses and handshakes. More cars began to arrive, and boots were unloaded of folding picnic tables and chairs. Cool boxes were brought out, lavish lunches laid on the tables, and bottles of wine uncorked. Some cars even pulled little trailers stacked with plastic tables, chairs and parasols. Soon the green resembled an open-air restaurant.

Véronique, freshly discharged from hospital after her asthma attack, was drafted in as hostess to a dozen lunchtime diners, friends and various members of the extended family to which she belonged, in her modest kitchen. She had baked a range of savoury and sweet pies and tarts, roasted numerous chickens and boiled a variety of green vegetables. Bowls of salad were assembled. A delivery of a sackful of baguettes arrived from the *boulangerie* and a selection of cheeses was delivered by the *alimentation* van.

Back on the green, droves of Lycra-clad cyclists pedalled into the hamlet, unwrapped foil packages of sandwiches from their saddlebags and tucked in, swigging juice from their plastic bottles. Groups of walkers appeared from all corners of the hamlet, trailing dogs on leashes, or wheeling children in pushchairs, and stood about watching and waiting for the anticipated arrival of the procession around midday.

When it happened it was rather like the Tour de France, which I remember witnessing one year when the world-famous cycle race ventured onto English soil and passed through Tunbridge Wells where I had my office: the build-up far outweighed the actual event. David, Dennie and I had been chatting with various neighbours and other strangers when suddenly, from the far end of the communal green, there came a horde of walkers, marching three, four or more abreast. The majority were dressed in waxed jackets or lightweight anoraks, having walked throughout the previous night. Most wore stout walking boots, although surprisingly some wore wellingtons – not a natural choice of footwear when faced with a fairly brisk 54-kilometre overnight march. Nearly all members of the procession carried walking sticks or tall canes, and many wore badges on ribbons around their necks or pinned to their clothing. These badges were given to all members of the procession, having once completed the route, and featured an effigy of the saint and green ribbons with a white border, the traditional colours of Saint Maximin. Staunch supporters of the procession, elders who had completed the walk over a duration of thirty years, were awarded a golden medal at a special ceremony presided over by the priest of the parish. All of the walkers looked tired, bedraggled and hungry.

Joining the head of the procession as it entered the hamlet was Monsieur Cédric, proudly carrying a banner on a long pole. The banner, green edged with gold tassels, was emblazoned with the words: '*Les Processionneurs de Magnac-Laval à leur St Patron*'. It featured the symbols of a crown and shield, identifying the *Fédération des Confréries Limousines* (Union of the Limousin Brotherhoods), whose members organised the procession each year. Contrary to David's assurance, the cowman had not changed his attire and still wore the grubby green boiler suit, frayed shirt and wellington boots. His hair, however, exposed by the removal of the cap, had been plastered down over his skull with wax, and shone brilliantly. His expression was stony, serious and pious. The man's faith was clearly more important than his physical attire. As he approached the flower-bedecked cross, Cédric dipped the banner and several children placed floral wreaths on the pointed top. Without pausing, he raised the banner again and strode off towards the Pentecostal way that led past our back field, on the way to the neighbouring farm, Sejotte. A huge red-and-white striped marquee had been erected in a field at the back of the farmhouse to accommodate the hundreds of walkers in need of shade, liquid refreshment and a hearty lunch. Some time later they would again set off to return to Magnac-Laval and the end of their procession.

Many scores of walkers filed past the cross and headed off down the path, after pausing to make the sign of the cross on their chests, or to kiss their badges with a bow of the head. Some sang religious songs as they passed through the hamlet. Others simply walked by without even appearing to glance at the flowery cross. Towards the end of the procession the bespectacled priest of the parish, attired in long, flowing robes with a huge metal cross around his neck, yet wearing green walking boots, approached the cross and recited a melodious prayer while the surrounding walkers stopped and bowed their heads.

It seemed that no sooner had the procession appeared than it had gone, leaving behind only a trail of flattened grass and a few dozen picnickers, who then started on their own lunches, some even lighting portable barbecues. Véronique's lunch guests followed Monsieur Jérôme to her little house, where she was waiting to feed them, exhausted after her supreme and single-handed efforts. Hundreds of walkers had passed through Le Mas Mauvis within a matter of only ten minutes, yet the sound of their voices was carried on the air for another half-hour as they gathered at the neighbouring farm. Bringing up the rear came a group of 'sweepers', whose job it was to ensure no walker met with difficulties en route, or was left behind.

Some of those who had been loitering around the cross began to pluck roses from it before drifting away to their lunches. David rescued Jolanda's wreath before it disappeared, and hid it away for safekeeping, intending to return it to his neighbour. When everyone had departed, David, Dennie and I retreated to the shade of the linden tree and consumed a hearty barbecue, listening to the excited chatter of the other picnickers gathered in the hamlet.

Later, when the picnickers had departed, or were sleeping off their meals in the shade of the trees, I left David and Dennie to their own *sieste* and strolled down the Pentecostal way. The long grass had been trampled flat by the passage of hundreds of feet. I walked up to the end of the track, which was normally blocked by a wire fence to contain the cattle that usually grazed in the fields beyond. The fence had been rolled back and the cattle were elsewhere. Although I could not see them, I could hear their bells jangling in the distance. I was just able to make out the top of the marquee beyond the farmhouse, and could hear the hum of excited voices as the *processionneurs* relaxed after their lunch, ready for the continuation of their march.

On the way back to the communal green I noticed Madame Météo scrutinising the cross. It had been stripped bare of its roses, leaving only the elderflower and foliage.

'Where's my *couronne*?' she demanded angrily.

'I think David has kept it to give to you later, Jolanda.'

'*J'espère!*' she rasped. 'It took me ages to make and it looks like people have taken just about everything else. Vultures! So David has it, you say? Good. I'll get it later. Anyway, what are you doing?'

'Just taking a stroll.'

'*Alors!* You can stroll with me, then!' she half shouted, slotting an arm through mine and dragging me off towards the communal green, which had by then emptied of picnickers.

'Where are we going?' I asked.

'For *un petit quatre* with Véronique, of course!' came the growled response.

'Does she know?' I asked, thinking that perhaps Véronique had crashed out after her luncheon guests had departed and would be in no mood for our company.

'She will when we get there!'

Véronique, in fact, welcomed us with open arms. Our presence gave her a good opportunity to moan about her lot in life, especially the deplorable state of her legs and the fact that she had been rushed off her feet ever since her release from hospital. The lunch, however, had been a roaring success and virtually every scrap of food had been eaten by the twelve ravenous guests (except for a crisp lettuce, fresh from her garden, and a substantial wedge of *tarte aux pommes*, which were donated to me for later consumption).

After politely extricating myself from the company of the ladies I set out on a lengthy run in the warm evening sunlight. As I headed south along the back road to Magnac-Laval I could still discern the sound of wine-fuelled jollity emanating from the marquee in Sejotte's field. Three-quarters of an hour later, as I rejoined the main road by the hamlet of Beaubatou on my return journey, I encountered a dishevelled party of a dozen or so *processionneurs* weaving their way along the grassy verge – and occasionally stumbling into the ditch – as they brought up the rear of the resumed march. Having obviously benefited from a hearty liquid lunch, they saluted me with half-consumed baguettes and called out words of encouragement as I trotted past.

'*Bong-goo-raj mossieur! Bong route! Ov-war!*' they slurred. I somehow doubted that these well-meaning souls would ever succeed in reaching their goal, the church in Magnac. But I was sure their efforts would be appreciated by the saints that doubtless watched over them with a twinkle in their pious eyes.

Chapter Seventeen

Trouble at Source

The Yorkshireman did not function well in the mornings. It took him a good few hours to become fully conscious. So, like a good many folk, he preferred to take his time to rise from his bed, take a shower, dress for the day ahead, drink a couple of cups of coffee, eat a leisurely breakfast and smoke several cigarettes – not necessarily in that order, and frequently at the same time. If called upon to function before this process was complete, things were likely to go awry. Take his new job, for example. He was skilled and competent. He took immense pride in his work. The fact that he fell off a ladder during his second week of employment, leaving him suspended upside-down from the rungs, should have served as a warning. But it did not.

One evening when David returned early from work, I popped round to cadge a beer. He looked a wreck; a far cry from his usual impeccably turned-out appearance. His hair was standing on end and he sported rough stubble on his normally smoothly shaven chin. A bent cigarette hung limply from his lips. His eyes were glazed and his eyelids baggy. He appeared disoriented.

'Sit down, kid,' he slurred, proffering a little bottle of shandy (not exactly what I had been hoping for, but still …). 'Well, you know I've been suffering a bit from backache?' he said, stretching his shoulders and grimacing. 'Ever since I fell off t'ladder at work. So I went to the doctor and he said he thought it was muscular. Not a bad guess, considering. He gave me these tablets. Muscle relaxants. Take one per day when you go to bed, he said. No more than one, mind.' David paused to swig from his shandy. I opened mine and took a glug. It tasted sugary sweet, but was quite refreshing.

'Go on,' I said.

'Well, kid. You know I'm not good in t'mornings. Need a bit of a boost, I do. So I bought these kind of pep pills from the pharmacy; give you a bit of a kick-start, they do. Anyroad, I overslept this morning. I'd taken a muscle relaxant the evening before as the doctor instructed. Came down to get a cup of coffee, really groggy. Didn't have me specs on, see. Reached for pep pills, took two. Went off to work. Arrived at the house we were working on and young Johnny, t'labourer, remarked about how rough I looked. Cheeky sod, I thought. Take a look at yourself! Anyhow, I kept bumping into things, tripping over stuff, couldn't focus on owt. Had to sit down. I fell asleep on the lounger in the front room for two hours, while t'others worked around me. Good job the client didn't turn up! Silly sod, I'd only taken two muscle relaxants instead of pep pills – two of the buggers as well, mind you!'

After I'd stopped laughing, I pulled myself together and adopted a serious pose. 'You're damn lucky you managed to drive to work without crashing, actually. That could have been nasty. You're a liability really, aren't you?'

'Aye, lad! You're right there!' he laughed.

After that incident, David was more vigilant as to what pills he popped, and when he still complained of lethargy, aching limbs and a tightness in his chest, Dennie, Al and I bullied him into agreeing to visit the doctor again. Although he protested, he was clearly worried, and eventually succumbed. In truth, he was reluctant to go for a physical examination because he was frightened of what might be found: for it was true that he was rarely without a cigarette in his mouth or stuck behind one ear and was apt when full of *bon viveur* to sup one too many glasses of wine.

During Dennie's absence in Bordeaux, Al accompanied David to the doctor's surgery to act as a translator in case the French should flummox him. He came away with numerous boxes of tablets and bottles of lotions. The diagnosis was that he had strained an intercostal muscle in his ribs. We sat him down and went over the dosages with him several times until the information appeared to have sunk in.

It was highly likely that David's aches and pains were exacerbated by the widely known stresses of moving house. Not only had he cut his ties with England (although his daughters still lived there) and moved all his possessions over to France, but he had also entered into lengthy and fraught negotiations to buy the house near Mailhac-sur-Benaize. Happily, contrary to the expectations of the long-suffering *notaire*, who had presided over a dozen or more failed attempts to wrest the property from the grip of the bickering siblings, the house purchase had eventually teetered to its successful conclusion. It had been touch and go, with two of the elderly brothers starting a slanging match and almost coming to blows in the *notaire*'s office on the day when the contracts were due to be signed. Even as the accusatory brothers squabbled over items of furniture (or rather, pieces of woodworm-infested junk) that had allegedly been stolen by one brother, thus robbing the other of part of his inheritance, David was signing his cheque for the balance of the purchase monies and surreptitiously sliding it across the desk to the elderly *notaire*. The old boy was glad to complete on this particular purchase because he was due to retire the very next week. This troublesome sale would be his swan song.

With the house in their possession, David and Dennie could at last make plans for their future, which involved Dennie giving up her teaching job in Bordeaux and moving to the Limousin. While David was at work one day, Al and I went with Dennie to view the property. Hidden behind the jungle of saplings that had sprung up since negotiations for its sale had commenced over a decade ago, the house was typical of the region. Broad and relatively narrow from front to back, it featured stone door and window jambs with rough rendered walls beneath a substantial clay-tiled roof. It would make a fine home for the couple and, while it required new electrical and plumbing systems and some interior alterations, there were few major structural jobs that needed to be carried out.

The first job, however, was to remove the bulk of the sapling forest and bramble-choked wilderness that was once an elegant kitchen garden. For this, David had enlisted the aid of Monsieur Bonnard, a local farmer who owned a magnificent earth-moving vehicle. The next time Al and I visited the property, the machine was marooned in the centre of the vast open space it had created by tearing out most of the saplings and scraping away the brambles. Oil spilled from the exposed engine of the beast, for it had inconveniently broken down halfway through the task. What it had exposed, nevertheless, was a can of worms in the form of a water source.

Although our friends had known of the existence of the water source – a quaint little grotto in the centre of the garden, which babbled merrily with crystal-clear liquid – it seemed that the sudden removal of the ten-year-old saplings had the effect of uncapping a vast underground river (this liquid sustenance was presumably why the young trees had shot up so rapidly during the time the house was neglected). The ground had swollen with the released water, which had then bubbled forth like a geyser to rapidly fill up a soggy dip in the ground a few metres away so that it became a small pond. Another branch of this rivulet headed off across the garden and poured into the neighbouring field.

'There's always been a source at this house,' their aged neighbour told David and Dennie. 'I myself have rights to take the water. And your other neighbour over there has the right to water from the source entering his field! In fact, you won't be able to divert it, because of these rights.' The neighbour might live to regret this particular right if the water source continued to pour into his prize pasture, turning it into a marshland.

'I don't know what we're going to do about it,' said a rather worried Dennie. 'It could be a real problem. We think the water source might run right under the house. There's even a huge bulge in the concrete kitchen floor. There's probably a river running underneath!'

'Well, lass,' remarked David fatalistically, drawing on a cigarette. 'I were going to 'ave a water feature in any case ...'

Perhaps the muscle relaxants, lotions and other tablets he had been popping had worked their magic. The Yorkshireman finally appeared to have achieved a French state of equilibrium.

Charlie the floppy-eared hound had been born and bred in Le Mas Mauvis. In fact, he had been born in one of the barns owned by that English bloke, the Writer, and his unusual wife, the Olive Oyl lookalike. He was one of a third-generation litter produced by Monsieur Jérôme's bitch, one of the hounds that had originally been incarcerated in the ancillary barn when the farmer sold the property. Luckier than his siblings, who seemed condemned to a life of constant hunger (to keep them 'sharp', ready for *la chasse*),

Charlie ate well, slept in the house and had Aimie, a human child, to play with. Charlie lived with English residents Jeff and Amanda in the cottage across the communal green from the *grange*, next door to '007' Bruno Bussiere and his spooky wife (she who always shouted at him and threw stones whenever he chased their ducks or scared the hell out of their mangy cat Margot). Charlie could wander wherever he pleased in the hamlet, and he was always friendly and docile. (Some would say downright sloppy, but what did they know? He knew how to play to a crowd.)

Charlie always liked to give the Yorkshireman a hard time whenever he came to visit and would purposefully and repeatedly stick his nose in the man's groin, knowing how much it irritated him. What a laugh! No matter how Amanda tried to pull him away, he was a strong dog and usually succeeded in disappearing between the Yorkshireman's legs, almost dragging her through with him. It was all good fun. And at night, during his rounds of the hamlet – when he wasn't pinching a chicken from that grumpy farmer, Monsieur André – Charlie might go and deposit a nice, fresh, steaming turd on each of those neat little garden uplighters the Yorkshireman had installed at each side of his brother's driveway. Or perhaps he'd go and leave a similar present for the Writer, just in the entrance to the hangar where the idiot would invariably step in it when going to hang out his washing the next morning. Maybe he'd just go and wake up Cédric and Émile's poor excuse for a dog – it was more like a bottlebrush than an animal – and set the little twit off yelping for the rest of the night. Now that would be *really* irritating!

Yes, living in Le Mas Mauvis was terrific fun. At least it had been. Most of Charlie's loutish acts had of necessity been carried out under cover of darkness. But now what had they gone and done? It all started when the Writer got the mayor to divert the rainwater flow away from his buildings. All this modernisation was not good for a backwater hamlet like this. Already there were telephone lines sending email messages back and forth;

satellite television dishes fixed to the sides of the houses. The next thing you'd know there'd be ...

'Streetlights!'

'What was that?' asked Al, turning to me from the stove, where she was involved in preparing a meal. The camping stove was roaring and she could not make out what I'd been mumbling about.

'Streetlights,' I said, raising my voice. 'I can't get used to the fact that they've put streetlights in the hamlet. It puts a whole new perspective on things.' Folding my arms, I leaned forward and peered through the window towards the communal green. I could plainly see the skulking figure of Charlie the floppy-eared hound returning from dumping on Vic and Anne's uplighters, a chicken dangling from his jaws. He was trying to keep to the unlit areas lest he be spotted and apprehended. It was not difficult for the dog, though: his dark colouring gave him a ready disguise, and in any event the authorities had only installed three streetlights at strategic points in the hamlet. One was fixed to the pylon just outside Veronique's house, another at the corner leading past Gordon and Maureen's house and a third at the entrance to the little row of cottages where the family of Messieurs Cédric and Émile lived.

At first I had been concerned that the lights would ruin the clarity of the magnificently dark night skies resplendent with stars, but their subtle orange glow exuded minimal upward light pollution. Although I would rather they were not there, I had to admit that the lights did make the elderly residents feel safer and meant it was easier to walk through the hamlet at night without the need for a torch. The lights would certainly discourage prospective burglars from chancing their arm.

This new view of the night-time hamlet would take some getting used to, however. Standing chatting to David on his driveway one evening after a drink, my friend had remarked about how his uplighters were becoming a little faint due to the ingrained dog mess that coated the lenses. He suddenly caught sight of a figure in the little orange pool of light cast by the streetlight across the green. The man was walking backwards and forwards under the light.

'Look, Rich, there's Jeff taking Charlie for a walk,' he said. 'He's late tonight. No. Hang on a minute. That's not Jeff. Or Charlie. Who the hell is it? It's a bloody big dog, Rich, but it's right obedient! Look how it's following the man from the car to the little workshop and back.'

Suddenly the man, who had been unloading something from the boot of his car, changed direction and set off towards the row of cottages, followed by the big dog. The next thing we knew the poor man was being set upon by the dog! It leapt onto his back so that we could no longer see him. Then, as our eyes became accustomed to our newly illuminated environment, all seemed to fall into a true perspective. We saw that the man was being followed not by a large and ferocious dog, but by his own shadow cast by the new-fangled streetlight! We shuffled our feet, feeling rather foolish, then shook hands and said goodnight. Suddenly we both burst into fits of juvenile laughter.

'Daft pair o' buggers!' said the Yorkshireman. Waving, I wandered off down the lane, followed closely by my own shadow.

Other changes were due to beset the hamlet of Le Mas Mauvis and its environs that were far more serious and wide-ranging than the installation of streetlights. During an evening run, I came upon a scene of utter devastation, which left me shocked. On the route to the hamlet of Le Poux, the tunnel-like avenue of trees through which the dappled sunlight filtered – the 'bunny hole', as Al cutely described it – I was saddened to find that on one side of the lane there were gaping holes where a row of mighty oak trees had been felled. The mature trees, which must have each been two hundred years old, lay in the field where they had been cut. The exposed metre-wide diameters of their trunks had been spray-painted with a garish blood-red number. That is what these majestic trees had been reduced to: a number, a commodity. I stopped and stared, breathing heavily and finding it difficult to absorb the scene of carnage. I started to run again and as I ran I counted the trees. There were twenty along the road frontage and half as many again on the field side, their stout branches still rustling with leaves and dangling with acorns.

Perhaps the trees needed to be felled for winter firewood. This was a fact of life: we stored logs ourselves for future use, and would buy more when we no longer had any fallen trees on our own land to consume. But I could never imagine felling any of our own trees: their presence was one of the many reasons we bought the farm. However, it was true that the French government also encouraged farmers to selectively remove trees and hedges between the traditionally small fields of the Limousin to create larger fields that would produce higher yields of crops. Although this undoubtedly resulted in fatter profits for the landowners, it was a policy that was forever changing the age-old face of this rural *région*, and depressingly sad to witness.

'Aye, kid,' said David sympathetically, when I told him of the felled trees. 'I was talking to the farmer just the other day. He told me he was going to fell four hundred oaks on his land. He hasn't had the farm long, he's got hundreds of hectares of land, probably has a lot of debts, and he sees trees as a means of making money.'

To the farmer, the land was his livelihood, and his decision to cut the trees was understandable. But I could not imagine that the trees felled on the farm would ever be replaced with new saplings; there appeared to be no policy of reforestation. And even if they did replace the felled trees, it would be merely cosmetic in the eyes of a farmer, and centuries before the young trees reached anything like the size of their predecessors.

The sea of change, which that rural area of France was experiencing, was not all for the worse. Some innovations were sensible, others just plain practical. Take the subject of rubbish disposal, for example. Normal household waste was collected and disposed of, but for the bigger bits of debris that couldn't be collected (redundant refrigerators and washing machines; old furniture and crockery; garden waste), the trend in the past was to simply dig a big hole and bury it (or, in some cases, leave it in a prominent heap). But with the new millennium there came a wholly modern innovation. Springing up in communes all across the Haute-Vienne was a flurry of *déchetteries*, organised municipal tips. Simply drive up with a trailer or boot-load of rubbish, deposit it in the skips provided and depart.

One day an important flyer was delivered to every home in the commune, which described the huge investment that had been necessary for the establishment of these facilities – the figure of 255,325,087 euros was quoted, which probably made as much sense to the French, who had enough trouble coping with meaty figures in francs, as it did to someone who still remembered the farthing with some fondness. In addition to the half-dozen skips devoted individually to garden waste, cartons, general junk and building waste and *à tout venant*, 'all comings and goings', there were recycling points for packaging, magazines, glass and batteries. So long taken for granted in the UK, the introduction of this simple system in our part of France was a godsend.

As soon as the tip was declared open, I filled the back of the car with the pile of debris that was threatening to block the entrance to our hangar and set off to make my deposit. I pulled off the road into the neat new compound and waited until one of the skips became free, then approached the ramp, reversed and stopped at the top. I became aware of a man in blue overalls waving at me from the little supervisor's hut. What friendly staff! I thought, and waved back, opening the hatchback of my car to reveal the sacks of debris, chunks of concrete, twists of iron piping and coils of old electrical cable that were placing a considerable strain on the Peugeot's suspension, squashing the tyres.

Just as I was about to start unloading, the supervisor – a rotund man with a stubbly chin and bushy black moustache – came wheezing up the ramp, looking flustered. 'Are you local, Monsieur?' he panted. He mopped the sweat from his balding pate with a big handkerchief. How charming, I thought, that the man had taken the time to come and greet me: that wouldn't happen at the local tip in England.

'Why, yes, I am as a matter of fact. This is a fine facility you have here, Monsieur! Very welcome, I can tell you.' I stuck out my hand to shake but the man, who I had to admit looked a little stern, put his hands on his hips and adopted a somewhat macho pose.

'Your *dernière facture d'ordures ménagères, Monsieur*,' he snapped.

'My what?'

'You can't make a deposit without your last rubbish bill, Monsieur. It's simply not possible!' He mopped his perspiring brow again.

'My rubbish bill, Monsieur? I'm afraid I don't have it with me,' I apologised. I realised that the bill in question was probably neatly filed away back in England. Fat lot of good it did there. 'It's not something I normally carry around. I've never been asked to produce it before, you see. I do have my driving licence and my supermarket loyalty card, however.' I fished my loyalty card out of my wallet but the supervisor did not look impressed.

'That proves nothing, Monsieur! How do I know that you have the right to dump your rubbish at this facility? You could be from another commune for all I know! I'm sorry, Monsieur, but you will have to leave and take your rubbish with you!' He folded his muscly arms across his chest defiantly.

In my peripheral vision I noted other law-abiding citizens pausing in their refuse disposal to stare at me; some shook their heads at my effrontery. A queue of cars had formed behind me and the occupants were getting fidgety: my British numberplate was a giveaway. I was a marked man, guilty of attempted illegal flytipping. As innocent as my mistake was, I felt like a cad. And so it was with extreme embarrassment that I was turned away from the municipal dump with my tail between my legs and a carload of illegal rubble.

'Crikey, the flippin' veterinarian 'ee ees late and I am a bit 'eld up,' apologised Bernard the llama breeder, sounding a bit harassed.

Al and I had arrived at his property half an hour earlier and I had made the necessary introductions. Jaffa the dreadlocked dog immediately adopted my wife as a lifelong friend and decided to stick close to her legs. She bent down to give him some attention and he rolled over onto his back (although so thick were his dreadlocks it was hard to tell which was his back). We had arranged to pay Bernard a visit so that Al might meet his herd of llamas and perhaps begin to understand my growing attraction and affection for these placid animals. Like me, she had visited the llamas at commercial English farms, but had never been this close to the creatures. Already we had been introduced to a pack of frisky and inquisitive males in the nearby paddock, and now were commiserating with the two poor inmates of a quarantine pen, after the foot-and-mouth outbreak in the UK had prevented them from crossing the channel to join their new English lady owner. One was a placid, extremely woolly, caramel-coloured individual with wonderfully beguiling black eyes, while the other had a thinner coat of brown fibre with white blotches, and a somewhat startled expression. The animal was clearly fed up and frustrated with being confined to his prison cell, but the law prevented him from being released into a field or even moved from his present quarters.

It seemed that we had arrived at Bernard's farm at an inopportune moment. The vet was due to arrive in order to inject some of the llamas with a microchip inserted in their ears, which would lessen the risk of theft of the animals. The microchips would identify the animals and their owner in the event of them being stolen.

'Look, Richard, you know where the other guys are. Why don't you go and introduce them to Al and meet me back 'ere for some lunch?' A van pulled into the farmyard. 'Oh, 'ere ees the vet now! Look, I will see you back 'ere in 'alf an hour, *non*?'

I led Al towards the little house Bernard was converting: it did not seem that he had progressed far at all since my last visit. We peered into the ground-floor area, which had been stripped back to its bare oak beam framework and had a beaten earth floor. There was a wonderful, capacious fireplace with a somewhat grand oak mantle surround in the main room whilst, in an adjoining annexe, Bernard's computer sat on its little table, protected from the dust and debris within a zip-up cover. A broad, dark staircase rose at a sharp angle from the centre of the ground floor, directly into the steep roof space.

The house was compact, quaint and truly delightful, resplendent as it was with period features, yet it was in dire need of a considerable input of time and money to complete its restoration. At that moment in time Bernard lacked both ingredients. As a llama breeder with a substantial UK clientele, he had been hit badly by the foot-and-mouth epidemic. Sales of llamas to England had ceased abruptly during the spread of the disease and the restrictions that had been imposed, and had not yet recovered since the disease had been eradicated.

Al and I wandered down into the lower paddock, which was intersected by little streams feeding a pond. Two male llamas were tethered there. We hauled in the animals in turn and spent a few minutes stroking their thick coats and chatting to them. Both animals were a little flighty due to the fact that they could see and no doubt hear the activities unfolding in the farmyard, where the vet was attending to some of their companions. We released them and allowed them to pace impatiently back and forth, ears pricked attentively towards the goings-on up at the farm.

Adjoining the farmyard was another paddock that contained a group of young male llamas also eager to see what fate was to befall their companions who were held in the stables nearby. They need not have been concerned, however, as the vet had forgotten to bring the microchips with him and had been obliged to arrange another visit. Bernard shook his head in disbelief as the vet drove away.

'All that excitement and preparation for nothing!' he moaned. 'I don't believe eet! Bloody 'ell!' So Bernard was able to accompany us visiting the other llamas after all, and while we made the acquaintance of the herd he rattled off their names. 'The only way I can remembere their name ees by the alphabet. Each year when crias are born, I use the next lettere.' The youngsters were jostling us for our attention, rudely pushing each other aside and spitting.

'Charming!' said Al, as one of the spitters managed to reach her and was able to receive her undivided attention by poking his face directly in front of hers.

'Oh well, spitting ees about all thees boys can do now they 'ave 'ad their fighting teeth removed,' said Bernard, laughing.

'Fighting teeth?' queried Al, stroking the soft muzzle of her new and persistent young friend who was now kicking out with his back legs to fend off his companions, who were also eager to reach the front of the group.

'Oh yes, the llama 'as sharp fighting teeth 'ere at the back,' replied Bernard, grabbing the head of a nearby llama and pulling back his lips to reveal the blunted stumps of yellow teeth at the back of the lower jaw. 'The boy llama could use these teeth to castrate anothere llama, if they were fighting over the lady llama, for instance. Yes, they do thees! So eet's usual to 'ave the teeth removed. Eet's a good idea, I think, *non*? Safere.'

'Sounds good to me!' I said. I wondered why conversations with Bernard invariably reverted to the subject of genitalia. Bernard then turned the conversation to the safer subject of aesthetics. Or so I thought.

'So what type of llama do you like the look of, Al?' asked Bernard, standing back and surveying his curious herd. 'The classic? The woolly? The not-so-woolly?'

'I don't mind about woolliness,' replied Al. 'So long as it's a kissy-kissy llama.'

'Ur? A what?' Bernard looked to me for help. 'What is that she's saying Richard? What ees thees kissy-kissy malarkey?'

'It's simple. I want a llama you can kiss, right here on the soft muzzle,' Al explained, demonstrating the kissability of her close friend, previously the Spitter, now apparently the Snogger. The other llamas looked on, jealous. The Snogger gave a few well-aimed back-kicks to keep them at bay. 'It's so warm and soft and kissy, kissy, kissy,' purred Al. The Snogger pulled an expression of unbridled ecstasy, batted his huge eyelids and even made puckering, kissing actions with its top lip. The animal's huge dirty yellow incisors were just visible where they poked from the front of its lower jaw. The Snogger's banana-shaped ears twitched with pleasure. Bernard looked quite aghast.

'Bloody 'ell! You'll have to watch this woman, Richard! She'll ruin all your young boy llamas! They get too much of thees stuff, they go soft. They'll not listen to you. They can be real trouble for you, thees juveniles! The next thing you know, thees boys they try to mount you when your back ees turned! Now that's not so pleasant, I can tell you!'

'Perhaps you'd better stop with the kissy-kissy stuff, Al. Bernard's worried about his personal safety.' Al relinquished her passionate embrace with the Snogger, who sauntered off, followed by some of his pals. He had assumed the role of Lothario and I could imagine the other young bucks asking, 'Hey, dude, what's it like kissing a girl?' 'Oh, you know, *comme ci, comme ça*,' he'd respond aloofly.

'So when are you going to be living here in France permanently?' asked Bernard as we sat down at his big circular table in the barn to eat the delicious lunch he had prepared. 'At first I theenk you talk about anothere three or four years, *n'est-ce pas?*' He produced some rustic, crusty bread which had a very open, holey texture. He cut it into thick wedges and then took a little round baking tin from his oven, which contained a smoked salmon and egg tart in a wholemeal pastry base. He served it with spoonfuls of diced baked potato and fine green beans.

'Well, Bernard, we've been looking at our move with a kind of renewed perspective,' I said, tucking into the food with relish. The tart simply melted in the mouth. 'It seems likely that I'll be able to work quite easily on my writing and editing from France.'

'Oh blimey! With the Internet and the email eet's much easiere to do thees!'

'So we think it could be as soon as next spring or summer,' put in Al between mouthfuls. 'At least for Rich. I might commute from the UK for a while. Or maybe I could find a job in Limoges, Poitiers, or even Paris. The TGV train is fast and efficient. It couldn't be worse than the trip I already make up to London and back.'

'So you work in the office, Al?'

'Yes. In the music industry, licensing music.'

'Thees ees interesting, *non*?'

'Yes, very. But I could be content working anywhere. I used to be involved in competitive equestrianism, training young horses, showjumping, but I'd be just as happy teaching basic riding skills at a riding school.'

'Crikey! Then we might be neighbours soon enough, eh?' exclaimed Bernard with an expression of unbridled glee.

'It looks that way,' I said, smiling across the table at Al. That, at least, was our shared dream. I reached out and squeezed her hand affectionately.

'Then I must pay a visit to your place in the Haute-Vienne and look over your land. Perhaps I explain what you need to do to prepare for the arrival of the llamas.'

'That would be good, Bernard,' I agreed. 'I could certainly use your advice.'

'Hey, no problem, mate!' said Bernard, sitting bolt upright, slapping both hands on the table. 'And then you can cook the flippin' lunch, huh?'

'Yes!'

'But meanwhile, eat up, because there is the second course!' Bernard rose and went to the kitchen, returning with yet another hot pan, this time stacked with dozens of little lamb cutlets. He placed the tray in the centre of the table and sat down again. 'Dig in, chaps! Eat eet all up!'

'Bernard, you've excelled yourself this time!' I said, taking a few of the beautifully tender cutlets. Bernard may have assumed some of the ways of the English, including his colourful dialogue, but it was clear that he had not lost one iota of the ingrained French ability to 'do lunch'.

'Oh, eet's nothing,' he said modestly. 'A simple lunch, that's all. And aftere thees lamb, some *fromage*, some fruit, some *café*!'

'And then a long walk afterwards!' laughed Al.

Chapter Eighteen

A Minor *Effraction*

'Hiya love, I'm afraid I've got some sorry news,' announced David gloomily down the phone line from France. Al's face turned ashen.

'What's happened?' she asked, sounding shocked.

'I'm afraid you've 'ad a break-in, flower.'

'A break-in? Oh no! What's been taken, David?'

'Nowt.'

'Nothing?'

'Aye, nowt. It's not that simple, lass. I know who broke in.'

'Who was it?'

'It was your builder, Monsieur Fugère.'

'Monsieur Fugère? I don't understand.'

'Me neither, lass. Thing is, he was supposed to come to collect the key from me, as arranged. Only he never turned up. Maybe I was out or sommat. But instead of going away and coming back another day, he just went over to your place, jemmied the locks and went in. Knocked three flippin' great holes in the back wall of the house and then buggered off leaving the door wide open, with scaffolding, ladders and such leaning up against the walls. Anyone could just walk in and take what they like.'

David emailed digital photographs of the break-in to us so that we were able to witness the desecration of our home after Monsieur Fugère's alleged *effraction*, or forced entry. One photograph showed the locks brutally levered off, smashing part of the door itself. Another showed a ladder leaning invitingly against one of the upper windows at the front of the *grange*, which had been conveniently left wide open. Other pictures illustrated the horrendous debris that was scattered about the interior of the *grenier* – although this was to have been expected – and most shocking of all there were three enormous, uneven and uncovered holes roughly bashed through the back wall for the rest of the windows. Pairs of adjustable metal props were wedged under scaffold boards, holding the roof up where the openings had been formed. A big pneumatic drill lay abandoned on the floor, its cable curling like a snake through the open window at the front to where it was connected to a compressor. At the rear a scaffold tower offered easy access from ground level to anyone interested in pilfering our possessions.

'Ooh, this has really got my shackles up!' said Al, forthrightly. I decided to let the Alism go. She telephoned the residence of Monsieur Fugère. Madame Fugère answered with a bright '*Allô?*'

'Madame Fugère? *Bonjour, Madame*. This is Al Wiles, telephoning from England.'

'Ah, *bonjour* Madame Wheels. *Comment ça va?*'

'*Ça va, ça va.* I'm sorry to disturb you at the weekend, but is your husband there?'

'*Oui, Madame*. He is.' There was a long pause. Al could hear Madame Fugère breathing in France. What was she waiting for?

'Could I speak to him please?'

'*Oui, certainement!*' There was a fumbling at the other end of the line, and then Monsieur Fugère spoke.

'*Allô?* Madame Wheels? *Bonjour, bonjour. Comment ça va?*'

'*Ça va, ça va*. But, Monsieur Fugère, we understand that you have broken the locks to our house.'

'*Oui, oui, oui …*' Ah, so he didn't deny it!

'But why?'

'I could not get in, Madame Wheels.'

'But Monsieur Fugère, we had arranged that you collect the key from Monsieur David.'

'*Oui, c'est ça!*'

'But you did not collect the key from Monsieur David …'

'*Non*. I could not, Madame Wheels.'

'But why not, Monsieur Fugère?'

'Monsieur David was not there, Madame Wheels.'

It was clear that this conversation was going nowhere. Our builder seemed to have no comprehension that he had done anything remotely wrong, nor suffered remorse for his actions in breaking and entering. Al decided to divert the course of the conversation to the general progress of the work. It seemed pointless to force the issue. When she came off the phone, her mood had sweetened.

The immediate problem of our open house was solved by David, who replaced the locks and removed the ladder from the front. He could do nothing, however, about the scaffolding at the rear of the property or the three gaping holes in the back wall (which Monsieur Fugère had originally promised to temporarily seal against intruders and the weather). I was due to travel down to France the following week, so David determined to keep a watchful eye on the property, which at that time contained the entire contents of his English house.

I had arranged to chauffeur the Count and Countess down to their abode in the Creuse, and carry on to Le Mas Mauvis in order to commence installation of the second set of window frames. I was keen to get the openings sealed: if a strong wind was to blow directly from the west, as it sometimes did, there was little to prevent a gust entering the exposed *grenier* and blowing the roof off.

When I entered the *grenier* for the first time since the openings had been created, I was amazed at the amount of light that now flooded into the vast, open-plan space. It completely changed the perspective on the building in a dramatic and uplifting manner: whereas the building had previously looked towards Veronique's house and vegetable patch, and the common land to one side, it now offered a westward outlook that encompassed our own land, the line of majestic oaks at the boundary and the rolling fields beyond. The three apertures on the front façade were now duplicated on the rear, enabling us to track the movement of the sun from dawn until dusk. Overlooking the dust and debris that still remained, even after Monsieur Fugère had packed up his tools and left, at first I could only stand and stare with a feeling of immense contentment that our previously dilapidated barn was now very definitely a beautiful home with a glorious panorama of the countryside. I overlooked the fact that the fields at the back of the property were shabby and overgrown: I could, in my mind's eye, already see a colourful garden and imagined myself happily toiling therein, while my darling Al busied herself in the kitchen making chutney (OK, so *that* was still an image I had trouble bringing into sharp focus). I wished Al was with me now to share this latest major development, but I was equally determined to get the windows fitted so that she would be able to see the transformation complete on her next visit.

Grateful for their lift and understanding my plight in getting the house sealed, my brother and sister-in-law had kindly volunteered to assist me in fitting the frames. All went swimmingly well until, after I had delivered my helpers back to their house, I stood at the opposite end of the *grenier* to study the three new window openings. Something looked wrong, but I could not quite work out what it was. I squinted and peered. Something was definitely wrong. I fished out my extending tape measure and checked pertinent dimensions. My fears were confirmed. The central opening was off-centre by a good foot. After the debacle with the break-in, I could not believe that Monsieur Fugère had also perpetrated this monumental blunder. But he had. And now that I had identified the problem, it was glaringly obvious. I went outside and looked up at the three openings with a different perspective. The central window opening was definitely off-centre, destroying the overall symmetry of the façade.

Depression set in when, during a hefty downpour that same day, I noticed that the guttering Monsieur Fugère had also installed while creating the window openings did not appear to be attached to one of the downpipes, causing copious litres of water to cascade down the walls of the *grange*.

Monsieur Fugère stood back and studied the central aperture, shaking his head. He murmured to himself. He stood to one side, murmured again, took out his tape measure and noted down various dimensions. He went to the cab of his van and returned exuding renewed composure. But still he looked worried.

'*Non, non, non,*' he purred. He took more measurements and marked a point on the sill of the opening that appeared to be the true central point. It was thirty centimetres adrift. '*Pas beaucoup, pas beaucoup.*'

'Not much?' I echoed. 'It's off-centre enough to ruin the symmetry of the façade, Monsieur Fugère. It must be central! Our architect's plans show it as being central. Our *permis de construire* demands that it is central.'

'Oh, *non, non, non,* Monsieur Wheels,' he countered, soothingly. '*Pas de problème* with the *permis de construire, pas de problème!*'

'Ah, *c'est possible*, Monsieur Fugère. But it is very important to us. The window must be in the centre. When we install the arched entrance below it, this would look off-centre as well. No, I'm sorry, but the window must be central, as we originally instructed. I'm afraid you'll have to move it.'

'*D'accord*, Monsieur Wheels. *Si vous voulez, si vous voulez.*'

'And Monsieur Fugère ...'

'*Oui*, Monsieur Wheels?'

'Please also take a look at the gutter,' I pointed through the off-centre opening. The builder poked his head out and craned his neck to the left, where there was a sizeable gap between gutter outlet and downpipe. Turning to me, he slapped a hand to his forehead and lowered his gaze. His shoulders sagged. With this hang-dog expression, he appeared on the brink of tears.

'*Je suis un idiot*,' he murmured, shuffling off towards the staircase, plodding down to his van, where he lingered for longer than usual by the glove compartment. Then, humbly apologising for his gaffes, he promised to rectify the errors at his earliest convenience and drove off at an unusually sedate pace. As I watched him leave the hamlet I actually felt sorry for the old boy.

By the following month, August, when Al and I next made a trip down to France, Monsieur Fugère had still failed to make good the off-centre window, despite his assurances to the contrary. According to his wife, the builder had felt the need to take a holiday – 'It's the only five days he'll take off this year,' she said, pleading his case, so that we ended up feeling sorry for him again – and other jobs had bottlenecked. Apologising, she promised that he would arrive at the beginning of the second week of our stay to make the repair. This was not altogether convenient, because for three days during the middle of that week we were to be descended upon by a delegation from England, namely Al's parents, her father's 83-year-old cousin Hope (known to family and friends as Hoppy), and her mother's elder sister Janet. The Doctor and his wife were keen to see recent developments at the property, as it had been some two years since they had last visited.

On leaving Mauvis the previous month, I had temporarily sealed the three window openings with sheets of polythene to prevent the worst excesses of the weather infiltrating the *grenier*, trapping the material within the unglazed casements of the two outer windows. The central, off-centre opening – lacking its frame – I merely sealed with a drape of polythene held in place by wooden battens. This had been fine while I was there by myself, for there had been little or no wind. However, the first night Al and I settled down to sleep in the tent, a gale whipped up from nowhere and proceeded to catch the polythene and shake it so that it vibrated noisily from dusk to dawn. At four o'clock in the morning, fed up and irritable at being woken every few minutes, we rose, made ourselves strong coffees and commenced an urgent bout of glazing the casements. We made a solemn pact to get all twelve panes puttied into their rebates by the end of the day, and the casements hung in the outer frames, or risk another sleepless night. In the central opening we wedged large sheets of expanded polystyrene insulation.

Al had never glazed a window in her life but, after I had explained to her the basic principles involved, she soon got the hang of kneading the linseed oil putty until smooth and pliable. I, meanwhile, an old hand at glazing, pressed the pre-cut panes onto Al's bedding putty, retained them with panel pins and applied the outer putty seal. I then shaped it into neat mitres with my putty knife. The job was not as neat as I would ordinarily have accepted in my quest for perfection, but we managed to complete our task with a little time to spare for celebration with a bottle of wine, and that night slept the sleep of the righteous, so exhausted yet satisfied were we. Even the neighbourhood canines, who normally roused me at an ungodly hour of the morning with their persistent, grating yapping (and which I would frequently threaten to strangle with their own leashes) failed to wake me on that occasion.

We had learned from Bruno and Jolanda, who had called round with a gift of a carrier bag full of ripe tomatoes, that Véronique was in hospital again. She had been in the major hospital in Limoges for a fortnight, where she had undergone a lengthy operation for the installation of a ceramic knee. The initial prognosis was that the operation had been successful and Véronique had been transferred to convalesce for a week in the hospital in nearby Le Dorat. Al rushed off to visit her adopted aunt, while I, with a publishing deadline to meet, settled down to some serious writing. Al was eager to help out our friend. Was there anything we could do to tidy up her vegetable patch, for example, as it had become rather unruly during Véronique's three-week absence?

'Non, merci, Al. Jérôme's promised to look after the garden,' replied Véronique. 'But promise me you'll help yourself to any vegetables you like?' she pleaded. 'Don't let anything go to waste!'

Afterwards, Al ventured into the depths of Véronique's sizeable vegetable patch opposite our *grange* and re-emerged half an hour later, having uprooted several large carrots; a basketful of potatoes; dozens of shallots (which proved to be incredibly strong-tasting and quite luscious); numerous varieties of rather limp lettuces which had escaped total decimation by the slugs; a bitter-leafed chard; and a couple of cauliflowers, whose white spongy tops were beginning to harden and turn yellow. Al had also discovered several plants heavy with huge green tomatoes, and was tempted to pick them for a scrumptious fried green tomato dish, but resisted the urge: we had quite enough tomatoes after the Bussieres' kind gift. Although she had messed about in the garden as a child with her sister, this was the first time that Al had ever picked vegetables straight from the ground, and she was hooked. She arranged the shallots on a windowsill to dry out in the sun and artistically displayed the potatoes, cauliflower, chard and carrots (complete with their frilly green tops) in a wicker basket by one of the new windows adjacent to the kitchen sink. That evening, while I tapped away on the computer, Al concocted a gourmet supper of fish pan-fried with garlic and olive oil, served on a bed of steamed chard with green beans and potatoes fresh from the ground.

'Tomorrow I'm going to make a sauce from Bruno and Jolanda's tomatoes and Véronique's shallots and I think I might make a lovely thick soup with the carrots and potatoes for tomorrow's evening meal – and I'm going to take some in to Véronique in hospital,' Al said breathlessly as we sat down to consume the delicious meal. It was wonderful to see her so enthused, with all the innocent excitement of a toddler having discovered that she can walk, and that things previously out of reach were within range and able to be grabbed.

'It won't be long before we have our own vegetable garden,' I said, hoping upon hope. For I knew that this dream was becoming well within our grasp.

The next day, Al concocted her all-natural soup and took a container of it into the hospital when she visited Véronique. She returned a few hours later, her face slightly downcast. '*Merci beaucoup*, my dear Al; I'm sure the soup is delicious,' Véronique had said sadly, patting Al's hand. 'But I can't eat it.' Her strict diabetic diet forbade the poorly lady from consuming anything not on her prescribed list of ingredients – even if it was a lusciously healthy, preservative-free, natural soup.

'I know!' said Al, brightening up. 'I'll take the soup to the Bussieres! After all, it's got their tomatoes in it!' She returned an hour later, beaming from ear to ear. Bruno and Jolanda had been touchingly grateful for the gift. So grateful were they that they appeared at the *grange* the very next day with the container emptied of soup but filled with ripe, sweet, cherry tomatoes.

Refreshed from his brief vacation, Monsieur Fugère arrived one morning with his smiling assistant Jean-Jacques in tow. Together they assembled rickety-looking access equipment on the rear elevation of the *grange*, which consisted of a pair of aluminium triple-extending ladders positioned at each side of the troublesome central window opening, spanned by scaffold boards that rested precariously on big metal angle brackets hooked over the rungs. I remarked about this dangerous-looking and lopsided structure to David.

'Aye, kid. They're called cripples and they're banned in England. Obviously not here in France, though. Bloody risky if you ask me! You wouldn't get me up on one of those!'

The workmen set to with jackhammers to move the window opening over thirty centimetres to the right, after first propping up the roof so that they could slide the oak lintels across to the new position. There followed much use of the word '*merde*' over the next few hours. Monsieur Fugère would make frequent trips to the cab of his van for inspiration.

Once the opening had been repositioned, rudimentary shutter work comprising wooden planks was nailed around the reveals and held in place with an ingenious little tool widely used in France but rarely seen in the UK: the *chevillette*, from the verb *cheviller*, which means 'to peg'. This neat and simple device consists of a long metal cold chisel with a bracket attachment: the chisel section is hammered into the surface against which, for example, a batten is to be held and the bracket slid into place to secure the batten. Once removed, the hole left by the *chevillette* is simply filled with mortar or filler. Starting at the bottom, the shutter work was fixed to form the new reveals and concrete shovelled in behind it and tamped down. When the shutter work was full, another section would be added and the process repeated until the lintel was reached.

Al and I stayed well out of the builders' way: she to brighten up the frontage of the *grange* by painting the decrepit barn doors, which now served only as decorative shutters (I had previously constructed a huge, heavy door to seal the cart entrance) and me to glaze the casements for the central window, ready for hanging once the remodelled opening was complete. Monsieur Fugère had positioned his ancient and noisy compressor right outside the barn doors, near where Al was working, and I was amused to see my wife painting while wearing a pair of ear defenders. These not only warded against the sound of the infernal machine but also the stream of expletives that issued from the grumpy builder each time his temperamental compressor broke down – which it did frequently.

Chapter Nineteen

All That Jazz

Flying in to Limoges' Bellegarde Airport from London Stansted, our family visitors were collected by Al and immediately whisked off (at my mother-in-law's plea) for an educational tour of one of the major Limoges porcelain manufacturers. While Sheila, my mother-in-law, and Hoppy got their hands dirty by throwing a few lumps of the fine china clay, Janet flunked out halfway to adjourn for a quiet moment with a cigarette: the pace of her life was not as frenetic as that of her younger sister. Meanwhile, Al and her father (a dedicated lover of the institution of teatime) discovered the pleasantries of the factory shop's café, and chatted over interesting pastries and cups of tea.

Since the nineteenth century Limoges has been world-famous for its fine and unique porcelain, after a pure supply of kaolin was discovered nearby in Saint Yriex-la-Perche. This extra-fine clay is used in the production of the distinctive and exquisite hard-paste porcelain. Today there are many chinaworks centred around the Vienne River, the kilns of which – firing day and night – earned the city its name, Le Cité Rouge (the Red City) and created what is a thriving industry.

Suitably worn out, but satisfied, the visitors were transported to the Café de France in the main square at Le Dorat, where they had been booked to stay. We dined in the hotel's restaurant that evening and, after an early night, Al collected our guests the following morning to bring them over to Le Mas Mauvis. To say they were suitably impressed was an understatement. No sooner had they clambered out of the car than their camera shutters were clicking away as if our *grange* was a world-famous tourist attraction. After this photo-frenzy, they settled down to a more leisurely guided tour of our property with a running commentary by Al on the renovations currently underway and our plans for the future.

At times during the afternoon, Sheila, a keen oil and watercolour painter, would be found lying stretched out on the dusty floor of the *grenier* squinting through her camera's viewfinder into the oak beams of the ceiling, or else wedged into a cobwebby corner while she framed a number of unusual angle shots.

'Are you OK there?' I asked, helping her to her feet on one occasion.

'Yes, Rich, look!' she enthused in her typically highly animated way (rather like a female Frankie Howerd, I often felt). 'No! You might laugh! But these are the basis of my future paintings. There's *so* much here! I'll be kept busy painting for months! Which is good, because I've got an exhibition coming up later in the year. My horses are going to think I've deserted them, and so is my husband! No, dear! These are my arty shots. I just love all these angles, these textures, don't you? It's *so* lovely, Rich! *So* wonderful!'

'But you're all covered in dust!' I said.

'Oh, so what's new? Get a life, Rich! Do you think I care about a little dust? No, dear! Rich, listen, life's too short to worry about a little dust! I mean, just look at my kitchen. You know me, I'm usually up to my neck in horse's whatsits, aren't I?' And off she flitted, this time precariously leaning out of the open upper-floor windows to capture the interesting angles our barn offered.

My mother-in-law was a woman who possessed boundless energy. Happiest when casually dressed in jodhpurs and sweatshirt, her grey hair frequently in disarray and covered in hay, she was obviously a person who spent much of her time outdoors. She had an animated face with a beaming smile and the same quizzical expression her daughter Al had inherited. She waddled with a pronounced limp caused by a tricky hip replacement that left her with one leg shorter than the other. Whilst this operation had taken place some years ago, it had not slowed her down and she lived for her horse riding, where her gait was immaterial.

Her mornings would invariably start with a pre-breakfast ride on Ashdown Forest with friends, whatever the weather, after which she might attend a life class at her art club; then there would be the endless bagging of home-produced, well-rotted horse manure (sold at the gate, proceeds to charity); jump judging at a local horse show; a pony party for young riders; or one of the many other charitable activities she was involved in. On quieter days she would scour the charity shops for useful items and had filled a spare bedroom in her house with knick-knacks that she thought might find a home with us in France.

'Sheila never did sit still as a child,' commented her sister Janet dryly, lurking in the smokers' corner with Al. 'When we were at boarding school together, I used to pretend she wasn't my sister. I suppose I don't have that luxury now.'

'Now, Richard. Tell me which is my window. Is it this one? I contributed to one of them, but I don't know which it is!' said Hoppy, drawing me aside. Hope, although tiny, white-haired and frail-looking, was in fact an active long-distance walker who would think nothing of scaling one of the Lake District peaks before breakfast, although she was always modest about her abilities. 'Anyway, don't worry; it doesn't matter, if you're busy. Sheila has the plan. I can check later. Now are we going to have time to walk around the property after lunch, or do you think it would be best to go before lunch, in case it rains?' she asked.

'I'm not going anywhere until after lunch,' decreed the Doctor firmly. Taking the initiative and claiming his right, as elder of the family, he lowered himself into the seat at the head of the table we had laid out in the centre of the *grenier*. There was to be no argument. There were few activities that would be permitted to get in the way of the prescribed time for lunch.

The Doctor was a tall, quite portly man, and, while age had stooped him slightly, he was nevertheless a formidable figure. Each day, week in, week out, he would be impeccably dressed in collar and tie, waistcoat, tweed jacket and smart trousers; his once dark hair was now pure white and thinning and he wore tortoiseshell horn-rimmed spectacles. He possessed a round, inquisitive face with smiling, somewhat mischievous eyes and ruddy cheeks. He was every inch the traditional country doctor. A man for whom routine was sacrosanct, he rose early each morning – four-thirty was not uncommon – and retired to bed early in the evening, rarely after ten o'clock (an arrangement that suited his perennially busy wife admirably).

Advancing age was not about to stop the Doctor from indulging in his love of travel and meeting people. When he and his wife were not jetting off to see friends in Slovenia, or taking a cruise down the River Danube or along the Norwegian fjords, they might be enjoying a leisurely trip by steam train to Cumbria, Wales or Norfolk with one of the companies that operate lovely restored trains.

During the Second World War he had served as a ship's medical officer on the *Île de France*, where one of his patients had been the crooner Bing Crosby, who was suffering from a throat infection. The Doctor had fond memories of the hours he and the celebrity would spend chatting below deck in those difficult times. The Doctor was rarely happier than when allowed to explore an airport. He loved not only to watch the aeroplanes, but also to see and meet the mixed bag of travellers from all over the world. After retiring from general practice he had taken a part-time position at Gatwick Airport, working for the Area Port Health Authority. In his element, he would be called upon not only to examine and treat ailing foreign travellers but also, if they were unfit to travel alone, he would accompany them back to their country of origin. One of his tales concerned a dishevelled traveller who asked the Doctor to arrange transportation to Buckingham Palace, as she had an urgent appointment with the Queen.

Although one day we planned to furnish the central section of the *grenier* with a huge dining table, on this auspicious occasion we had to improvise with a sturdy wallpaper pasting table donated by David. Al had covered it with a white paper tablecloth, concealing its practical origins. For seating we had borrowed David's own dining chairs, released from their dust-protecting wrap of clingfilm. We all sat down to dine on a fine spread of ham, sausage, various colourful salad leaves, luscious tomatoes from the Bussieres' garden, several ripe and runny cheeses, a crusty round loaf and a *pain périgordien*, which Al had managed to pick up from the speciality *boulangerie* in Bellac. Wine was opened and toasts were offered to our guests and to the future of our home at Le Mas Mauvis.

After lunch Al and I escorted our guests around our property, first visiting the Ugly-Bugly to look for signs of fish or coypu. Striking off down the grassy path that skirted alongside the woodland, we came across a curious sight. Just within the boundary of the communal pond and the rivulet that ran into it, someone had been excavating and had uncovered a stone-lined circular well. The well was full to the brim of clear water and had been superficially cordoned off by a length of rope between two canes.

'I wonder who's been digging this out,' I said, examining the exceedingly deep well.

'I don't know, but it's a bit dangerous left open like that,' remarked Al.

'Ooh, my gosh, darling!' said Sheila, peering into the abyss. 'That's *so* deep! Keep Father away from that or you'll be fishing him out, I'll bet!'

'Don't get too close, Sheila,' warned the practical Hoppy. 'The ground's terribly slippery! You'll end up falling in yourself, dear!'

Janet merely narrowed her eyes and smiled as if she was plotting naughty schoolgirl pranks and methods for torturing younger sisters.

'I'll ask Bruno about this. He's always down here chopping logs, so he's bound to know who's dug this out.' I made a mental note to consult our lumberjack friend about the mysterious well when next I saw him. Ushering our intrigued guests past the gaping chasm, we carried on to the back field and into the copse where the local children's camp had been. Now the ground was covered with mushrooms rather than broken beer bottles. After returning to the *grange* for a welcome cup of tea, the weary travellers were returned to their hotel for a *sieste*, while Al and her mother paid a visit to Véronique in hospital.

On our visitors' last evening we dined at a much-recommended restaurant, the amusingly named La Marmite, in Le Dorat. We were joined by David, Dennie and, visiting for the weekend from London, Dennie's 22-year-old daughter, Marianne. This attractive and effervescent young lady – who Al rather aptly described as 'a real babe, just like her mum' – had opted for the comfort of the train on this brief visit, rather than the brand new 650 Ducati motorcycle she had roared up on some months previously, the mere sight of which turned her mother into a nervous wreck.

The evening spent at La Marmite was a fitting end to a successful visit. Al left two days later. I had decided to stay on in France for another month or so: apart from the fact that we both missed each other dreadfully and hated our frequent bouts apart, we both agreed that there were few practical reasons why I should be in the UK at all. My new-found ability to stay on at Mauvis while carrying on with my writing career meant that I could time-manage my efforts wisely to progress with the renovations. The *grenier* now boasted six new windows and a wonderful aspect on our future garden and llama paddocks (if one saw beyond the tangle of weeds).

Our next priority was to install a form of heating that would allow us to spend Christmas and New Year at our own home in the Limousin for the very first time. Fortuitously, a commuting acquaintance, Gerald, on hearing about our French property and the fact that it was unheated, had offered us a wood-burning stove which currently languished in his garage, unused, for a very reasonable price. The Jøtul stove had proven far too powerful for his own house: it had not been possible for him and his family to even sit in the same room as the ferocious beast, and so he had removed it. Al and I duly collected the monster, an incredibly weighty appliance, and transferred it to storage in her parents' garage.

In what would amount to the first stage of our eventual total relocation to France, Al and I planned to transport the stove over from her parents' house in a horsebox owned by Roy, a good friend of the family. It was Roy who first mooted the idea of using the horsebox as a removal van: he was in the process of renovating the van, which had space to accommodate seven horses, with the intention of selling it on.

'Look guys,' he said. 'I'd love to come down to France to see your gaff. So why not bung as much gear as we can in the old horsebox and lug it down there?'

'We sleep in a tent pitched inside a barn,' I reminded him bluntly. 'We don't have guest rooms up and running yet.'

'That don't matter, mate. I'll kip in the van. No worries.'

Although I imagined that I might wake up in the morning, creep from my tent and discover a frozen corpse on the little shelf above the cab of the horsebox, it was agreed that we would load up the vehicle with as many of our possessions as possible, except for the few items we would need to make our rented UK home habitable in the interim. Our booty included two stables' worth of furniture and appliances, and the contents of Al's old bedroom, boxes of crockery, ornaments, books and bedding.

Our first stage of relocation was proposed for mid-October, a time when the weather could be inclement and the temperature in the as yet unheated *grange* decidedly icy. So, in preparation for the arrival of the stove, I was to prepare a concrete hearth on which we could stand the beast at the kitchen end of the *grenier*, ready to be connected up to a flue.

Until the stove could be shipped over and fitted, however, I was faced with the immediate problem of how to keep warm. The September weather had been generally hot but in the closing stages of the month I saw a distinct change. Autumn had arrived with a vengeance. A bitter wind from the north-east blew through every gap – and there were many – in the unheated *grenier*, and the temperature dropped like a stone. I reluctantly abandoned my usual outfit of shorts, T-shirt and sockless moccasins in favour of multiple layers. I wore a pair of my Lycra running shorts, denim jeans, thick thermal socks, boots, a running vest, two T-shirts, a heavyweight denim shirt, a sweatshirt, a fleece, a padded jacket and a baseball cap. This helped to keep the cold out, but only marginally. It was fine while I was moving about, but when I sat in front of the computer, which now occupied the pasting table in the centre of the room, a chill penetrated my core. A tiny electric convector heater thoughtfully donated by David helped to keep my kneecaps warm while I sat huddled at my computer, icy fingers tapping the keyboard, as I worked on the magazine articles I had been commissioned to write.

The mornings were generally misty and, although I was at first reluctant to crawl from the relative warmth of the tent, had a peculiar beauty. Some days a heavy frost covered our unkempt fields. Once the sun had risen, the mist had evaporated and the frost had melted, the days were generally fine, although there was a distinct bite in the cooler air. The leaves on the oak trees were showing the first signs of turning colour, fading to yellow, and our grapevines were assuming a dry, crumpled texture. Likewise the twin wisteria, which had now grown enough to meet in the centre above the cart entrance, were beginning to brown and lose their leaves. Soon they would be no more than a tangle of stems, and I made a mental note that winter pruning would be necessary to encourage the plants to form thicker trunks and a more compact habit. In their first year of growth, I had permitted them to run riot across the face of the building.

Monsieur Jérôme's fields at the back of the *grange* glowed with a rusty hue as the stems of buckwheat turned a vivid red. In other fields surrounding the hamlet, crops of sunflowers which, a few weeks before, had still possessed their bright yellow heads, were now shrivelled, blackened and bowed as if in shame at having lost their previous beauty.

By the afternoons, if pillows of cloud had not tumbled in from the Atlantic, the air was noticeably warmer outside, while in the *grange* it remained chilly. The metre-thick walls kept the building cool in summer but in autumn and winter, without any form of heating, the temperature would plummet. I pulled the duvet from the tent and laid it over my chair, then sat down and wrapped the corners around my body, so that just my head and hands protruded. In this way, I discovered with some satisfaction, I was able to type while remaining cosy, warm and free from draughts.

'You can't work like that, kid!' said a concerned David, when he and Dennie paid me a visit. 'You can't sit with the duvet wrapped round you, lad! It's not the Dark Ages you know! You need some kind of insulation.' With that, he nipped downstairs and started to rummage around amongst the furniture we were storing for him. He reappeared with an offcut roll of carpet tucked under his arm.

'This is what you need, kid. A nice piece o' carpet under your feet while you're sitting at the computer. You'll feel much warmer. This is good quality stuff, mind you. Industrial quality Berber. Used to have this all through the house in England.'

'No, really, David. That's not necessary. I'm quite comfortable with the duvet. The floor isn't at all draughty, actually,' I said. But there was to be no telling the man. He started to release the strings securing the roll but, when at last the carpet sprang loose, half a dozen mice spilled out and scattered in all directions. One of the little buggers headed straight for my open tent. Another scuttled under the fridge.

'Ooh, bloody hell, sorry Rich!' said an embarrassed David. 'I've let mice in t'barn!' More of the rodents spilled from his roll of carpet and darted for the nearest cover.

'I haven't seen a mouse in here for over two years!' I exclaimed.

'Oh, they're so cute!' trilled Dennie, watching the little rodents scarper. Then, thinking better of her comment, added, 'But they are vermin and they do eat your food and you don't want them in your house, of course!'

'Well, I don't think I brought mice from England!' said David with a touch of panic in his voice. 'Ooh, bloody hell! There's mice everywhere, Rich!'

I ran to zip up the flap of the tent, hoping that I had not trapped one of our unwanted visitors inside. The others seemed to have exited the *grenier* via the gaps in the floor at the perimeter, and were now scuttling amongst David's possessions. The immediate panic was over. But now I knew the mice were there. I saw visions of the first nights Al and I spent in the barn, shivering within our tent, as the mice practised their skiing techniques. We had come a long way since then. Or had we?

During those autumn evenings, when the sky had depressingly darkened just after seven-thirty, the temperature in the *grange* actually appeared to increase. This phenomenon enabled me to remove some of my layers while I cooked a lonely meal for myself. I slipped into the habit of listening to Radio France in an attempt to perfect my French by a process of osmosis. (It was just possible to receive a crackly Radio Four from the UK, but somehow I thought of this as cheating. How was I ever going to learn the language if I did not immerse myself in it?) Although translating the rapid-fire speech of presenters was incredibly difficult, I loved the wonderful diversity of programmes broadcast by Radio France – the interviews with politicians, musicians, writers, actors from all over the French-speaking world – and particularly the music. This was a mixed bag indeed. One evening there might be a classical orchestral offering, the following evening traditional French folk artists, the next the pulsing rhythms of rock (such as a splendid concert and bilingual interview with David Bowie). Saturday evenings usually offered a live concert broadcast of world music and I was introduced to the prodigious, soaring vocal talents of Algerian musician Idir, the harmonious melodies of Corsican band I Muvrini, and the guitar-based ballads of Brazilian singer Marcio Faraco.

Afterwards there would be a programme of my favourite music, jazz, and I was moved to take my own tenor saxophone from its somewhat dusty case and play. I had played the sax for over a decade and took the treasured instrument everywhere with me, even on holiday. I had achieved what I regarded as a modest proficiency, which I knew I could not hope to improve without daily practice: something I looked forward to when living at Le Mas Mauvis permanently. Playing a range of scales and arpeggios helped to warm up my fingers, and then I played some smooth jazz to soothe my spirit. The cavernous barn offered rich, utterly gorgeous harmonics, and I was able to play with a volume that would be deafening in a more confined space: in our UK lodge house, I usually had to stuff a sock down the bell of the sax in order to mute its sound.

David and I discovered that we shared a love of music and were both particularly fond of jazz. The Yorkshireman had himself played violin and piano since his childhood, although he was self-effacing about his skill. As a saxophonist, I had always sought other musicians with whom I could play and would, when the opportunity arose, improvise with the Count, a jazz aficionado who played keyboards. Unpractised and slow at sight-reading, I tended to play by ear, priding myself on my ability to pick up any tune and run with it. A competent reader of music, David nevertheless found it difficult to veer from prescribed notation and needed gentle persuasion – eventually succumbing to pressure from Dennie and me – to indulge in the occasional musical evening together.

These musical soirées proved suitably diverting from thoughts of how numbingly cold it was becoming in the *grange* (not least because I could escape to the warmth of Vic and Anne's centrally-heated house for a few hours), but it was obvious that the installation of our wood-burning stove was vital if our French home was to become more than just a summertime retreat.

However, until this could be done, there was the knotty problem of a recently discovered leak in our plumbing system, which had been pouring hundreds of litres of valuable water into the ground. It was infuriating and hard for me to admit that smart alec Monsieur Jérôme might have been correct in his initial diagnosis, during our trench-digging episode, that we had sprung a leak somewhere.

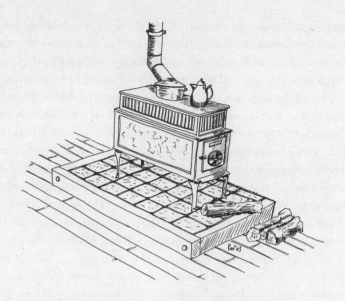

Chapter Twenty

Home is Where the Hearth is

The discovery of the leak had occurred quite by accident after Al had made bold strides into the bed of nettles that had grown around and concealed the inspection chambers where our water supply entered the property. She was attempting to clear up the patch of grass in front of our *maison du pain* in preparation for her parents' visit and had slashed a broad path into the undergrowth with the scythe.

'There's a lot of water around the base of these chambers,' she said. 'Is that normal?'

I looked. It was not normal. I lifted the heavy concrete lid of the smaller chamber, which housed the three meters for the main *grange*, the *maison de cochons* and the *maison du pain*, and could see that this too was full of water. I baled out the chamber but it filled up again within a few minutes. I lifted the lid of the other chamber, the one Monsieur Laborde had forbidden us to touch, warning us: 'You don't need to do anything in that chamber. That only contains the water authority's main tap and meter. Don't touch anything in there!' As I lifted the lid I was squirted in the eye by a fierce, needle-sharp jet of water that made me stumble backwards, slithering in the muddy earth. The second chamber was full of water, too. The jet of water was coming from a valve inserted in the pipework next to the water authority's meter, the dial of which was racing around at a frantic rate. I could see the digital read-out scrolling before my very eyes as water poured into the ground, and most probably filtering along our pipe runs to the soggy patch at the back of the hangar. And we had dug a 65-metre-long trench in order to eradicate our excess of water. Could we really have just been draining our own water supply into the stream all these months?

While our relations were visiting we decided to ignore the leak, but once they had gone Al put through an urgent call to the water authority, which sent out an inspector immediately. After all, the source of the leak was within their inspection chamber, the one our plumber had told us not to touch on pain of death.

'*Non, Monsieur*. That's your *supape*, not ours,' said the spotty youth who had been sent along to investigate the leak.

'*Supape?*'

'*Le truc, là*,' he pointed at the pissing valve, which was sending a graceful arc of water into the air. 'It's your *supape* because it is on your side of our tap.' He bent down and turned off his company's main stop tap. The leak subsided. 'It's your responsibility. You need a plumber. OK? *Au revoir!*' And with that the insolent young pup climbed back in his van and sped off.

Al's telephone call to Monsieur Laborde's establishment revealed the shockingly sad news that the poor man had been taken seriously ill and was unable to work. His wife was distraught. His son was already overloaded trying to keep ahead of his father's considerable workload. Al apologised for the disturbance, explained that we would solve our little problem elsewhere, and asked Madame Laborde to please pass on our good wishes to her husband. David recommended our neighbour Jeff as an alternative plumber.

'Bloody hell!' exclaimed Jeff when I urgently called him out to examine the leak. 'You're losing water by the gallon! Look at that gauge! You've wasted more water than I've used in five years' living here!'

Despite the fact that Jeff only lived across the communal green, Al and I had only ever met him briefly two years ago, when he had been cycling past with Charlie the floppy-eared hound in tow. People in Le Mas Mauvis tended to respect each other's privacy, and would not presume to foist themselves on neighbours. Jeff was a general builder, plumber and electrician from the north of England, who made a tidy living mainly working on English holidaymakers' houses. He seemed amused by our water fountain.

'Of course, Richard. I can replace the valve. No problem at all. I'll go to the *quincaillerie* tomorrow and see if they've got a matching one. If they haven't – because it looks like an unusual one to me – I'll be going to Limoges the day after tomorrow and I'll be able to get one there for definite.' And so I left the repair to Jeff and returned to my writing deadline.

One of the problems (or benefits) of being a do-it-yourself writer is that you're always writing about repair jobs but rarely have time to tackle them yourself. It was more important that I earn some money – and fast! – because there was no telling what horrendous water bill we would next receive. And my main priority was to keep Monsieur Jérôme from confirming the existence of a leak! I could just imagine the ribbing I would get.

I had been sitting in the *grenier* at my computer when I heard the sound of an unfamiliar tractor rumbling along the lane. Peering out of the window, I was greeted by the sight of Monsieur Cédric driving his ancient vehicle with Bruno Bussiere perched on one of the big rear wheel rims. Behind the tractor was a large trailer. I went down to greet the pair. Bruno removed his tartan cap and bowed theatrically.

'*Guten morgen, mein Herr!*' he called above the drone of the elderly tractor, talking in German for some obscure reason. 'Goot mornink, ewe underztand? *Wie Sie heute sind?* 'Ow are ewe?' Bruno pulled the well-chewed stick of liquorice root from his mouth and carried on with his ridiculous accent: 'Vee haff come for zee logs, meester. You helfen?'

I followed the tractor down the path to the pile of logs Bruno had cut and stacked and the three of us loaded the trailer. Reverting to French, he began to tell us of his exploits when he was a young gendarme, and the fine time he had experienced when stationed in Berlin. Bruno had the best of both worlds in the Gendarmerie, because rather than being on active service, he was a cook. Thus, he was excused from a lot of the physical stuff but still got to wear a uniform – and to impress the local girls.

Bruno continued with his bawdy reminiscences, revealing that on one occasion he had been entertaining the *Fräuleins* when he should have been cooking and, caught by his superior officer, was made to swim fifty lengths of an icy-cold outdoor swimming pool as punishment.

'*Bussiere! Nager!*' Bruno said, repeating the words of his officer. He saluted extravagantly, then mimed diving into a pool followed by an impressive crawl action. '*Pas de problème pour Bussiere!* I swim *sehr gut*. Pworr! *Idiot officier!* At ze least I got to kees zee girls, *non*?' He gave me such an enormous nudge with his elbow that, taken by surprise, I dropped a hefty log on my foot. 'Ouch!' I cried, hopping on one leg. And then the three of us were laughing, with the irrepressible Private Bruno Bussiere guffawing the loudest and performing a dainty little jig.

When we had calmed down, I remembered the mystery of the well we had found exposed the other day, and asked my companions if they knew of its existence. At first they shook their heads. I led them down the path to the site.

'*Non!* I have never seen this before!' said Bruno, thankfully reverting to French. He clambered down the little incline, past the string line marking the presence of the well, and peered into the clear, still water. 'Did you know of this *fontaine*, Cédric?'

'*Oou-i-i, nat-urelle-ment.* This *fontaine* I rem-em-ber as an *enfant*! My *mère* would come here for *l'eau, j'crois*.'

'I think it's on communal land,' I said. After consulting the cadastral plan, I had worked out that our path ran along the side of the parcel of land where the well was located, and which I assumed was communal.

'*Oou-i-i, c'est communal,*' confirmed Cédric. '*Vraiment.*'

'But I wonder who has exposed the well?' I posed the question.

'Pworr! I don't know this either,' said a flummoxed Bruno. 'But it's certainly dangerous left open like this! So we will find out! *C'est une mystère, certainement!*' With 'Inspector' Bruno on the case, I was sure we'd soon get to the bottom of this little mystery!

On the afternoon of Véronique's release from hospital, during *un petit quatre* – caramel tea and several lemon butter biscuits – my neighbour hoisted her skirt and showed me her *genoux*. My eyes widened with a mixture of horror and surprise at the sight of the knees I was being asked to examine. The right knee, thankfully somewhat obscured beneath the thickness of her stockings, bore a livid 30-centimetre-long scar stretching above and below her kneecap.

'Wow, that's some scar!' I remarked. 'Does it hurt?'

'Does it hurt?' she echoed. She held a hand to her forehead. 'Oh, Monsieur Richard. *Je m'en souffre! Je m'en souffre!*'

'Early days yet, though!' I said. 'It will get better!'

She flopped down wearily on the chair opposite me, pulled something out of a large envelope that lay on the table in front of her and handed me the x-rays of her knees. 'These are *avant*,' she said, handing me the 'before' shots. 'And these are *après*.'

'Oh Véronique,' I said, handing back the x-rays and feeling queasy. 'Now you have a new ceramic knee you'll be able to join me when I go for a run!'

'*Peut-être un autre jour*, Monsieur Richard!' she said, laughing.

Changing the subject, I asked Véronique about the presence of the mysterious well, and she admitted that she was not aware of its existence – she had not lived in the hamlet all her life, unlike Cédric – and she had no idea who could have exposed it. 'I never go down that path,' she said. 'The ground is too uneven for me, even with my new knee, and there are many brambles. I might slip! But I will ask Jérôme if he knows about the well. If anyone knows about it, he is sure to.'

Just then, Dennie turned up for a chat and was immediately drawn into the sweltering heat of Véronique's kitchen for tea and a biscuit. She politely declined the biscuit, so I was obliged to eat it. David had returned to England to attend a friend's wedding and would be gone for five days. Dennie, who could not take time off work to join him, was at a loose end that coming weekend. Al, likewise, had headed off back to work in the UK, leaving me to finish off painting the new windows and to carry on with my writing. Dennie and I discussed what to do with ourselves. Véronique handed us a flyer for an event taking place at the weekend in Le Dorat.

'*Grand Concours Hippique*,' I read aloud. 'A horse show. Fancy that, do you?' Dennie agreed and so the next day I collected her and we headed off for the town.

We arrived to a scene of chaos. Cars were parked on pavements, verges, and even in the middle of the road. Hordes of people were milling about. In a cordoned-off area was a practice ring, complete with jumps. Riders smartly dressed in red or blue hacking jackets and crisp white jodhpurs were guiding their steeds over the jumps in the cramped little ring. A strong smell of horse dung pervaded.

Horse boxes and trailers were parked higgledy-piggledy in every available space, having disgorged their equine passengers. Over a crackling tannoy we could hear an announcer broadcasting the next rider to compete and, following the sound, we made our way to the open-fronted marquee. The sand arena was framed on the two sides adjacent to the marquee by rows of tall, rustling chestnut trees, and on the fourth side by a terrace of town houses. The householders sat at their windows or on their balconies, taking in a grandstand view of the proceedings.

The marquee housed a bar, a stall selling fine wines, and an equestrian supplier. Games had been set up for the youngsters: one involved tossing metal boules at a fresh egg perched on an upturned log. Another game involved guessing the weight of a Shetland pony. Animated chatter issued from the crowd at the bar, set against the tinny music that accompanied each rider's attempt at the course. The repertoire of music ranged from saccharin-sweet Euro-pop to, quite bizarrely, Greek bouzouki music, including a rendition of 'Zorba's Dance'.

Fascinated spectators lined the fencing that surrounded the arena. Some die-hards had clearly been here since the early morning, and their weighty programmes were dog-eared and scrawled with scores and comments on the riders' and horses' performances. We squeezed close to the fence and watched the next few riders jumping a somewhat complex course. Few competitors managed clear rounds, and it became apparent that we were watching the novice category. Some riders appeared over-horsed (one skinny man's legs barely stretched over the girth of his cart-horse-sized mount), others just the opposite (another man's feet almost touched the ground as he entered the ring sitting poker-straight, looking like an old-fashioned wooden clothes peg rammed on the animal's back). Some riders came a cropper at the most daunting of jumps, slithering out of their saddles under the bellies of their horses, or being flung unceremoniously over their mount's head as the animal skidded to an abrupt halt in front of a jump. One game competitor tore around the course with little regard for her own safety and, on leaping an awkward wall, was rocketed out of her saddle and stirrups in a spectacular star jump. Amazingly, she landed heavily back in the saddle and exited the arena at breakneck speed, clinging onto her horse's mane for dear life.

After watching the outcome of the somewhat shambolic but entertaining novice class, Dennie and I adjourned to the bar across the square for a leisurely drink, sitting at an outside table where we could watch the horses and riders making their way back to their transport and home, before heading back ourselves to Le Mas Mauvis. It had been a thoroughly enjoyable afternoon, which had given Dennie and me an opportunity to witness firsthand a largely unseen aspect of French culture.

'Blimey, thees ees some place you 'ave 'ere, Richard!' said Bernard, sauntering from his car, hands casually stuffed in pockets, as I came out of the *grange* to meet him. It was a delightfully sunny day in late September, with a light, cool breeze. Bernard had come, as promised, to inspect our land and advise on the containment needed for llamas. 'But what potential you 'ave!' he trilled in his musical voice. I led him into the coolness of the barn and up the stairs to the *grenier*. 'Oh, but thees ees wonderfool, Richard!' he sang as we emerged into the cavernous room.

'It's starting to look like a home now,' I admitted. Bernard loped across to the newly installed back windows and surveyed our overgrown fields. I indicated the boundary, demarcated by the line of oaks.

'My, you need the bloody 'erde of feefty llamas to clean up thees field, I theenk! Oh, but don't worry! Slowly but surely they eat the grass down.'

'Would you like to take a walk around the property before lunch?' I suggested. Bernard agreed, and we set off down the path. The sides of the little track and the perimeter of the communal pond were choked with a variety of saplings that had self-seeded, notably hazel, the woody stems of broom, and a leafy shrub that I had been unable to identify, which Bernard confirmed was a common water-margin tree, which farmers normally cut down each year. The grass track was still damp with the morning dew, and the stems of brambles tripped us as we walked. Bernard paused to pluck blackberries from the spiny stems and toss them into his mouth. 'Perhaps you should pick theese berry and make the pie, *non*?'

'You're right. But to be honest, the brambles are the bane of our lives. They multiply so rapidly.'

'Oh, blimey, but thees ees nothing! The llama, 'ee will eat thees plant.'

'They'll even eat brambles?'

'But of course! Not the whole thing, though. The bramble grows by sending out this stem, which roots, say a metre away, and thees also send out the stem and so on and so on, *et voila*, the bramble 'ee spread! Monsieur Llama, 'ee come along and nibble the leetle growing tip and the bramble 'ee cannot spread. So 'ee die back. In time the bramble ees no more.'

'What else will they eat, then?' I asked. 'Will they eat broom, for instance?'

'Well, they eat many, many things, Richard. But they will not eat the broom. No, no. Not the broom. Maybe eet's too tough for them. They don't eat buttercups, eithere, but they love the clover. My guys don't like the white clover, though, only the mauve colour: picky, huh? Perhaps eet's not so tasty, though. The thistle are your main probleme, I theenk. Thees big field 'ere ees great. The llamas will love this field. There ees not too much thistle and the grass ees lush. But the othere field behind your 'ouse 'as much thistle. Maybe you need to theenk about ploughing up that field and starting again.'

'You could be right,' I admitted. The thought had crossed our minds already. I looked a little downcast. There seemed so many obstacles to overcome. Bernard slapped me on the shoulder reassuringly.

'Don't worry Richard! In time, I theenk, even just a few llamas would eat thees thistle. There is no 'urry, aftere all, eh?'

'No, no hurry!' I replied, brightening up. He was right. Everything would happen in its own time.

As we strolled, I indicated the areas I was intending to fence off, and Bernard suggested that I could ignore for now areas where the tangle of shrubs, brambles and holly was especially thick, as the llamas would take several months to eat their way through to freedom. I discovered with relief that my fencing task was to be less wholesale than I had feared, as the existing stretches of low-level sheep fencing could merely be supplemented by a few strands of barbed or plain wire fixed to separate posts above the *grillage*, preventing the llamas from jumping over. The back field required the most attention where it ran alongside the Pentecostal way – a distance of about three hundred metres – as the existing fencing was either missing or had been strangled by years of rampant undergrowth.

'Where does thees path lead, Richard?' asked Bernard, as we wandered along the Pentecostal way towards its boundary with Sejotte. I explained about the religious significance of the track, the annual Whitsun procession and the presence of Le Polissoir, the ancient stone that had caused us so much anguish in the past. We stepped over the rickety fence at the end of the track into our neighbour's field and I pointed across the pasture towards the ominous stone. The field was full of cattle grazing on the clover and sweet grass. Intrigued by our presence, they began to approach.

'Ah, but these are not the Limousin cattle!' exclaimed Bernard. 'I theenk eet's the breed l'Aubrac. You see their colouring, eet's palere than the Limousin, almost yellow. They are very beautiful cows, *non*? But look at their long 'orns! Blimey, they're sharp!'

The herd of doe-eyed cattle had stopped a few metres away and were regarding us with interest. Bernard looked down at the electric fence that separated us from the beasts. 'Ees thees thing switched on?' He reached out and grabbed it, held if for a few moments, then released it. '*Non!*' He looked at me. 'Anyway, we give the old stone a miss, I theenk. I don't like to go in the field with the cattle, especially with theese big 'orns, eh!'

'As you like,' I said, absently brushing against the electric fence. A sudden, sharp electric shock shot up my left arm and pounded into my chest. 'Shite in hell!' I yelped, recoiling from the live wire, my cheeks wobbling shakily, the hairs on my arms and neck bristling. My heart was thumping wildly and my arm tingled disconcertingly. 'Bollocks, Bernard! I thought you said it was switched off!'

'Well, crikey, eet nevere 'urt me! Maybe I'm not surch a good conductere as you, eh?' He chuckled roguishly. Then he adopted a more concerned attitude. 'Do you need to sit down for the moment, perhaps, Richard? Do you feel unwell?'

'No, don't worry,' I moaned, giving myself a touch of heart massage. 'I'll be OK, I expect.' The pounding in my chest was considerable. 'Jesus, Bernard, I can't believe I used to deliberatcly grab electric fences when I was a child – and for fun, too! What madness! It gives you quite a punch, I can tell you!'

'Well, I expect eet does, Richard,' agreed Bernard. 'Aftere all, eet 'as to be able to stop the big cow, *non*?'

On the other side of the fence the herd of cows kept their distance and, batting their big, dark eyelashes, seemed to be smirking at me.

While I prepared lunch, Bernard leafed through my book on wild flowers and trees in an attempt to identify some of the specimens we had collected during our walk. He steadfastly refused to partake in a glass of wine, protesting: 'Don't tempt me, Richard! I 'ave given up the booze. I theenk I 'ave the gout! Just give me a glass of watere, that's all.'

I laid the pasting table with plates of coarse pâté and *saucisson*, served with fresh, crusty walnut bread and we sat down to eat. While we ate, we discussed the number of llamas I should buy to start off my modest herd. My guest recommended restraint, having started off himself with about twenty animals, which in hindsight had been far too many. He had known nothing of llama husbandry and had made many mistakes along the way.

'Look Richard,' said Bernard, carving off a chunk of the sausage. 'Identify your reason for 'aving the llamas. First and foremost, you want to go trekking, *non*? So perhaps you start with just two llamas. Young males, maybe two years old. One for you, the othere for Al. Maybe you also 'ave a young pregnant female, who stays on the farm and increases your 'erd slowly. Of course, you 'ave to keep the males separate from the lady ...'

'That sounds like a workable plan,' I agreed, slicing a chunk of pâté.

'And perhaps you 'ave a few sheep. Some 'ardy type that can live outdoors all the year. They will 'elp with the grazing.' As he spoke, a vivid image of our farm began to form in my mind, and my dream came ever closer to reality. While Bernard continued to outline my options, I prepared a second course of thick avocado soup – the soft green flesh blended with chicken stock and crème fraîche – served with fillets of lightly poached pink salmon floating in the centre. As I laid the dish before him Bernard's eyes widened appreciatively.

'Flippin' 'eck, Richard! You outdo me, I theenk! But thees ees a splendid feast you 'ave prepared!'

We both tucked in, eating both fish and soup with only a fork: the kind of soup I adored. After a little break, we consumed a selection of cheeses. After fresh coffee, we felt the need for a further stroll, and set off through the hamlet, past Gordon and Maureen's abandoned house and onto the stony track that led between Monsieur Jérôme's fields. According to the local map, the track eventually split into two, one arm eventually rejoining the tar road to Le Dorat, the other arm crossing pastureland to emerge in Le Poux. The tracks, however, petered out after a short distance: unused by the local farmers for many years, they had been allowed to merge with their surroundings and disappear forever. Bernard remarked about the wonderful proliferation of oak trees in the area, far more than existed in his neck of the woods.

'And the acorn, eet ees so large, *non*? I have not seen acorns thees large before.'

The sun was starting to dip in the sky and the shadows lengthened. I could detect a distinct nip in the air. We strolled back to the *grange* and, after taking tea, Bernard bid me farewell and headed off back to his own barn-home and the herd of llamas that were patiently awaiting his undivided attention. As my guest sped out of the hamlet, waving from the open window of his car, I looked forward to further meetings with this humorous, warmhearted man.

I was due to leave for England in a few days and had yet to construct the fireproof hearth on which I was to mount the wood-burning stove we planned to ship over the following week. The hearth was to be a chunky concrete slab edged with oak, its top inset with *tomettes*, the 16-centimetre-square rustic clay tiles that were commonly used as flooring in many old French houses, and often used to floor a *grenier*. We had plenty of spare tiles stacked in the *maison de cochons*, where they had once been used, and I had gathered the 48 I calculated I would need to tile the hearth. Sitting outside the *grange* on my log seat, I felt rather like an aged peasant from a bygone age, cleaning his *tomettes* outside his hovel before replacing them on the dirt floor. First I used a bricklayer's trowel to hack off the dried soil that clung to the backs of the tiles, then I washed them to remove the years of dirt ingraining them. I used two bowls: one containing warm, soapy water, the other clean water to rinse them. Dipping the scrubbed tile in the clean water revealed its rustic beauty and true, rich colouring of mottled reds and yellows. After washing, scrubbing and rinsing each tile, I laid them in the bright sunshine to dry.

For the oak surround I had selected an aged and stout flooring joist from one of the ancillary barns. We were going to be obliged to replace this floor in any case, due to its advanced state of deterioration, and I had cannibalised the structure on other occasions in the cause of renovations elsewhere.

David had offered to help me in my mission to construct the hearth and duly arrived with his special tool known only as 'the Whizzer', which he boasted was the ideal implement to clean up any unfinished beams, revealing their attractive grain patterns and underlying colour. The tool was basically a triangular-shaped abrasive disc fitted in an angle grinder, and it made short work of removing the rough, discoloured exterior face of the tough oak beam to reveal its rich, glowing patina. I imagined a day when, equipped with my own Whizzer, I would race through the grange transforming the filthy beams to a lustrous sheen. David and I took turns sawing the incredibly dense beam into three sections – a front piece and two sides – which would contain the concrete while it set, while providing a decorative facing for the hearth.

If I experienced trouble understanding French, it was nothing compared to the hard time I had trying to understand the Northern colloquialisms of my friend.

'We need to broddle t'ole through front piece, don't we, kid?' he said, when we had positioned the three pieces of oak in their allotted positions against the wall of the *grenier*.

'We do?'

'Aye, kid. But we might want to frag it across the top a smidge,' he went on. He was clearly in a world of his own.

'Will that be necessary?' I asked innocently.

'Aye, of course it will! If you don't frag it, bloody thing might cockle out, mightn't it?'

'Oh yeah, of course.' I felt foolish, although I did not know why. How could I have missed that one? It was bloody obvious, wasn't it? To a Yorkshireman, perhaps. But to this lapsed Geordie, it was sheer gobbledegook. 'I guess we don't want it to cockle, eh?' I laughed. David peered at me poe-faced over the rim of his spectacles.

Having subsequently established by sly questioning that broddling was necessary to form holes through the front piece of oak to connect it to the ends of the two side pieces, and that fragging would be called for to brace the side pieces to prevent them from cockling (splaying outwards) under pressure of the wet concrete, I felt I was finally on the same wavelength as my colleague. Angle brackets secured the beams to the floor, while we laid thick polythene material on the base, lapping up the sides, and added chicken wire to this formwork mould to reinforce the concrete mix.

Later, when mixing concrete in David's electric mixing machine, he grumbled that I was responsible for creating a 'reet pother'. I checked my clothing and smoothed my thinning hair, but nothing seemed to be too amiss. What building malpractice could I be guilty of, I wondered? Then it was adjudged that my inexpert shovelling technique was to blame for the said pother. My do-it-yourselfer's forward-tossing action with the awkward, long-handled French shovel seemed to break all the rules of professional concrete mixing, in which the over-the-shoulder backward-toss was deemed to be more accurate. In my defence I blamed my dicky left eye for my lack of accuracy in shooting the cement, sand and gravel into the drum of the mixer without half of it ending up on the ground. But my technique, described not only as 'cack-handed', but also 'arse-about-face' and generally 'piss poor', resulted in me flinging the dry cement into the mixer so that it created a pother, or dust cloud. This, of course, made it difficult for Master Mixer to see into the drum and to determine the quality and proportions of the mix.

Despite my shortcomings as a mixing assistant, however, we succeeded in ferrying several weighty bucketfuls of concrete up the stairs to the *grenier*, where we poured the mix into the mould formed by the broddled, fragged, non-cockling beams. After compacting the mix and levelling it off to a smoothish finish, we stood back and admired our handiwork. We had expected that there might be some seepage of water from the mould, despite the polythene lining, but nothing like the deluge that started to gush from the corners of the hearth and dripped through the floorboards, dangerously close to an electrical fusebox mounted just underneath.

'Ooh, shit! Quick!' yelled David. 'Get some sand tossed on t'floor to soak it up!'

We skidded back and forth like Laurel and Hardy, flinging buckets of sand around the seeping mix, and eventually succeeded in stemming the flow.

When the concrete had been allowed to go off for a few days, I laid the *tomettes*, butted up edge to edge. The rough-edged tiles fitted together snugly, with a pleasant blend of rustic colours. A pair of oak wedges rammed into the bolt holes at the front of the perimeter beams and chiselled into neat domes completed the structure. David and I stood back and admired our handiwork, satisfied that the hearth would make a fitting stage on which to mount the monster stove.

'Stove's going to weigh an absolute ton, kid,' said David in his spare phraseology. 'Absolute ton!'

'Aye, it is that,' I murmured (I had a habit of speaking with a Yorkshire accent when conversing with David), reflecting that I had not yet worked out how we were going to get the appliance up the stairs: it had taken three of us to lift it into the back of the car, and the suspension of the poor vehicle had never recovered from the strain, to say nothing of our backs. But, I consoled myself, where there's a will there's a way: we'd just have to cross that bridge when we came to it. First of all we had to bring the stove, and all our possessions, across the Channel and the five hundred miles to Le Mas Mauvis.

Chapter Twenty-One

A Moving Experience

I returned to England eager to see Al, for we had been apart for almost a month. While I had been concentrating on my writing in the draughty *grange*, she had, as she admitted, 'gone into Mauvis mode', a self-imposed form of hibernation during my solo spells in France which involved steeping herself in the pages of exciting novels, dining minimally on microwaved frozen dinners, and falling asleep on the sofa in front of the television. They were diversionary tactics that seemed to work well for her.

Another reason for me to return to the UK was that I was due to run in a road race, a personal challenge for which I had been training for months. With Al worrying about my sanity and whether or not I would survive the event, I participated in the gruelling 55-mile London to Brighton Road Race on my first weekend back. Al was my faithful seconder, following in the car and keeping me supplied with water, energy gels and bananas. I was happy that my intensive training on the lanes of rural France had stood me in good stead during my first ultra-distance race, and I completed the route in eight and a half hours, coming forty-first out of 122 runners.

The following weekend I was to help our friend Roy load his horsebox with the furniture, appliances and various effects that we were to take to France along with the essential wood-burning stove. The day before we were to head off to France, Roy and his brother Paul rumbled up to Al's parents' place with the horsebox which, although it looked externally rather tatty, had been adjudged mechanically sound. Roy's younger sibling Paul was to accompany us to France as co-driver of the vehicle. The brothers were physically and temperamentally poles apart: Roy was a tall, rotund man with broad shoulders, wayward hair and a bristly moustache; Paul, by contrast, was slight of frame with close-cropped hair. While Roy was shy and softly spoken, his brother was the joker of the pack, a raucous and practised mickey-taker (with his brother and especially me as the butt of his endless jokes). It was going to be an interesting five-day trip.

The stables were an Aladdin's cave and contained a wealth of items Al and I had either never seen before, or which we had entirely forgotten existed, and unloading them onto the driveway in front of the stable yard yielded many surprises. Hugely generous friends had, during their own home renovations, donated serviceable beds, mattresses, tables and chairs, and in one instance an entire fitted kitchen which included a tumble dryer, dishwasher, refrigerator, freezer, electric oven and gas hob. These hardly-used windfalls were far more than we could ever hope to squeeze into our little Sussex lodge house, but they would be swallowed up with room to spare by our French home, and we were extremely grateful for our friends' kindness. We were also to receive the rather unusual but highly practical gift of a five-bar gate, including posts, which had been salvaged from Sheila's paddock and meticulously treated with creosote by the Doctor. This would take pride of place as part of our plans to corral the patch of grass in front of our intended llama and horse stables, the *maison du pain*.

We had finished loading the lorry by the early evening and the brothers decided that we might as well set off there and then for Dover to catch an early ferry to Calais at one-thirty in the morning. We had previously discussed catching a boat at a more civilised hour later in the day (partly, it seemed, so that the Lads could enjoy a pint or two in the local pub that evening), but even though I pointed out that the early start would require them to miss the hallowed evening session, they were not to be swayed. The trip was going to take a good twelve hours, they calculated, and driving through the night was not a problem with two drivers. They were a hardy breed, well used to trips abroad to bring back lorries and other vehicles in connection with Roy's trade, breakdown recovery. As Roy correctly pointed out, we would also have the benefit of arriving at Le Mas Mauvis in good time to unload before nightfall, leaving us ample time to sample the delights of the *bières de France*. There was, I realised, method to their madness.

As licensed heavy-goods vehicle drivers, the brothers would share the driving, taking turns to sleep. It was a good plan but it did not occur to me at first that, as their assigned navigator, I would be required to remain awake and alert for the entire journey. But, grateful for their assistance and the use of Roy's lorry, I decided to go along with their red-eye trip.

After stopping off at home to say farewell to Al, who had just arrived back from the London commute, I climbed up into the cab of the horsebox, a delicate rose sandwiched between two chain-smoking thorns, and directed Roy, the first-stage driver, on the route that wound its way through the orchards of Kent towards the port of Dover.

Although Al and I had become members of Eurotunnel's Property Owners' Club, which offered extremely affordable channel crossings, this facility was not open to the horsebox. Standard tunnel fares were horrendously costly, particularly as the weight and size of our vehicle obliged us to travel as freight. Ringing around the ferry operators, I plumped for Norfolk Line's surprisingly inexpensive channel crossing to Dunkerque, which would add little time to the usual journey.

Our vehicle was hemmed in and dwarfed by monster juggernauts in the bowels of the hulking ferry. The very last vehicle to roll off the boat, we arrived in France in darkness with rain pelting down and the wind blowing furiously, which caused the heavily laden vehicle to sway disconcertingly. A defective windscreen wiper blade, which left a smear in my line of vision, made my job as navigator particularly arduous, until daylight eventually came and the rain desisted. Roy and Paul took turns driving and sleeping, while I continued to glare through the windscreen, bleary-eyed, for hour after hour as the lorry rumbled its way along the autoroutes.

'Oi!' boomed Paul, roughly digging me in the ribs when at last my heavy eyelids began to flicker and close. 'Don't you bloody fall asleep, mate! I haven't a clue where I'm going!'

I blinked and examined the road signs. Snores emanating from Roy's hunched figure at my side instilled in me a niggling jealousy. Our in-cab entertainment consisted of a well-worn double CD featuring the dulcet tones of Mick Jagger and The Rolling Stones delivered at full booming volume over and over again throughout the journey, often accompanied by Paul tunelessly wailing the choruses. I was grateful whenever we pulled into the various service stations to take on more fuel (for the vehicle guzzled petrol with astonishing greed), as I was able to air my smoky clothes, stretch my stiff legs and consume sufficient strong black coffee to keep my attention on the route ahead. The rigours of the road were proving wearisome for my drivers, as both brothers felt the need to stop for a while and snooze. With both of them slumped in the cab, however, there was nowhere for me to snatch forty winks. Instead, I strolled around the service station shop staring comatose at the products, killing time until the Lads arose, suitably refreshed.

Continuing on our way, the miles rolled past for further long, drawn-out hours, until on one occasion Roy suddenly announced that the petrol gauge had failed and he had no idea how much fuel we had left. Pulling over once more, he poked a stick into the petrol tank and gloomily revealed that our supply was extremely low. We endured a nervous period during which we motored on through a particularly deserted stretch of countryside in search of a petrol station. Passing a few garages that were closed, we were forced to take a risky detour into a town, locating a service station just a few minutes before it was about to shut for the long French *sieste*.

As we trundled along the final stretch of autoroute past Châteauroux we received another scare as the temperature gauge suddenly shot into the red danger zone. We pulled up in a picnic area just before the water boiled dry. Having allowed the tank to cool before topping it up with fresh water, we set off once more, finally rolling into Le Mas Mauvis in the late afternoon. The Lads were undoubtedly tired after the long journey, despite the fact that they had been able to catnap frequently, while I had passed beyond tiredness into a zombie-like state in which I functioned purely by instinct. My first rational thought as host, however, was to sort out a place for my guests to sleep, although they had other, more pressing requirements.

'Let's get this lot dumped in the barn,' said Paul, talking of my valued furniture and possessions. 'And then we can get down to the pub.'

'There aren't any pubs,' I replied flatly.

'What?' said Paul, incredulous. He looked totally horror-struck. 'Whaddya mean, no pubs?' The concept was clearly alien to the lad.

'This is France, Paul. There aren't any pubs like in England.'

'B-but s-surely they sell beer somewhere?' stuttered Roy, struggling to maintain his calm exterior in the face of such terrible adversity, while wondering just what sort of rural backwater I had brought him and his brother to.

'Well, yes. In the *bar-tabacs*. But they're not really like pubs you're used to. They're often quite basic. More like a caff.'

'Don't matter what the place is like, mate. C'mon, let's get going!' said Paul, with obvious relief.

Calculating that unloading the lorry in its entirety that evening would seriously gnaw into valuable drinking time, the Lads became somewhat agitated. I calmed them down with the suggestion that we merely locate their bedding, then borrow my friend David's car and head off to the supermarket to buy essential provisions. After that there would be ample time for a pre-prandial or two in Le Trotteur, the pleasant little *bar-tabac* in Magnac-Laval, which I figured would be the nearest approximation of a 'pub'. In fact, as it was likely to be the only establishment open in the village, it would have to suffice.

'What do you fancy to eat?' I asked, as I wheeled my trolley into the icy cold atmosphere of the supermarket, with the brothers dawdling behind like a pair of stroppy kids being dragged off on a boring shopping expedition by their dad.

'Don't mind,' uttered Paul.

'Me neither,' affirmed Roy.

'Well, can't you suggest something?' I said, mildly ruffled. After all, I had no idea of their culinary tastes. 'You must have some idea of what you want to stuff down your throats.'

'Don't know what they have,' mumbled Paul, hands in pockets, like a truculent adolescent. 'Never been to France before.'

'Well, they have pretty much what you have in England, Paul. Beef, pork, lamb, fish,' I offered, leading them past the cold cabinets. 'How about chicken?'

'Naw, don't go much for chicken,' grumbled Paul. 'It's boring. What's that stuff?' He pointed at a pre-wrapped pack of four fleshy pink chops.

'What's it look like?' I said.

'Pork.'

'And what's it say on the label?'

'*Porc*.'

'Well, there you are then. Do you fancy that?'

'Naw ...'

'How about a nice piece of steak?' I held up a pack of juicy red sirloins. The brothers shook their heads.

'Turkey breast?'

'Ugh! No! Only eat turkey at Christmas.'

Lamb chops? 'Naw, too bloody small; not enough meat on them.' Rabbit? Horse? Or how about heart or other lumps of offal? Their blank faces told me that those were a non-starter, or perhaps they assumed I was cracking a joke. I was not.

'Salad? How about a nice, crisp, fresh salad?'

'Naw, don't be ridiculous, man! Salad's a garnish, not a meal.'

'What then?' I stood with my hands on my hips.

'Burgers,' pronounced the brothers in unison, shuffling their feet.

'Burgers,' I repeated sternly, somewhat deflated. I recalled that they had both tucked into burgers and chips at one o'clock that morning in the fast-food restaurant while waiting to board the ferry, when I could only face a cup of coffee. For lunch they had consumed hot-dogs and chips at an autoroute stopover. Clearly their tastes revolved around junk food, but I was not to be shaken. 'OK, we'll have these. Steak *hachés*,' I said, grabbing a pack of the burger-shaped patties from the shelf.

'I only eat frozen burgers,' said Paul, examining the juicy, 100 per cent Limousin beef patties. 'What's in these?'

'Beef,' I said. 'That's about it, though. No chemicals, colourings, flavourings or preservatives, I'm afraid.'

'Well, OK, we'll give 'em a try,' relented the younger brother.

By the time I had dragged my reluctant charges around the aisles and we had passed through the checkout and into the car park, I was ready for a drink or two. Le Trotteur was filled with chattering French folk, mainly men in their working clothes, a few denim-clad young ladies playing pool (the cramped surroundings requiring those standing at the bar to move aside each time a shot was played or else be poked in the ear with a cue), and a few tired-looking children clinging to their young mothers. The television set, mounted high on the wall, was tuned to a French gameshow, which no one seemed to be watching. Behind the counter at the end of the bar were rows of cigarette packs, which aroused some interest in my companions, calculating that the prices were a third less than in the UK. A large counter display case contained stacks of scratchcards.

'*Messieurs-dames*,' I said, nodding and smiling towards the assembled clientele, who each, without exception, turned to us and responded with '*Messieurs*', or nodded acknowledgement. This, I reflected, would rarely happen in an English pub. The patron, a smiling, friendly man in his mid-thirties, came up and shook my hand warmly, then asked what we would like to drink.

'*Trois pressions s'il vous plaît*,' I said, and ushered Paul and Roy towards a window seat. The patron returned with three stemmed glasses of draught beer and an empty ashtray. The Lads' eyes lit up and their previously glum expressions became animated.

'Don't they sell pints, then?' asked Paul, sipping his beer and studying the hue of the liquid like a wine taster examining a vintage claret.

'I think they do have some big glasses, but not in a pint measure, of course, and probably only for English visitors. They're metric here in France. Most people drink small glasses, though.' Paul shook his head in disbelief and tut-tutted.

'Like a bit of a gamble, do they?' asked Roy, gazing at the bar's décor. The room was furnished quite plainly, but with perhaps more panache than many *bar-tabacs*: simple wooden tables with bentwood chairs, and green-painted joinery with wood-panelled walls painted a paler, toning green. Posters advertising various brands of beer adorned the walls, while racks of *loto* slips featured quite prominently. Over eight thousand *bar-tabacs* in France have a strong link to the horse-racing fraternity. I gazed up at the posters and bunting festooned around the bar, which promoted a selection of the wide range of bets available.

'Yes, they're not averse to a flutter on the horses,' I commented.

The Lads began to chat about *their* particular passion: racing cars. Paul had been a mechanic who built TVRs, and the pair were part-time members of a racing team that regularly participated in events at the Brand's Hatch circuit in Kent. We dawdled over our beers, refilled our glasses and chatted, before returning to the *grange* to arrange beds for the pair and cook a meal.

'It's bloody freezing in 'ere!' announced fleece-attired Paul, shivering as he arranged a mattress on the floor next to my tent and laid out two duvets and numerous blankets. Roy, who also commented on the cool temperature of the barn, set up his bed on the other side of the tent and spread out not only a thick duvet, but also several layers of blankets. The barn resembled a dormitory. To my mind, the temperature was not particularly cold that evening, although I accepted the fact that I was more conditioned to the climate in the unheated *grenier* than my guests were. I wondered, however, how on earth the pair would have coped had they slept in the horsebox, as they had originally planned. Despite being forewarned of the likely weather conditions in France, the brothers had not come prepared. Roy, who had neglected to bring a jumper with him, sat swaddled in his polo shirt and padded jacket, while Paul crouched over the little convector heater in an attempt to keep warm.

'Gawd, look at your quilt!' said Paul, when he caught me stuffing my duvet into a clean cover. 'I'll bet that's the highest bloody tog rating you can get!'

'Actually, it's about fifteen years old and all the feathers have bunched up in one corner,' I revealed. This was the wrong thing to say.

'Feathers? Bleedin' 'ell! Roy, he's got bloody feathers in his quilt! Lucky bugger! I might be nicking that in the night, mate!'

The steak *hachés* – fried until all vestiges of blood had been eradicated – had passed the burger test, and with the addition of boiled potatoes and chunks of bread, made a welcome meal. Even Paul relented that frozen burgers did not hold a light to the fresh French versions, although the sight of my oozing flash-fried patty turned his stomach.

It was time to turn in. I had not slept for almost thirty hours and was beginning to wilt. The Lads, too, were keen on hitting the hay, although vociferously doubting that the intense cold would enable them to experience deep sleep. Lying in my tent in the darkness, however, I heard a guttural rumble coming from one side.

'It's started,' came Paul's sleepy voice from the other side of the tent, as his brother's deep, exuberant snoring roared into action.

'Yeah,' I murmured, cupping my hands to my ears.

'It ain't me,' mumbled Roy straight off, as the snoring ceased abruptly. There was a momentary silence.

'Who the bloody 'ell was it, then?' said Paul. 'There's only three of us in here, and it sure wasn't me!' The three of us sniggered, despite our tiredness.

'How did you do that?' I said at last, quite impressed by Roy's rapid transition from deep sleep to full wakefulness. But there was no reply this time, just a reverberating rumble from Roy on my right, and a nasal whistle from his brother on my left. Soon enough, however, I too was asleep.

The next morning I awoke to the irritating sounds of 'I cain't get no-o satis-faction' blasted out from my stereo, one speaker of which was positioned a foot or so away from my pillow on the other side of the tent. The noxious fumes of tobacco wafted into the open front of my boudoir, as Paul lit up his morning cigarette while making the coffee and Roy, languishing on his mattress, smoked the third of the six or so fags he claimed that he required before even thinking about putting one foot on the floor each morning. Somehow my romantic vision of living in a dream home in rural France had become a touch obscured.

After we had risen, showered and dressed, the Lads swore blind that they would never shower again until they returned to England: it seemed that stepping out of the hot shower into the chill of the bathroom was not an experience they intended to repeat.

We soon emptied the horsebox of its load and I arranged items of furniture in the *grenier*, while the boxes of ornaments, the kitchen components and appliances were stacked in the central hallway, which had been partially cleared of David's belongings during my absence in England.

The monster stove was hauled up the staircase on a sturdy sack barrow given to Al and me by her parents as an early Christmas present. Its wheels ran up oak floorboards laid the length of the flight, while Roy, at the top of the flight, grasped the barrow's folding handle and tugged, and Paul and I pushed from below. It was a far easier process than we had feared, and Paul decided to celebrate the stove's installation on its hearth with a well-earned bottle of beer. I was so pleased that I joined him in a tipple.

Later, I gave Roy and Paul a guided tour around the property, but I could sense that these townies could not quite see its potential with my eyes. Nevertheless, they did admit that the *calme* of the village and surrounding countryside held a vague attraction, a relief from the hubbub of the city they were more used to. But it was short-lived, for the call of the statutory Sunday Lunchtime Drinking Session in the pub was too strong for these London lads, and we set off in the lorry for Magnac-Laval. Le Trotteur was closed and so we drove on to Le Dorat in search of another watering hole. Although the town was largely deserted, the Café de la Poste was a veritable hive of activity, and we settled down at a little corner table with a few glasses of beer. Still not sated, the Lads insisted that we move on to another establishment and we drove into Bellac, some ten kilometres distant. After wandering the pretty, cobbled streets in the drizzling rain and finding a number of *bar-tabacs* firmly closed, we settled in a brightly lit, rather brash bar which seemed to be populated largely by rowdy English people holding their own lunchtime session, and which lacked any kind of French character that I could detect. Thankfully, we stayed there only briefly before returning to Magnac-Laval to find that Le Trotteur had at last thrown its doors open. We, however, were the only customers. I tried to explain to my companions, who were obviously totally baffled by the lack of drinking establishments and drinkers, that the pub culture prevalent in England simply did not exist in this part of France.

'What do people do, then?' asked a bewildered Roy from behind a cloud of cigarette smoke.

'Well, remember this is a farming community; they work horrendously long hours. Go to a city, such as Limoges, and you'll find bars, nightclubs, restaurants. But people here in the sticks are perhaps more family orientated,' I said. 'Having said that, though, in their spare time they probably do what most people seem to do the world over nowadays – they watch telly.'

'Ah! Now that I can understand!' Paul said, obviously au fait with the slovenly ways of the couch potato. It was a sad fact that television had contributed to the demise of traditional social life in many villages. Pre-Second World War rural communities, generally poor and isolated, had been more closely knit in the face of adversity, but with peace, relative prosperity and new forms of mass entertainment, families had become insular. While elderly men would still meet daily at cafés to play cards and talk, or to congregate in the village square for a game of boules, the days were gone when families would regularly get together to play folk music and sing songs, and when grandparents would recount traditional tales to delight their grandchildren. Harvest time had traditionally been a communal affair and an excuse for rowdy get-togethers, but mechanisation had changed all that: haymaking could be tackled by a few men and a combine harvester rather than dozens of workers with pitchforks. Summertime fêtes, often lasting all weekend, were still popular events, when the spectacle of folk music and dancing with traditional instruments and costumes would lure families from their television sets. The magnetism of the small screen, nevertheless, had largely sounded the death knell for the future of folk culture.

'Where's your telly anyway, Rich? I didn't see one back at the barn,' asked Roy, wrenching me from my musings.

'I don't have a television.'

Paul shook his head forlornly. 'You're just weird, mate,' he decreed, and lit another cigarette. Weird I might be, but I had not once missed the television during my prolonged periods in France: there was always so much to do. In England Al and I tended to use the television as a means of zoning out after a hard day's work. Everyone had their own means of relaxation, of course, and I knew that Al and I, when resident in France, would be able to find other, more absorbing ways to chill out. It wasn't as if nothing ever happened in Le Mas Mauvis after all. The ever-present intrigue of feuds between our neighbours added spice to daily life that was far more interesting than TV soaps, and there were many little mysteries that required solving. For example, the phantom well-digger had still not been identified, despite enquiries all around the hamlet, and I was determined to get to the bottom of this particular puzzling occurrence. No, life would certainly be rich and varied, even in this quiet corner of France.

The following day the brothers and I ventured into La Souterraine on the thinly veiled pretext of taking in the medieval splendours of the town. I took my companions on a whistle-stop tour of the historic landmarks, past shuttered houses behind which the gabble and clatter of lunchtime sounded. There were few people on the streets and the shops had closed, as many did on Mondays. The weather was overcast but mild and we settled at a table on the outside terrace of a narrow little bar squeezed into one corner of the square overlooked by the turreted La Porte Saint-Jean. A printed notice posted in the window of the bar revealed that the key to the interior of the historic gate was available to interested visitors from within and I made a mental note to take up the offer on another occasion. Having witnessed enough culture for one day, we crawled on to another *bar-tabac* before returning to the *grange*, whereby I received a telephone call from the Count, also in France at the time. He offered me the welcome opportunity to return to England with him the following weekend, rather than leaving midweek with the Lads. This was a fortuitous suggestion, because it had become apparent to me that installing the stove's flue and chimney was likely to be a more complicated and lengthy task than I had at first thought. Access to the giddying height of the *grenier* roof was going to require more than my triple extending ladder.

Without my presence in the cab as navigator, the brothers decided that their work in France was done and announced their decision to depart the following morning, a day earlier than planned. Equipped with a detailed route description I prepared for their return journey, they left after a modestly early rise, several cups of coffee and numerous cigarettes. Their plan was to load the horsebox with as many crates of beer and cartons of cigarettes as they could afford, before heading for the ferry home.

Although I was immensely grateful for the Lads' help, I was glad to be left alone in the *grenier* to sort out our furniture. After clearing away the makeshift beds I was able to arrange our armchairs, tables, mirrors, standard and table lamps, and laid an assortment of rugs on the bare wooden floorboards. Eventually I settled down in a comfy armchair to survey the fruits of my labours. With the placement of these items, the vast open-plan room finally seemed to have achieved its transformation from a utilitarian barn to a habitation and I was able to witness its true character taking shape. I was truly at home.

Realism kicked me up the backside when I realised that, despite our well-appointed furnishings, the lack of heating facilities was set to make the *grange* uninhabitable as the autumn weather started on its downward spiral towards winter. The Count's scaffold tower, which he had brought over and which we erected alongside the stove's hearth, was found to be just too short to comfortably reach the apex of the roof. With our return ferry trip from Le Havre to Portsmouth already booked for three days' time, it became clear that we were not going to be able to complete the installation of the stove in time. I decided to call in our neighbour Jeff and persuade him to take on the job. Not only would he fit the flue pipe and chimney outlet but he would also connect up the stove's integral copper water tank to a modest heating circuit serving two chunky school-type radiators positioned at each side of the open-plan room. Christmas promised to be warm and snug in the *grange*, even if our makeshift cooking facilities would challenge our culinary ingenuity. However, Al and I looked forward to utilising the wood-burning stove's in-built facility for smoking chicken, fish and other foodstuffs over logs of oak. With our pioneering spirit, these hurdles were all part of the rich tapestry of our French renovation in rural Limousin. With the New Year would come not only our fifth anniversary as owners of the property, but also the commencement of our last year based in England and the start of our new lives together in our adopted country.

Epilogue

Sleeping in the Open

I was restless. I stared up into the all-encompassing blackness, feeling a little exposed. It was also a mite chilly. Perhaps Al and I had been foolish to sleep out in the open. It was coming up to our fifth anniversary since purchasing the property, but in all our time here we had never before dared to sleep outside, even in the height of summer. No, this was an experience I had dreamed of. I should savour it. I gently nudged Al's sleeping form. She grumbled and absently elbowed me in the nose. I stared around me again but could see nothing. Then something flopped from nowhere onto my face. I screamed, scrabbling at my unseen assailant, and sat bolt upright.

'What is it? What's wrong?' said Al, waking in a panic. 'Did you have a nightmare, darling?'

'No! Something attacked me!' I shrieked, wiping some horrible substance from my forehead. What hideous creature of the night had tried to make me its prey?

'What was it?'

'A bat, I think …'

'A bat?' she said doubtfully.

'It could have been. Or some kind of huge poisonous spider. I don't know. But it didn't half give me a shock!' I could still feel the horrible tendrils of my mysterious foe clinging to my face. 'Maybe sleeping out in the open wasn't such a good idea …'

Al clicked the bedside light on. She sat up in bed and rubbed her sleepy eyes, then glowered at me. She laughed.

'And what's so amusing, I might ask?' I said, examining myself for signs of blood, perhaps oozing from twin fang marks on my neck.

'You've got a huge cobweb on your head,' Al said, giggling. 'A bat indeed! Now can we get to sleep? It's four in the morning.'

I peered up into the rafters where the long trails of cobwebs hung, heavy with years of accumulated dust. Another one dropped from the beams and landed next to the bed with a plop. I clambered off the mattress. It seemed a long way down to the floor of the *grenier*. It had been a fair while since I had slept in a proper bed rather than the mattress on the floor of the tent. I tottered over to the central window overlooking the fields at the back of the *grange*. Opening the casements, I sat on the window sill and peered into the gradually lightening sky. I could make out the line of majestic oaks on the horizon. An owl screeched as it headed for its roost.

Al clambered out of bed and shuffled over to join me at the window, nestling under my arm. The air was crisp and fresh, but not too cold.

'Don't catch a chill,' she murmured.

'No, I won't. I'm just not sleepy,' I said, somewhat dreamily.

'What are you thinking about?'

'Oh, just how satisfied I am, living here with you …'

'That's nice. Thank you. I'm happy too,' Al declared. 'Big day today, Lol. I'm going to make chutney! What are you going to do?'

What *was* I going to do? Where would I start? When it got light, I would make two huge bowls of coffee for us and we would breakfast sitting next to the window that overlooked the front of the *grange*, where it received the morning sunlight. Perhaps we would hold a polite chat with Véronique toiling in her vegetable garden. I would set out on a long run, exploring new routes, and return in time for a long, leisurely lunch. Then in the afternoon, while Al busied herself with her experimental chutney, I would perhaps continue my project of mapping out our garden at the back of the building. It was to be a fluid design of meandering pathways traversing the area set aside for cultivation, intersecting and connecting orchard, herb garden, herbaceous borders, and rose garden. One of the first jobs was going to be to plant some of the larger trees and shrubs that would give structure to the scheme.

The majority of the boundary fencing was in place and very soon Al and I would pay another visit to Bernard with the intention of selecting the llamas that would become our companions and helpers in clearing the land, bringing some order to the somewhat unruly terrain. And then I would start on the process of training the animals to walk on the halter in preparation for the treks Al and I had discussed.

But here I was getting ahead of myself again: the establishment of the garden, the llamas, the exploration of our newly adopted country, that was another story. Today? Well, I would just have to see where the mood would take me.

Acknowledgements

I would like to thank Summersdale Publishers for their guidance in the production of *Bon Courage!* and for releasing this smart new edition. I could not have written this book without the help and understanding of certain selfless individuals. Special thanks to our French neighbours for accepting us so readily into their fold and their country, particularly our 'adopted aunt' for her kindness, friendship and endless petits quatres; to Bernard Morestin for his long lunches while dispensing inspiration and invaluable advice on raising llamas; to my old friend John Cansdale for his loyalty and building expertise; to Lee Bassett, David and Dennie Wrightham, and Kenny Clements for their warm companionship; to Phill and Stephanie Wiles for their endless support; and lastly to Al, without whom there would be no *Bon Courage!*

GRAPE
EXPECTATIONS

'a beautifully written tale of passion and guts'
Alice Feiring, author of *Naked Wine*

A Family's
Vineyard Adventure
in France

Château
Haut
Garrigue

Caro Feely

GRAPE EXPECTATIONS
A Family's Vineyard Adventure in France

Caro Feely

ISBN: 978 1 84953 257 1   Paperback   £8.99

When Caro and Sean find the perfect ten-hectare vineyard in Saussignac, it seems their dreams of becoming winemakers in the south of France are about to come true. But, rather than making a smooth transition from city slickers to connaisseurs du vin, they arrive in France with their young family (a toddler and a newborn) to be faced with a dilapidated eighteenth-century farmhouse and 'beyond eccentric' winery. Undeterred by a series of setbacks, including mouse infestations and a nasty accident with an agricultural trimmer, they embark on the biggest adventure of their lives – learning to make wine from the roots up.

'A must-read for anyone who's dreamed of owning their own vineyard, at times gritty, at times joyful, Grape Expectations is an inspiring story of how one couple changed their lives.'

Jamie Ivey, author of Ten Trees and a Truffle Dog

'Captivating reading for anyone with dreams of living in rural France'
DESTINATION FRANCE

'... worth reading and a great introduction to a winery, tourism destination and family that deserve our attention. I shall be on the lookout for a bottle of their wine in the very near future.'

thirstforwine.co.uk

SERGE BASTARDE ATE MY BAGUETTE
On the Road in the Real Rural France

John Dummer

ISBN: 978 1 84024 770 1   Paperback   £8.99

When ex-blues drummer John Dummer decamps to France to start up as an antiques dealer and live the simple life, he doesn't count on meeting Serge Bastarde. The lovable (if improbably named) rogue and brocanteur offers to teach John the tricks of the trade in return for his help in a series of breathtakingly unscrupulous schemes.

As the pair trawl through antiques markets and old farmhouses looking for hidden treasure, they get into more than their fair share of scrapes: whether they're conning hearty lunches from unsuspecting old peasants, secretly manufacturing priceless collectibles or losing a Stradivarius to gypsies.

'Dummer describes a very different France... Bastarde certainly lives up to his surname, cruising the countryside in his battered van tying to cheat clueless peasants out of their heirlooms. But Bastarde grows on you, with his imaginative lies and unexpected generosity.'   THE FINANCIAL TIMES

'Get a copy. You'll love it.'   ANTIQUES DIARY

'Filled with eccentric characters and unlikely adventures, this is a highly amusing romp through the real rural France.'

LIVING FRANCE

Have you enjoyed this book?
If so, why not write a review on your favourite website?

If you're interested in finding out more about our books,
find us on Facebook at **Summersdale Publishers** and
follow us on Twitter at **@Summersdale**.

Thanks very much for buying this Summersdale book.

www.summersdale.com